GROSS
MISCONDUCT

GROSS MISCONDUCT

MY YEAR OF EXCESS IN THE CITY

VENETIA THOMPSON

POCKET
BOOKS

LONDON • SYDNEY • NEW YORK • TORONTO

First published in Great Britain by Pocket Books, 2010
An imprint of Simon & Schuster
A CBS COMPANY

1 3 5 7 9 10 8 6 4 2

Simon & Schuster UK Ltd
1st Floor
222 Gray's Inn Road
London WC1X 8HB

www.simonandschuster.co.uk

Simon & Schuster Australia
Sydney

A CIP catalogue record for this book is available
from the British Library.

ISBN: 978-1-84739-770-6

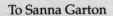
To Sanna Garton

CONTENTS

PROLOGUE

Farewell happy fields
Where joy for ever dwells: hail horrors, hail
Infernal world, and thou profoundest hell
Receive thy new possessor: one who brings
A mind not to be chang'd by place or time.
The mind is its own place, and in it self
Can make a heaven of hell, a hell of heaven
What matter where, if I be still the same

(Paradise Lost 1.249–56)

The City got hold of me, drawing me in like a gilded bog. For fourteen months I enjoyed sinking – head down, heels up – deep into its folds. I became an inter-dealer bond broker, and took all that the job had to offer as I descended into the abyss: the eight-course tasting menus, the £900 bottles of wine, the champagne-fuelled nights at strip clubs, the Chanel handbags, the meaningless sex, the friendships.

Then, as easily as I had slid in, I was catapulted out. There were no pristine cardboard boxes to aid my transfer back to society; no emotional leaving drinks; no desperate calls to headhunters. I had just sat on a bench and watched people as

1

they rushed past for a while; I was another nameless suit absentmindedly fiddling with a BlackBerry. Then I got on the Tube and made my journey home away from the ivory towers of Canary Wharf for the last time.

At the time, the so-called 'credit crunch' had been quietly gnawing away at the bowels of the City for about six months, marked only by the occasional headline that filtered through to the outside world. We all still believed in the future and the little green lights flashing on the screens in front of us; we believed that the market would have bad days or months, but that it was ultimately infallible and would resurrect itself as it always had previously. And to that end, we pressed on – Gatsby's boats, borne back ceaselessly into the past. We carried on drinking, blacking out, grasping strippers' talc-swathed buttocks as they writhed around on our laps, blissfully unaware of the tide turning beneath us.

I was fired for gross misconduct at the end of February 2008 for an article I'd written for *The Spectator* while working for one of London's biggest broking houses. When Lehman Brothers collapsed, on 15 September 2008, I saw the lights begin to flicker along with the rest of the market; I was within yet without. Images of former Masters of the Universe staggering around Canary Wharf and Wall Street holding cardboard boxes stuffed with gym kits, stationery and condiments were plastered all over the front pages of the newspapers. The Dow and the FTSE tumbled to unprecedentedly low levels. It was no longer possible to carry on in blind faith.

This memoir will document that final year of excess before I made one final trade and got out, before the market and the future of banking subsequently changed irreversibly and hundreds of others made that mid-morning journey home as the market shook and their jobs disappeared.

CHAPTER 1

THROWBACK

Now a name that saved you has a foreign taste
Leonard Cohen

There is always a trade to be done, but I never thought that the transactions completed away from the trading floor would be the ones that would become the most significant. I also never expected to be standing alone in July 2008, exactly a year after my first visit, at the Cartier International Polo, motionless, holding a glass of lukewarm champagne, feeling the prick of tears from behind oversized sunglasses, surrounded by inescapable ghosts.

I hurriedly sipped, breathing and blinking heavily, my eyelashes brushing against the inner lenses of my glasses. I knew that Giles would be here, but I still felt a wave of nausea and became short of breath when my eyes settled on the back of his white linen jacket. He was standing a few feet away, with Allen, an American trader our age, who was once a client of mine, and his girlfriend Cecelia. Every broker hopes to find a client who becomes a good friend, and Allen had quickly become Giles'. We'd easily formed a perfect foursome, attending concerts, dinners and football matches together on a weekly basis. Here they were at the polo, laughing and dancing as we had this time a year ago, but now with two new playmates, while I, the voyeur, watched from the other side of an invisible door to which I no longer held the key.

The night that I was suspended, banned from the trading floor until further notice, Giles became unreachable, cutting the rope and continuing on his way to the summit without me. Weeks later, I received a text: 'so are you really never coming back?' and by that time I wasn't – not to him, not to broking and not to the City. Game over.

Suddenly there was a flick of polished brunette hair and a pair of lithe, tanned arms around my neck: Cecelia. I hadn't noticed that she'd left the group and approached me. We walked over to join the guys. More hugs and kisses were exchanged, but soon everyone else had gone and it was just me, Giles and a bottle of champagne in an ice bucket. This was a scene that I knew so well, and had been a part of on countless occasions when we had lost clients at events or been left to our own devices. Yet now I was just passing through, lodged momentarily between Giles and the ice bucket like a piece of driftwood. We weren't colleagues entertaining clients any more, sharing private jokes and glances; we weren't even old friends sharing a drink; we were simply strangers with a shared history.

'I'm so sorry I wasn't there. I wanted to be. I just couldn't. But I read everything you write.'

His words tumbled out as he poured me a fresh glass of champagne. I was never in any doubt that he had read everything. We were unable to escape each other fully. Fragments of lost friendships lie embedded somewhere within, like minute shards of glass – virtually impossible to remove. Scar tissue forms and the skin heals, but the glass is still there, securely hidden beneath the skin's surface, and every so often it stings. He'd been my one true ally in the City, among the wide-boys, the whores and the coke addicts. He knew me well. And he'd let me down the way only a true friend can.

He introduced me to Pete, his 'very good friend', one of the new playmates, who bumped his way around us with a jug of Pimms.

'Ahh, so you're the new very good friend. Well, I'm Venetia. An ex very good friend of Giles'. Nice to meet you.'

Awkward laughter. Pete smiled sympathetically, with the warmth of someone who knows more about you than you do about them.

'Well, Venetia, he speaks very highly of you.'

He disappeared into the crowd. I turned to Giles. There were questions I'd tried to leave alone for the last six months, hoping that eventually I would no longer need to know the answers. I'd stopped thinking about the Company a long time ago – whether they all hated me, how my ex-colleagues were – but I'd never stopped thinking about Giles' betrayal. Why had he never called me back that night? Why had the only person who could have given me some sort of insight into what was going on at the firm when I was suspended, who could have come around that night and picked me up off the living-room floor, where I'd sat in the dark for hours, simply decided to forget about me?

The rapper Wiley was performing. His lyrics reverberated around the tent.

So what do we do usually drink usually dance usually bubble . . .

'So what the fuck happened?'

I stood staring at him. I wasn't sounding as calm and relaxed as I'd hoped I would. I was suddenly angry again. I thought that enough time had passed for me to forgive him, or at least not to be mad about it any longer.

'Venetia, it wasn't that simple. I knew that you were going to ask me to come to the disciplinary meetings with you. And I didn't think that I'd be able to say no if you asked.'

That's when I start promising the world to a brand new girl I don't even know yet . . .

'One fucking text message or phone call – that's kind of simple. And I never had any intention of asking you to witness the meetings. I didn't need you for anything practical, just a bit of support would have been nice. You were my best friend there. Just admit the fact that you let me down.'

'I know, and I'm sorry.' He grasped hold of my arms. 'V, I was shitting myself. They went through my entire computer, all our conversations over Bloomberg chat, all of our emails.'

His voice was pleading and high-pitched. I didn't know how to respond. I'd been so angry for so long that I had forgotten to think about whether, given the option, I wanted to recover our friendship.

'I had to get a lawyer to look over it all to check I was safe. You have no idea what a tonne of shit you managed to unload on all of us – everyone you ever spoke to. They had all their emails, all their Bloomberg messages checked. It was a fucking mess. They told me that if I spoke to you I would be fired on the spot. I couldn't risk it. You blasted your way out and nearly took us all with you.'

Next thing she's wearing my Rolex . . .

'Oh, come on. They had no access to your mobile. You could have sent one text or made one quick call to tell me what was going on, but you did nothing. And it's fine. It's fucking fine. You were spineless, but it's fine. I had other people to speak to, other friends. My entire family was out of the country, but, you know, I had my friends. People I'm not even that close to stepped up and called me. Clients fucking well called me to check if I was OK and if there was anything that they could do. You didn't, but it's fine. I was fine.'

'I know, but you should have had me. And I know it doesn't really help or count for anything now, but I'm sorry.'

Fine. Of all the words that I could have used, the only one that I managed to spit out was 'fine'. People never mean it when they use the word fine. It never is fine, and they never feel fine. It is perhaps the most misused word in the English language.

What would we do, usually drink, usually dance, usually bubble . . .

I knew he was sorry, but he was right: it didn't really help, and it wasn't fine. I knew that he would've gone out every night as usual, got drunk, got home at 3 a.m., got up at 5.30 a.m. and soon no longer noticed the empty chair where I'd sat or the set of drawers that I'd never had the chance to clear out.

My legacy was pathetic. I'd left behind a company fleece left over from a race meeting at Ascot with dried piccalilli all over one sleeve, two jars of pickled onions – both gifts – a tie and a rugby shirt that were handed out on Charity Day, a box of lapsang souchong, and several plastic dragon toys from Kinder Surprise eggs sitting on the top of my three computer screens. I sometimes wondered what had happened to my sad collection of possessions, and whether the dragons were still silently observing the chaos below.

Despite the fact that it was starting to get dark, I pulled my sunglasses off my head and covered my eyes, turning away from him, and frantically sipped more champagne. The tears were intercepted by the thick, black wraparound frames, but they still found their way onto my cheeks.

'So, everyone definitely hates me then?'

'They just didn't really get it. The whole thing was incomprehensible. They started thinking that maybe you had planned this the entire time.'

'What the fuck?'

'I know – that you were some sort of mole. It's funny that it all started with us just talking about jobs we would rather be doing. No one could have predicted that you'd wind up getting escorted out of the building having been fired for gross misconduct.'

Gross misconduct. We started laughing.

'I've really missed you.'

I rested my chin on his shoulder for a while, gazing out at the mass of unruly emaciated blondes stumbling around the dance floor, steadying themselves on the ice sculpture. Wiley had left the stage and the music had returned to polo-friendly house music.

I knew it was time for me to leave him and return to my table, and to remember that I wasn't here as a broker this time.

I couldn't cling to his shoulder and get wasted, knowing he would always be nearby to peel me off the floor. He had other people to look after, and I was no longer one of them.

Some of the people I'd driven down with that morning had resurfaced, and were sitting at our table, swaying to the music in their chairs. One of the girls was sitting on her boyfriend's lap, laughing and whispering into his ear. I sat down and poured a large shot of vodka from the bottle sitting capless, flanked by two unopened bottles of wine, in the centre of the table. I downed it, quickly poured another one and went to find Greg, who had invited me to the event, and whose date I was supposed to be – although whether it was actually a date or not, I wasn't entirely sure. Considering how long he had been gone, I doubted it. There was no great history between us. He was a broker at another firm whom I'd known when I was in the market and always ran into at market parties. After he heard I'd been fired, we'd gone out for dinner a couple of times.

Now I was bored and stuck in the middle of Windsor Park having to make small talk with Greg's friends while he roamed around the room looking for people he knew. It had been awkward for everyone. I had therefore been hugely relieved to see Giles as I staggered back from a trip to the bar, lost in the dark, but now I had to find my 'date'.

At some point in the last few hours, Greg had apparently managed to drink, and possibly snort, more than anyone else combined. He was now barely able to walk and was flailing maniacally in the middle of the dance floor. Seeing me, he grabbed me by the hand and swung me around, and we danced. He was drunk, I was tear-stained – an unhappy couple lost in a messy tango. Everything was spinning: the smiling faces of people I'd once known – a trader I'd slept with to a Bryan Adams soundtrack (which, along with Kate Bush's *Greatest Hits*, were the only CDs he seemed to own); the guy my friend Lena used to sit next to at her bank – and numerous smiling blondes. I kept thinking that I could see the American, in his uniform of chinos and deck-shoes, lurking in the corner.

Even now, every time I walked down the street or entered a restaurant, I would see someone, and for a few panicked seconds think that it was him. It never was. I hadn't seen him once since describing him as 'my boss, the most hated man in the City', and I probably never would again. He haunted me nevertheless.

When I'd had enough of having my arm pulled from its socket, I went to sit down, leaving Greg to dance with a drunk brunette X-ray in a green silk dress. The tent was suddenly a blur of drunken barefoot girls bumping into each other and men in incomplete suits – shirtless, tieless or both. Bottles of vodka and champagne lay strewn across tables.

I caught sight of Jimmy, whom I'd drunk Cristal with in my second week at the Company. He had been the first broker to take a chance and take me out with his clients. I hadn't seen him since I'd been fired, yet instinctively I got up and went over to him, like a dog hearing its lead jangling. We kissed on the cheek and he introduced me to his wife.

Formalities aside, he was different. He looked at me warily, like a head-shy horse, asking distantly how I was and what I was doing now. His head was at an angle that I'd never previously seen it, set back away from me, his chin firmly pointed upwards. There was none of the conspiratorial leaning in and whispering that there had been when we were out with his clients or at a broker party. Now that I was standing there, I didn't know what else to say. Luckily his wife saw me floundering, and warmly told me that she'd liked my article, making some joke about now knowing what her husband's workplace was really like. We all laughed awkwardly. Jimmy then wished me well and I casually told him to send my love to Dory and the other guys.

Sending love somehow seemed a little pathetic, however much I meant it. As the words came out, I knew that it was far too late. I'd written about their world, their language – a life that I'd only ever been briefly lent. None of it was ever mine to reveal – yet I had, carelessly. Now I was on my own, out at sea, and there was no going back to that strangely comforting trading floor, the lighthouse sitting high above Canary Wharf, with its roars and expletives and its jars of pickled onions. Everything had changed irreversibly. My once familiar role and the people I played alongside had become alien to me. Our paths now had no reason to cross, and I had no right or claim to them or their friendship.

I sat back down and looked around for Giles and the others, but they were gone, so I drank and waited. Then I wandered around in search of food, letting the drunken barefoot girls bump into me. A guy in a suit jacket far too big for him abruptly turned around in front of me, his nose a few inches from mine. I told him that I was hungry, not knowing what else to say and because I was, and he opened his suit jacket and produced a pack of Thornton's toffee cake bars from his inside pocket. He handed me one and asked for my number. It seemed like a fair exchange.

Someone grabbed my hand in the throng as I turned to walk away. It wasn't the cake-bar bearer. Suddenly I was being dragged off by Giles towards the hotdog stand, after a pit-stop for two bottles of water. We stood, crushed against each other in the queue, until finally we were standing by the exit, sharing a Cumberland sausage, my face covered in ketchup and mustard. For a few minutes I forgot about everything that had happened; it was like that blank moment between waking and remembering the events of the night before. Maybe if we were able to break bread together, there was hope.

After a couple of hours of everyone traipsing along carrying their shoes while Greg tried to find a fourteen-foot Hummer in a field, we were on our way home. In the back, everyone was sprawled out fast asleep. I lay in the darkness watching the tree-tops flash past the window, a half-empty carton of Tropicana left over from the morning's breakfast Buck's Fizz sploshing around beside me. The car suddenly came to an abrupt halt. Everyone sat bolt upright to see that the driver had driven straight over a T-junction, very nearly crashing into someone's porch. I lay back down. Greg weakly fumbled for my hand.

I had no idea whereabouts or how far from London we were, but I'd started counting streetlights instead of treetops, and assumed that we were going in the right direction at least. I wasn't tired, despite having got up at eight that morning to get ready and having spent the entire day in the sun, drinking continuously. I couldn't stop thinking about the people I'd bumped into, and I was soon going back over all the things that I might have done differently if I were given the chance again.

I had never really decided to leave the City. Things had spiralled out of control as a result of one email and 1,150 words that I'd written following a particularly bad few weeks. I doubted I would ever have resigned – I would have been leaving a well-paid job, good friends and a lifestyle I would never be able to afford again – yet something had shifted sufficiently to make me write, and the words had come splattering out onto the page with ease. Before I knew it, I was ripped out of the City as unwittingly as I'd stumbled into it, and there was no going back. The trade was done. I'd folded, and no amount of nostalgic encounters with old friends would change that.

CHAPTER 2

RUN LIKE HELL

He who makes a beast of himself gets rid of the
pain of being a man

Samuel Johnson

My alarm sounded, providing a cheerful calypso soundtrack to accompany the beams of blue light emanating from the muted television set. It was 5.45 a.m., Thursday morning. January 2007. I was lying semi-naked on the floor beside my bed, a half-eaten matzo perched atop my right breast, my Chanel handbag lying faithfully at my feet, its contents strewn across the floor. I rolled slowly onto my side and hit snooze on my BlackBerry, waiting for the familiar pounding above my left temple and the waves of nausea to begin, as the cracker crumbled into the stained beige carpet beneath me.

More calypso signalled 6 a.m. I had to get off the floor. I found a three-day-old glass of water above me on my bedside table, downed it along with some painkillers, and pushed myself upright, waiting for my head to settle once again before

making the final effort to get to my feet. More calypso. I somehow made it into the shower and leaned against the wall until
the thick crust of make-up and alcohol from the night before
began to dissolve around me.

It was still dark outside as I flitted along the street, a
drunken moth heading for the comforting glow of Starbucks.
Steadying myself against the counter, I ordered my first double
espresso of the day, and knocked it back before asking for a
skinny cappuccino with three extra shots for the journey.

The barista smirked. 'Ma'am, are you sure? That would
make it a small cappuccino with four shots of espresso. That's
too strong, no?' He chuckled, looking at me in disbelief.

It was 6.30 a.m., I had one of my worst hangovers in recent
weeks and I was late for work; I simply wasn't in the mood to
be told how I wanted my coffee. I felt a surge of rage, making
me want to lean across the counter and grab him by his green
apron before throttling him with it.

'Yes, I know it's strong. Just make the coffee. Please. I don't
feel well and I need you to make this process as pain-free as
possible. Now, how much is it?'

I grabbed a bottle of water, and flailed around looking for
some cash in the bottom of my bag. He eventually handed me
my drink and I continued on my pilgrimage to the Tube station, furious that Starbucks were trying to be prescriptive about
my coffee intake. Maybe I did have a caffeine problem.

As I walked, I attempted to recall the events of the previous
evening – the restaurant, the various wines, the club, then the
inescapable stench of talc and the stripper called Keisha who
studied psychology at Westminster University, and my
pathetic attempts at a normal conversation while she sat next
to me, naked, bored and desperate.

15

It was a routine Tube journey. I focused on the floor and sipped from my bottle of water, the cappuccino long gone, trying not to move my head, while taking deep breaths of the early morning stale air to counteract the nausea. I knew that alcohol was seeping from my pores, and no amount of perfume could disguise it.

I was always glad to reach Canary Wharf without having thrown up or fallen over. The hard part was over. I was awake and had made it to my destination. Now once I'd made it upstairs I could sit in the comfort of my chair, maybe trade something, take my commission and go home at 5 p.m. If the market was quiet, I might even attempt an afternoon nap. Today was going to be fine. My headache had begun to ease. I was still a little drunk and in dire need of my second hit of caffeine and something to mop up the alcohol, but I was ready for work. It was a feeling that I'd grown accustomed to: being vaguely anaesthetized, amused by my own drunkenness, but with an underlying swagger. I was a broker, and however horrific I was feeling I was here to make money.

Different desks employ various tactics at the end of the week to ensure that everyone makes it in to work, whatever state they may be in. At one broking house, there were desks that made whoever was last in pay for steaks to be delivered for the entire desk from Gaucho Grill, even keeping everyone's credit card numbers on file so that if anyone called in sick with a hangover they could still be made to pay. This resulted in most of the desk being in by 6 a.m. just to err on the side of caution. Others made life so difficult for anyone coming in late – by hammering phones on desks, roaring expletives at them and hurling cricket balls at them every time they stood up for the next week – that it simply wasn't worth having a lie-in.

'Nowhere does fucking drip coffee in this fucking town. I only like drip coffee. Do you even know what I mean by drip coffee? Course you don't.' It was the American: *cawfee. faacking*. He was ambling through the foyer. 'You're supposed to open at 7 a.m. You never do. What are you doing cleaning now? Why is there no drip coffee ready?'

He turned around, having lost interest, and was slowly walking towards me, frowning. 'Fucking hell.' It wasn't an invitation to enter into a conversation; it never was. He ambled past, his face fixed somewhere between a scowl and a half smile. He was focused on something in the middle distance, his rucksack slung over his shoulder, his open-necked striped Gant shirt tucked into belted beige chinos. I don't think he even saw me.

He had a strange range of expressions: deranged, furrowed fury, pleasantly surprised for no reason and the inane halfwit smile. This morning had been furrowed fury swiftly followed by deranged when he moved away from the counter. If I didn't know him, I would probably have assumed long ago that he was insane, dangerous or both.

There was no turning around once you were in the lift to the nineteenth floor, unless you wanted to stumble out into the backwater offices of a large British merchant bank that occupied the lower levels. They had a canteen that we would occasionally infiltrate uninvited, but other than that sharing a building was our only common ground. Their employees were never to be seen in the morning, but they could usually be found in the lift en route to their statutory hour-long lunch breaks, frumpily clutching the sad-looking salad boxes from their canteen, mystified by the surrounding hordes of junior brokers struggling under the weight of enough pie and mash to feed their fifteen starving bosses.

You were immediately visible on exiting the lift, with only two thin glass doors standing between you and the trading floor. The latter was split into two, separated by the bank of lifts. One side was slightly smaller than the other, but from the lifts they looked identical, and I always turned the wrong way. The only noticeable difference was the large cupboard on my side that was visible through the glass doors. For weeks I would stand in limbo between the two sides, unsure which way to turn and waiting to see someone I recognized for fear of walking onto the wrong side.

'I don't give a fuck. Tell 'im he's done in ten. Try that again and I'll knock you out, you fat cunt.'

A broker on the CDS desk was standing and gesturing with one of his two uniform standard-issue phones, which we all had, both with inexplicably long cords. He spoke quietly into the other handset, held securely against his left ear the entire time, and paced around the desk, roaming as far as the long cord would let him, anchored like Leviathan. Suddenly he clicked out of the line and furiously hurled the black plastic phone at one of the screens in front of him, knocking someone's collection of toy soldiers and other figurines flying. He kicked his swivel chair and walked off, rolling up his sleeves as he strode, a dark patch of sweat clearly visible against the pale pink of his shirt between his shoulder blades. No one else on his desk looked up.

I stood in the doorway, a few inches from the discarded chair, which had come hurtling towards me. Someone was spraying a can of Lynx, and I was hit by wafts of deodorant, coffee and bacon.

It was 7 a.m. and the trading floor was already groaning under the heaving, testosterone-fuelled mass of several hundred Essex boys shouting a mixture of breakfast orders, greetings and prices. I walked across the room, narrowly dodging a bottle of ketchup being thrown from one desk to another, and made it to the relative safety of my seat next to the American, who was slowly chewing on a bagel and reading the *Wall Street Journal* online, his head cocked to one side holding one of his phones – a pose he often adopted, whether on hold for someone or not. He let out a chuckle all of a sudden. No one reacted.

Dory was squinting at his screens, a cup of tea in his hand, multi-coloured pens lined up and ready to be used. Stu was popping various different vitamins while flicking through the *Sun*, not yet logged into his system, and Wayne was loudly telling no one in particular about his new pool-cleaning mechanism, which had been installed the previous evening. Philippe was on the phone, head down, speaking quietly in French. The Ferg was nowhere to be seen.

I sat down, turned on my computer and took bites of toast while waiting for my three screens to start lighting up. I logged into Bloomberg, checking any emails that had come in overnight. An instant message window popped open: it was Lena, my best friend, who was a trader at a large European bank. Instant Bloomberg (IB) was a window that would stay open from 7 a.m. until I left at 5 p.m. – it was our lifeline. Knowing that she was at the other end of a Bloomberg terminal somehow made the job easier. When I sat, tears streaming down my face after being yelled at by the American or some client, I was able to focus on the small instant messenger box in front of me and type 'kunt' (with a 'c', the message bounced back unsent with a helpful reminder that it was inappropriate) as many times as I needed to, or at least until the anger passed and I could face the American again without the risk of bursting into tears.

> 07:11:35 LENA KLEIN: urrgh. Kunting hell today is already fuct. Morning meeting total fucking disaster. Stuttered all over the top line like a mong.
> 07:15:25 VENETIA THOMPSON: 2 secs. Need to print off price sheets. And get coffee. URGH.

At some point over the last couple of months, I had stopped flinching every time the phone rang or a trader's voice shouted down the 'squawk box' that was used primarily for all communication between us and them. I now took my suit jacket off as soon as I sat down to avoid sweating in endless layers of clothing, terrified of undoing a button or moving. The weeks of hurriedly gulping down mouthfuls of cereal when it was too early to be hungry and doing my make-up in semi-darkness at my flat had passed; now most mornings I waited in line with the other hungover brokers in Birley's Sandwiches for my Marmite on granary, my make-up was often done on the Tube, and my heels were kept under my desk. The transformation was complete. As for when I would resign, how long it would take for me to give up and go home? All bets were off. The probationary period was over. I'd casually slipped down the death-slide, and was lying in an alcohol-sodden mess at the bottom along with every other broker in the City. Yet the noise, sweat and panic of that first day never really left me.

I had stepped out of the lift wearing the same skirt suit that I'd worn during the job interview, wishing I'd at least firmly established in my head what a bond was. I made my way onto the trading floor, fighting my way through the endless clusters of new faces, avoiding eye contact, trying to look nonchalant, unimpressed by the view from the nineteenth floor.

That first morning when I reached the high yield desk – identifiable only by the piece of laminated white card suspended from the ceiling that read 'X-Over, HY' – there was nowhere for me to sit. I stood awkwardly, shaking various hands and introducing myself, as someone was sent to find a chair. He reappeared, all teenage skin, spiked blond hair and striped purple shirt, pushing one along between the two clusters of desks, apologizing for the Arsenal stickers on the back. He was a Spurs fan.

My skirt kept rising up, and every time I walked the slit in the back would make its way round to the side. I knew that hundreds of pairs of eyes were on me, looking up from their desks, from their morning calls, watching me awkwardly pulling at my suit, my cheeks moist with sweat. My hair was pulled into a ponytail so tightly that it was starting to hurt; the loose strands at the front were sprayed back with hairspray and secured with grips that seemed to be pressing into my scalp harder and harder. I imagined that they were all wondering why I hadn't taken my jacket off: 'She must be so uncomfortable, so hot under that suit – another awkward-looking bird who won't last five seconds.' I sat down.

'So where you from? This your first job? Why you here if you been uni? Devon? That ain't in Essex! How long'd it take you from Chelsea this morning then, eh? Posh are ya? Hard getting up? Watch out for the Ferg over there – 'e'll nick your phone. Don't you mean rape 'er?! Shut it, it's 'er first day. Sorry 'bout 'im, darling, he doesn't get to speak to women often, you

21

know? Last bird that sat where you are now lasted less than a week. You ever been down Faces? Been Southend? You don't want to, love, trust me.'

The onslaught had begun. I answered as many of the questions as I could, my neck craning in different directions to see who was asking what. Everyone was speaking at the same time, some from the other side of the floor. Then suddenly there would be a wave of commotion, and their focus would immediately shift to their screens, phones and each other. Numbers and fractions were being shouted out. 'It's going up at 8 and a quarter. At 9. Losing my offer.' People stood up as the crescendo increased. I could hear other mystery gruff voices coming from somewhere down a speaker. Half an hour must have gone by. Then something shifted. Voices became more urgent. 'Fucking hell. It's all fucking kicking off again. WATCH YOUR BIDS. CROSS IS GOING WIDER. TAKE MY FUCKING BID OUT. HIT ANYTHING YOU CAN.' I disappeared into obscurity for a few minutes, gasping for air. Then the wave would pass and all eyes were back on me. This cycle continued throughout my first few days, interrupted only by lunch and the rare moments the American decided to try to explain something to me, scribbling doodles on scraps of paper before resorting to telling me to get myself a dictionary of financial terms.

The floor was treacherous. Avoiding incoming missiles in the shape of half-eaten apples, cricket balls or empty bottles of water was as commonplace as the tea run. I would usually duck unnecessarily, as whatever object was hurled at me merely slapped against the back of my chair, but my reaction would be as eagerly devoured as a delivery of pies.

'It was 'im love. That nasty French fucker over there – see

'im? With the glasses. Sort 'im out. Go on.' The first time this had happened, I'd beckoned the said Frenchman over, waving his ball in the air flirtatiously, and made him walk across the floor to apologize. I felt myself tighten like a slingshot ready to fire. He had crouched down beside my chair, whispering that it wasn't him and he was terribly sorry. I'd smiled down at him and refused to give his ball back. Cheers and roars from the entire floor. It had been my first test, and as the guys left that evening, I felt a hand on my shoulder and heard the congratulatory words, 'Nice one, love – you handled that well, darlin'.' It was my first hit of that self-satisfied, smug pride that comes from being accepted. I'd wrung the neck of my first goose.

Acceptance always comes at a price, however, and nothing on a trading floor is ever quite what it seems. I later learned that it was never the quiet Frenchman with the glasses who sat on the new-issues desk who threw things. People just didn't like him, or his choice of jumpers, and he was therefore used as a scapegoat whenever possible. In the morning, he was frequently greeted by the growling chorus, 'TAKE IT OFF, TAKE IT OFFFFFFFF, TAKE IT OFFFFFF, YOU FRENCH CUNT', while phones were hammered on desks. Even the mystery voices joined in, the volume on the speakers turned right up.

Lena had warned me that, unlike in a bank, where I would be expected to complete a training scheme, on a broking floor the emphasis was on picking it up as you went along. The American had simply told me to write down everything I didn't understand and to ask him about it during a quiet moment, and to keep asking him until I understood. While this exercise worked in theory, nothing ever had a short answer and sifting through his complex theoretical explanations in order to pull together something succinct and memorable proved to be exhausting. It was often quicker to ask Lena over Instant Bloomberg. She could type an answer before the American had even begun explaining, and I would be able to refer to it later if I forgot immediately, which was likely.

I'd managed to establish that there was a basic pattern underlying the chaos around me. The phone would ring, or someone would shout down the squawk box and be answered by one of the guys. They would have a conversation, say nothing or merely 'sure, what size?' or 'gotcha' or 'yep', before hanging up and shouting out a number, usually in the 90s followed by a fraction, and then either the words 'bid' or 'offered' or sometimes just preceded by 'at'. Everyone else would then repeat the same number, clicking into various lines, making calls and giving the price to someone, somewhere.

Things then got confusing. Someone on the desk would usually respond with a different number, in response to the first figure. They would then have to wait for a response from the broker who had shouted out the first number. The response would be either another slightly different number or simply 'repeat'. This information would then be relayed back, before someone shouted either 'repeat', yet another number or 'work' and everyone on the desk then started shouting out the 'market' – the two different numbers in quick succession – down their phone lines. The numbers being yelled out were all prices at which traders would either buy or sell. To get a market going, you needed a buyer and a seller or several buyers and several sellers. My training consisted of passing comments in the midst of prices flying around, angry rants and tips over drinks after work.

'In a nutshell, a bid is when I want to fucking buy something and an offer is when I want to sell. If I say "mine", I want to buy; if I say "yours", I want to sell. You hit bids and lift offers. Don't ever fucking confuse any of these words. If you don't know, ask, and write down everything you hear.'

Nothing made any sense. I permanently had the expression of a dog being yelled at by its owner, failing to comprehend anything but knowing it has probably done something wrong. All I could do was sit still and wait for whoever was yelling to get distracted by something more important.

Thankfully, I was only allowed to pick up calls and pass them over to the American. It was when he was on a call and couldn't pick up that things became more complicated. He would make frantic hand gestures signalling that he wanted me to keep them on the line, get rid of them or take a message and relay it, but the various signals were often indistinguishable, which meant that I usually kept his gardener on the line but hung up on the head trader at Aggro Bank. Every time I picked up a call I prayed it wouldn't be someone saying a number, because I would have no idea what that number meant, what it related to or who was on the other end of the phone. For the time being, I was perfectly happy to remain a glorified secretary and avoid all interaction with fractions and decimals.

In addition to the hand gestures and an entirely new language that had to be learned, I was quickly realizing that I would need to work on my numeracy. The grade C I got in GCSE maths hadn't exactly left me in good stead for my new career. Numbers bored me. I had begun struggling in primary school to the extent that I had to get an after-school tutor for fear that I would fail entrance exams to whatever grammar or private school I might be sent. It was a constant source of amusement to my teachers that a pupil so capable when it came to English literature and languages was so mathematically challenged. As I got older and my GCSE exams approached, I once again found myself in the hands of a tutor, when the head of maths realized that I was going to fail the paper unless he intervened. I couldn't be the straight-A student who somehow managed to fail maths; it would be embarrassing for everyone.

My parents blamed glandular fever: I'd been out of action for months aged fourteen and missed most of the syllabus, and I was simply having difficulty catching up. This, of course, was bollocks; I just couldn't do it. When they try to read, dyslexics often speak of letters dancing around, rearranging themselves or changing colour. I experienced the same sensation with numbers; they jumped around on the page in front of me until I lost all interest and closed the book. I liked words. I was safe with words. I was able to write essays on any subject in various languages, but when it came to balancing an equation, I would have a panic attack.

Given my ugly history with numbers, choosing to embark upon a career in the City was perhaps unwise. I had never previously expressed any interest in pursuing a career in finance, and had even been put off law by someone mentioning the need for some sort of basic mathematical ability in order to pass the Legal Practice Course. Now here I was, becoming increasingly aware that I'd accepted a job that was largely based on numbers. It was career suicide.

Lena always maintained that maths weren't really involved in broking or trading; it all just came down to common sense and being able to think quickly. She dismissed my concerns about my mathematical shortcomings as ridiculous and was certain that I had nothing to worry about – but she had studied physics at Cambridge.

The night before my first day as a trainee broker, we met up at a sushi restaurant around the corner from her office, ostensibly to prep me with the basics of broking before I went anywhere near a trading floor. She had frantically scribbled notes on a couple of sheets of paper trying to explain what broking actually entailed, because I was still entirely unaware, even after various interviews.

'Look, it's easy. Say I'm your client. I ring you, say a name of a bond, or whatever the hell the guys on your desk actually trade, and then say a number, then the words "bid" or "offered". Or occasionally I might say "at" and then a number. This is the same as saying "offered". Those are the only words you really need to understand.'

I was already lost, but she continued, occasionally manhandling jewels of sashimi into her mouth.

'So, let's say I trade in Camembert. I want to buy some that's been aged three years that I can't get hold of through any other means. I ring a broker, that's you, and say "Camembert, three year. 98 bid", meaning I'll pay 98 for it. Now let's say Camembert usually trades in units of two million. So imagine two million whole cheeses. I will pay 98 cents on the dollar, or whatever currency it happens to be trading in – let's say the euro, as that makes more sense – for each one of those cheeses. The cheese might actually be worth 101 or 89 – whatever – it doesn't matter. Your job is just to take the price, and then work it around.'

She overdid the wasabi and started coughing, frantically downing beer.

'You following?'

'Vaguely. Can you even get three-year-old Camembert?'

'Just humour me. OK, so we have a 98 bid from me for two million Camembert cheeses. You now need to find a seller of Camembert, 'cos you can't trade without a buyer and a seller.

So off you go and ring around all your other clients to try and find me a seller. You hopefully find someone that will say "at 100" or "at par", as is sometimes said. You say "thanks" then ring me back and say, "Lena, I have a 100 offer in Camembert three year." I will then either improve my bid or say "repeat". If I say repeat, you scuttle off back to your seller and say "they're repeating". NEVER give away that I am female. Never say *"she's* repeating" as it will immediately reveal who I am, as there are so few birds in the cheese market.'

'Why does it matter if they know who you are?'

'Because they might not like me or my bank, because I don't want them knowing that I own any Camembert, because this information can be used against me. They're competition. Loads of reasons. It doesn't matter to you because you're a broker. It's just all about creating a safe environment for traders to do business in where nobody finds out who owns or wants what. Think of the Street as a financial *Eyes Wide Shut* party . . . you can have the filthiest sex ever and no one will know because you're wearing a mask.

'Anyway, let's say that I just repeat my bid. You then get the offer to repeat and check if everyone is happy for the market to be "worked". So I'll usually say "repeat and spin", and off my bookie will go to work the market around everyone else to see if the market can be narrowed. Often, if a trader sees a wide market they might tighten it, meaning less of a giant gap between bid and offer. The tighter a market gets, the closer you are to trading.'

I was still lost. She was speaking about it all so naturally, like she was speaking about the weather or a pair of shoes she liked. I wondered if I would ever get to that stage when speaking about trading became second nature.

'Now what happens after you trade the Camembert? Do you care how much that three-year-old Camembert is going to earn the owner? Do you care how much of a life it has left? Is it on the verge of being inedible? No. You don't care. You're a bookie: you are simply there to act as a middleman. It's my job as a trader to worry about everything else. You just take your commission and move on to the next trade. It's fucking easy.

'It doesn't matter whether you're trading cheese, cheese containers, bonds, kangaroos, houses, tuna, whatever, it's all the same shit. Just take the prices, narrow them down, trade and take your commission. And then take your clients out for dinner a lot. That's all broking is. Trust me, V, it'll be easy. You have nothing to worry about. You just need to be aggressive and tough as fuck, which you are. Just don't take any shit. Now let's go to salsa.'

That night I arrived home certain that it would be easy, certain that Lena was right, that I was perfect for the job and would love it. It had all seemed so exciting when I used to bump into her at salsa clubs during my final year at university and hear about her trading exploits, and I had soon decided that I wanted that lifestyle: the crazy hours, the adrenalin and of course, the money. I'd thought that because we were so similar – both blonde, both a bit ball-busting – that I would instantly take to it, but when I had actually started broking, everything had turned out to be far more complicated. I sat, in stunned silence, hearing numbers and words, unable to work out which was the bid, which was the offer and which was the cheese. There was so much going on at the same time that there was no analogy that could possibly be of any use, and I had totally lost my nerve.

I knew that everything had a price. Bonds, loans, CDS

(whatever the hell that was) and other random financial instruments would all have a level at which they could be bought or sold, unless they were worthless and untouchable. This level could change, much like the price of milk or exchange rates on currencies. Beyond this, I didn't have a clue.

My lack of understanding of the financial markets or basic economic theory notwithstanding, I wasn't even sure of basic fractions: whether 3/8 was more or less than 1/4, whether 11/16 was more or less than 1/2, or whether 7/8 was the same as 15/16. The idea that I would soon have to move seamlessly between fractions and decimals left me permanently in a state of panic. It was all very well neatly writing down the price next to the name of the bond on a sheet of paper, but if anyone had asked me what that price actually meant I'd have no idea.

Writing out all my fractions on a table that I kept in front of me at all times seemed like a good place to start. It would enable me to see instantly what a trader meant when he said, 'I'd trade in the middle' or at 'three eighths plus', or more simply to know which number was greater than another.

A 'plus' was loosely a sixteenth on our desk. Historically, it apparently had meant something else, but when Wayne, Stu, the American and Dory had all tried explaining at the same time, it had been impossible to understand a word anyone was saying. I had swallowed hard, on the verge of bursting into tears, and asked Lena to explain, but because she didn't trade in sixteenths (the bonds she traded were quoted in generally much smaller denominations), a 'plus' was as alien to her as it was to me.

I eventually established that because sixteenths were impossible to shout out with any urgency and without stumbling over the length of the word, we used 'plus' to indicate a sixteenth on top of whatever number we'd managed to reach. On high yield bonds and loans nothing ever traded in anything smaller than sixteenths, so my table covered all eventualities involving 'plus' and showed what the equivalent decimals and fractions were.

Whenever the American was bored, he would embark on a round of quick-fire fraction testing. We never shouted prices in decimals, only entered them into the computerized system in decimals, but it was still important to know in case there was ever any confusion about the dreaded 'plus'. Spot testing had been my greatest fear during school maths lessons. I spent the entire time keeping my head down and eyes tightly screwed up, praying the teacher couldn't see me. It never worked. I always got the answer completely wrong and the rest of the class would collapse into giggles. Now I was sitting next to a new, even scarier Quiz Master: the American. The tests went something like this:

Him: 5/8+?
Fuck, fuck, fuck, fuck, fuck.
Me: 0.6875 or 11/16
Him: 7/8+?
Argh, fuck, fuck, fuck, fuck.
Me: 0.9375 or . . . Errr. Fucking hell. 15/16.

'Fuck, fuck, fuck' had become my inner monologue, and it seemed to be permanently on loop. I used to hear whatever song I'd last heard in a shop or on the radio, but since starting work on the trading floor all I heard was an endless stream of obscenities. Every time the phone rang or someone said my name, all I would be thinking was 'fuck, fuck, fuck'. But I was, luckily, in one of the few jobs where swearing was expected.

While it's possible to rely on nothing but banter and a winning phone manner for a while, I knew that I would eventually come unstuck. When a trader told you he'd 'meet in the middle', meaning he would buy or sell at whatever figure was halfway between his current bid or offer and whoever was on the other side of the trade's price, you had to know immediately where the middle was, and that might well be halfway between 3/4 and 7/8+. There was never time for a calculator – not that a calculator would have been of much use as traders always expect to hear prices in fractions. Shouting out 'offered at 98 spot 875' instead of '98 and 7/8 plus' was as good as shouting out 'spot the fucking retard newbie'.

My survival as a broker came down to a few very basic elements: not fucking up my fractions, knowing when one number was higher than another, knowing the difference between a bid and an offer, and remembering to run like hell when I did my first trade and complete a lap of the trading floor – an old tradition. Fortunately, I had been warned by one of the sterling boys that when I eventually traded I should set off running immediately, before anyone had the chance to arm themselves with bottles of water and anything else they could get their hands on. This would limit how drenched I got.

When the day finally arrived, purely as a result of the fact that the American was out of the office and I had been left to cover all of his clients, I braced myself for the requisite soaking. I'd been sending out prices over Bloomberg without really thinking anything was going to happen, when I was suddenly hit by a trader in New York, who sent a Bloomberg message simply reading 'SOLD TO U' in reply to the bid I'd sent him five minutes earlier. With Dory's help, I managed to confirm the trade with the buyer and the seller, then immediately got up, making sure my four-inch heels were secured, all before anyone other than Dory and the Ferg had realized I'd traded.

Within seconds the floor had erupted. I was running, hair and shirt flying behind me, to the sound of hundreds of phones being hammered on desks; water was coming at me from all angles, along with missiles in the form of empty bottles and pens, and everyone was roaring. I'd stumbled into and was now bolting around the school playground at an East End comprehensive, wearing stilettos, and there was no head teacher on patrol – just dozens of men in their thirties and forties, throwing things at me, all the while trading millions of bonds. If I'd known I was going to do my first trade, I'd have worn a sports bra.

My elation was short-lived. I got back to my desk to find I'd also been hit in something else. Dory immediately realized that something was up – it was an obscure bank loan that hadn't traded for months. For a bid to be hit out of the blue meant one of two things: I'd either sent out an incorrect price that was too good to ignore, or my buyer had mispriced it. It quickly emerged that I had typed 96 instead of 95 – a whole point out. My heart was racing from my lap around the floor, and I immediately began to panic. I had no idea how much this was going to cost the desk.

'Neesh, you gotta immediately retract that Bloomie.'

'Retract? How?'

Dory ran around the desk and was leaning over my shoulder typing in a combination of characters that was the Bloomberg code for retracting a message.

'OK, now message the seller immediately saying it was a typo. He couldn't honestly have thought that was the correct price as it was a point out.'

I sent a grovelling message and one came flying back saying 'fine'. I was just starting to calm down again when a call came in.

'Neesh, line 2.'

'Yeah, Venetia?'

Someone was growling my name at the end of the line. It was the guy who had hit my incorrect bid. 'Listen, I understand everyone makes mistakes, and I know you're new to this, but you can't just whack out a Bloomberg telling me the price was wrong. You should have followed up with a call immediately. It's just good manners. Don't let it happen again or we will have a very short-lived trading relationship.' The line went dead. I couldn't believe he had hung up without giving me a chance to apologize again or explain.

'What was that about? Angry seller by any chance?'

Dory was chuckling.

'Just forget about him, he'll calm down. He's always been a grump. It's a fine line between success and disaster in this business. You just gotta roll with the punches. At least we didn't have to buy our way out of the trade.'

This wasn't fun. I was embarrassed, furious with myself and smarting from being told off by a trader for the first time. I couldn't believe I'd made such a stupid mistake and so soon after I'd finally made some money for the desk. The American was bound to be furious that I'd pissed off one of his biggest clients. All the surrounding desks had seen my fuck-up and were bound to keep reminding me about it. I wanted to resign immediately.

'Venetia. Pick me up a sec.'

I jolted upright, reminiscing over, relieved that I would never have to endure those first few weeks again, alcohol still surging around my body. I finished my toast, rolled the grease-proof paper it had come in into a ball and hurled it at the Ferg. I smiled, watching it bounce off the top of his head as I picked up the mystery voice. The ball of paper came flying back at me.

'What you got going on in Tylomed?'

'Jack shit. You wanna start something?'

What the fuck was Tylomed? I hurriedly checked the spread-sheet in front of me that had the last bids and offers we'd seen in all the bonds and loans we traded; it was often my only means of survival.

'Last saw it offered around 99 weeks ago,' I said.

'Stick a par offer out there and see what comes back. I've obviously got room but just see if there's any interest.'

'Tylomed Bs at par.'

'What account, Neesh?'

'Account 9.'

All banks were referred to by numbers, a code that only our desk knew, which meant that if someone were on the phone to another client they wouldn't know whose price was being yelled out if they happened to overhear us.

07:30:20 LENA KLEIN: so who were you out with last
    night?

07.52:19 VENETIA THOMPSON: sorry just faded out for a
    second. God knows. Someone's clients. Coulda been
    anyone.

07:53:48 VENETIA THOMPSON: I was too fukked by 9 to
    know. Was out with some guys from here after work
    and one thing led to another. I'm never getting that
    wasted again on a thurs night.

07:54:38 VENETIA THOMPSON: what's happening out
there? Busy?

07:55:22 LENA KLEIN: nah, just my Icelandics shatting
themselves, as ever. Need breakie. Hank. Want poached
eggs.

07:56:21 VENETIA THOMPSON: yum. Send someone to
retrieve? Be back in a sec, coffee not strong enough.

We wasted hours every day discussing what we were going to
have for breakfast, what we ended up having, what we were
going to have for lunch and then moaned about being hungry
all afternoon. We weren't the only ones. Most brokers started
planning what they were going to have for lunch as soon as the
mid-morning slump set in, when traders disappeared into
meetings and everything calmed down before kicking off again
at midday.

I'd always thought that trading was constantly, unerringly
fast-paced, but in fact there were prolonged periods of total
inactivity when everyone sat around doing nothing, reading
the paper or talking inane nonsense to no one in particular. It
could be the most boring job in the world when the market was
quiet. Topics of conversation among brokers could be divided
into four: football, loosely news-based trivia, food and home
improvements. There would always be someone somewhere
on the floor talking about BBQs, swimming pools, an animal
that saved its owner's life or Spurs' latest signing.

It was comforting to be surrounded by constant noise. I'd
always hated silence – ever since I'd lived in a barn conversion
in the middle of nowhere in South Devon as a child. There was
never any noise at night, apart from the occasional owl letting
out a screech, and I spent hours lying wide awake, my body

rigid, convinced someone was creeping through the fields into our garden, or worrying about what would happen to me if my parents died. I could only ever get to sleep if I left all the adjoining doors open and could therefore hear my parents clearing up in the kitchen or the television in the living room. I needed background noise to feel safe, and the countryside was always too quiet: the trading floor was bliss.

CHAPTER 3

CONTENTMENT

Amid the fuck-ups and the drunken nights, Christmas and New Year's Eve had come and gone unnoticed. The few days I'd spent in Devon and the usual festive fun to be had with my divorced parents were long forgotten, and I was hurtling towards February.

My first few months in the job had passed quickly, and the early starts were beginning to become routine rather than a daily shock to my system. My intake of caffeine was increasing, I had put on half a stone, and I had discovered a new capacity for falling asleep anywhere and at any time, but otherwise little had changed.

I was perhaps the closest I'd ever been to feeling content. People always seem to strive for happiness, but feeling content seems to be a more achievable goal. One of my exes, whose mother was a crack whore and brothers were all in jail, and who had somehow fought his way through med school and become a doctor regardless, had always maintained that he just wanted to be content. Perhaps he knew that he would never be happy, so contentment was the next best thing. He always told me he felt content when he was asleep next to me, but we never managed to achieve that state when we were both awake. We had simultaneous orgasms, but never simultaneous contentment.

For the first time, I could tick the various boxes we use to evaluate our lives: I had a new happy boyfriend, Mark, whom I'd started seeing just before I had taken the job, a nice flat-share, good friends and the beginnings of a career. It was the twenty-something graduate dream – on crack.

'Anything? Come on, find me a bid.'

Someone was yelling for me. At first all traders sound the same. Some grunt down the open wire; others shout your name if they can remember it, otherwise they resort to a mere 'yeah'. Their tone is rarely other than one of general annoyance that you, Broker Scum, have deigned to bother them when they are busy trying to send out prices to their own clients, yelling at their sales teams or trying to eat breakfast uninterrupted.

The American believed in perseverance, whatever the situation. He was frequently told by clients to fuck off, and never to call on the outside line (the trader's private line) with prices but to send Bloomberg messages instead. That way, if on rare occasions he did call on the outside, they would know that he had vital information and was worth speaking to. Calling on the outside is something usually reserved for traders' families, their favourite hedge funders, maybe a couple of their sales team and emergencies. Squawk boxes were for brokers, where they could be ignored or listened to at will, their volume turned up or down as desired like a public radio broadcast.

Along with their two phones, and maybe a headset and a

microphone, depending on preference, every broker had a squawk box, aka the 'hoot and holler' or dealer board in front of them. This was a large black plastic switchboard, with speakers built in at the sides, and buttons that could be pressed in order to 'click into a line' and be heard instantly by different clients, who were traders at various banks. The clients could choose whether to pick up the line and speak to you or to hear whatever price was being shouted and ignore you if they weren't interested. There was also a contact list, and further buttons that would speed-dial the traders' traditional phone line – their 'outside' lines.

Despite all traders preferring Bloomberg messages or a 'shout down the line', the American insisted on calling on the outside, attempting to have conversations to extract colour or, as he liked to put it, get traders to 'throw him a bone' just to get rid of him. He also fervently believed that shouting out prices on an open wire was a mistake, as other brokers might over-hear your prices if they happened to be speaking to the trader at that moment, and you had no way of guaranteeing whether the trader had heard your price. He spent much of my first few months attempting to instil this tactic in me: I should con-stantly be calling, never shouting blindly down an open wire, but if I had to, always to wait for them to pick up first before giving a price. His emphasis was on having conversations to try to find out what bonds or loans they cared about that day, even if I didn't manage to get any actual prices.

It was brutal cold calling, made worse by my suspicion that he had given me a couple of clients to harass who hated him and the Company and had brokers at other firms who were god-parents to their children and would therefore not respond well to being bothered by the new girl first thing in the morning.

The scale of responses and the tone of voice in which they were said varied considerably. They ranged from polite to funny, and to the very rude:

'Vanessa? Is that your name? I'm still drinking my morning coffee. Don't bother me when I have a coffee in my hand. How do you know if I have a coffee in my hand? Just always assume I do.'

'Still busy.'

'What the fuck do you want now?'

'I don't fucking trade chemicals. Why the fuck would I want to hear that price or "get involved"? Do you even know what it is to get involved?'

'Yeah, try me again when you guys aren't totally behind the rest of the market. It's offered two points lower away from you.'

'Who is this and why are you shouting my name?'

'Sorry, not right now.'

'Nothing to do. That bond is a piece of shit.'

'Do I care? No, I fucking don't.'

'Go away.'

'What is it now?'

'Thanks. Now stop.'

Inter-dealer brokers, or simply 'brokers', are at the bottom of the food chain. They are the frontline of the Street – the name given to the secondary market, where previously issued bonds, loans, stocks, options and countless other financial instruments are bought and sold between banks. Their job is to take prices from buyers and sellers, narrow down the price, and eventually get to a level where the product will trade. This process can happen within seconds or over the course of weeks, depending on the instrument being traded and the market, but the idea is that the secondary market always remains liquid, and buying and selling happens regularly and quickly through brokers, who take commission on every trade and provide a smoke-screen – on most products buyers and sellers never know who their counterparty is.

The Street provides the lifeblood of the capital market, and if it slows down and liquidity dries up, so does the primary market – deals get stuck on balance sheets, investors are slow coming forward and banks lose money. It is a fiercely compet-itive and often entirely commission-based business, and a trader's relationship with his or her 'bookie', as most of the market refer to inter-dealer brokers, is therefore eternally frag-ile. If a broker isn't providing a good enough service, there are dozens of others waiting to take over, and traders always have several brokers they trade through.

No broker is ever safe from having his or her line 'pulled'; this occurs when traders decide that for an often indefinite period they do not want to hear from you under any circum-stances and remove you from the board of flashing lights in front of them. It might be for a couple of hours or, in some cases, forever. You can no longer be heard and therefore don't exist. A trader will pull a line for any number of reasons. Traditionally, it will be because there has been a monumental fuck-up – a broker might have tried to be a little bit too clever, a bit too greedy and the trader has found out; or the trader might just suspect that he has, and paranoia will take hold.

One guy had his line pulled because he couldn't get the trader tickets to some film premiere the trader had decided he wanted to attend. Interestingly, it was the very same trader who was the first to call me a cunt and mean it. He'd moved around so many different banks and so many different products that most bookies had experienced his horrific behaviour and he had a lot of enemies – people just waiting for an opportunity to shaft him when he least expected it. He had all the characteristics found in most traders to a certain degree, but in his case they were present in abundance: paranoia, arrogance and aggression, but with an added hefty slosh of malice, which was what separated him from the others.

Most traders are not intrinsically bad guys. They won't go out of their way to 'hook' their brokers. This happens when the broker ends up taking a hit, having got caught in the middle of a trade, usually having lost a bid or an offer, and therefore has to step in as buyer or seller themselves as opposed to being merely the middleman, and it usually costs the desk a lot of money. But some people in the market go out of their way to hook bookies because it's good sport – probably the same guys who enjoyed burning the backs off woodlice as children.

Genuine mistakes happen, but most can be avoided if the desk works well together and deals with any problems that occur as quickly as possible. If someone loses a bid, whoever has the seller needs to know immediately in case the trader tries smashing the hell out of the bid the next second. Of course this isn't helped by the fact that it is standard broker practice to make up prices to get things moving, especially during quiet patches or first thing in the morning. Some shops (broking houses) were more prone to sending out runs of mythical prices than others. Making up a price is dangerous. You have to know where a market is and be sure that nothing has changed overnight, such as the company whose bonds you're whacking a value on hasn't revealed unexpected financial results that may have made the bond or loan worthless. As a senior broker at my firm once remarked to me, 'Your average bookie doesn't even know what sector the bond he'll make up a price for belongs to.'

There are too many brokers. For every trader, there are at least a handful of bookies clamouring for his business. Yet among the hordes of lazy, ineffective, overpaid City boys – the decidedly average bookies – there are the exceptional ones, the mystical Big Swinging Dicks. These are scarce, but their presence is always felt, and everyone wants to be one, be covered by one or be married to one. The Titans of the market were a mixed bag of ex-traders, ex-gangsters and ex-barrow boys. Jon Markham was one of them – which category he fit into was debatable, for his inscrutability was as famed as his love of gambling.

No one knew much about Jon other than he was one of the guys who didn't really need to work; he could cherry-pick whom he wanted to cover, pass off anyone he had neither the time nor inclination to be bothered with to his team of juniors and, like the House, he always won. Jon Markham looked like a High Street bank manager, but was a professional gambler, among other things. He cared about horses, bonds and golf. He could read the market instinctively and knew all of his customers' books so intimately that he could predict what they needed to shift or buy. He was so ahead of the market that he effectively could control his small part of it. No trader could afford to have him offside, and no one had ever pulled a line on him – at least, not in the last decade. Having the monopoly on a particular market meant that he could also charge whatever he wanted in brokerage. If traders wanted his prices, which were always the best in the Street, then they had to pay up. As one of the biggest earners at his firm (taking home in the region of 2 million sterling a year), the fact that he often had more than the odd position running for longer than it should have been was ignored. He was given carte blanche because his firm couldn't afford to lose him to a competitor.

This time when the roulette wheel had spun, it had landed on Lena. She'd inherited a book, and with it came Jon. She waited for his call. She had heard about his techniques for broking new traders. For the first couple of weeks he would ensure that anything that she wanted to buy or sell miraculously took place at the price she wanted. He was known to give new clients his undivided attention for a short intense period, to give them a taste of how it felt to be covered by the best bookie in the Street, then he would slowly ease off, like a bored lover looking for fresh untapped skin, and the trader would be left hanging, waiting to hear his voice down the line again.

It had been a slow morning; I desperately needed adrenalin. There were no phones ringing, no prices coming in – nothing. I had been staring blankly at the *Financial Times* online for the last hour, lost in my hangover.

Before I started getting up at 5.45 a.m., having had only a couple of hours' sleep, I had no idea what it meant to be truly tired. The mammoth effort it took every day to get out of bed and somehow keep my eyes open until I got safely back home at around 5 p.m. was something that I couldn't have imagined.

Staying awake is not an activity I would previously have associated with such extreme pain – when everything in your brain is urging your eyes to shut, just for a few minutes, and the only thing stopping you is a mixture of pre-emptive panic, the strange pain in your solar plexus and the inescapable fear that something bad is about to happen and it will be your fault for having your fucking eyes shut or not paying attention. Sleep deprivation on a trading floor is an underrated form of torture.

It was that feeling of impending doom and nervous expectation that not only kept me awake, but kept me coming back for more. Broking seemed to be nothing more than a giant game of Russian roulette, and survival came down to keeping your nerve while simultaneously developing a thick enough skin to repel even the most silvered of bullets as and when they were fired.

Fridays were always fairly quiet. Half the market would be struggling with hangovers or in meetings until lunchtime, when there was always a chance New York would wake up and want to get stuff done before disappearing to the Hamptons for the weekend.

Mark texted. He was reminding me about his gig later. All I wanted to do was go home straight after work and sleep. Fridays were no longer the big nights out they had once been – they now meant takeaway in front of the TV. I would be lucky to make it through the six o'clock news before passing out. It took all the energy I had to change my duvet cover, and having once fallen asleep inside it, I no longer attempted to do it in the evenings after work.

I'd fallen asleep everywhere: on the Tube, ending up in West Hampstead, having sailed on north and entirely missed my change at Green Park, and in Stratford on my way to work; in bars and clubs at the weekends with friends; in the bath; in taxis; and, most regularly, on Mark's shoulder. Because we got together just as I started broking, he had never known anything different – his girlfriend was a narcoleptic. He would come over to my flat to watch TV and have dinner together only to find me out cold on the sofa, so he'd have to spend the evening chatting to my flatmate. There was a decreasingly small window of time when I was able to remain lucid after I got home. I had to take my suit off immediately, otherwise I risked falling asleep wearing it, and then I had to avoid sitting down for as long as possible. I could currently manage about an hour before I was dribbling on whatever my head was resting on.

Mark was a bass player in a rock band, and spent his days attempting to get the band more gigs and writing songs. I wasn't entirely sure how he had enough money to live, but he somehow managed to get by and seemed content with his situation. He was an antidote to the adrenalin-fuelled frenzy I'd spend the rest of the week sweating my way through, and where I was immersed in money – the making, the losing and the spending of it.

Everything about the relationship was informal; our first date had been at a pub in Clapham where he played every Sunday evening. He'd borrowed money to buy me a drink – a detail I barely registered at the time, but which I probably shouldn't have overlooked so readily, like the good-luck text before my first day at work that he'd sent at 5.30 a.m. because he'd been out all night.

He was kind and comfortable, and as I was usually asleep when we were together, this was the perfect combination. When you get up at 5.45 a.m. every day and work in the City, you want someone with a large comfortable shoulder waiting for you when you get home. You don't want arguments, dinner parties or someone who is any effort to speak to.

There was none of the torment, uncertainty or crying silently into shoulder blades in the middle of the night of my previous relationship, and I was wonderfully content for a good few months. But I was simultaneously aware of two very distinct lives emerging and finding it increasingly difficult to live both with anything resembling authenticity. I imagined that one day I would slide down between the two parts, be too exhausted to get back up and just stay there – jobless and single. For the time being I was happy to have someone to pass out on.

I knew that it wasn't particularly fair on Mark that my clients and my colleagues got to see the best of me, and he got the unconscious dribbling version who was barely able to order takeaway, let alone cook, but I wasn't sure how I could do anything about it. Getting to my desk for 7 a.m. was the only thing that I was focused on. I had no energy for anything beyond that. When he occasionally broached the subject of my permanent exhaustion, I'd quickly dismiss it as part of a settling-in period; soon I'd get used to the early mornings and my body would adjust and be able to function perfectly on five hours' sleep a night. We would then have a social life again.

The American was on hold for Starbucks' head office. He had moved on from his bagel to low-fat seeded crispbreads. He normally got through two boxes a day, thus rendering the 'low-fat' part irrelevant. Someone must have finally picked up the phone, because he launched into an attack, wildly gesturing with half a cracker, sesame seeds dispersing across the desk.

'Yeah, good morning. Finally. I'm calling to complain about one of your branches – again. They are supposed to open at 7 a.m. I always get there at 7 a.m., ready to fill my thermos mug with drip cawfee. But recently they've been closed. I just don't understand why you bother having opening times when you don't stick to them. I can't hang around in some basement in

Canary Wharf for half an hour waiting for goddamn drip cawfee.'

Every now and again, as a result of his regular complaining, he would receive letters and vouchers for crème brulée lattes, which usually only made him angrier and were passed to me with disgust – it was drip coffee or nothing. The thought of anything flavoured repulsed him and was enough to trigger the complaint process all over again.

His complaint phone calls were legendary. Everyone from British Airways to the local BMW garage suffered the brunt of his rage if it was a quiet day and not much was trading. The rest of the desk would listen in to the conversation with their silencers clicked in so that they were free to snigger unheard in the background. He had a knack for somehow finding out the direct lines to CEOs of companies and would harass them until they took action to rectify the situation.

It became immediately apparent that no one would ever admit to liking the American. At best, they might have described him as an eccentric character they respected; I was in awe of him. He was smart, fierce and indestructible, with not even a vague desire to be liked. He more or less ran his business single-handedly, covering obscure products that no one else understood or had time to learn about, digging around in the mud to get prices in bonds that no one had ever heard of, and doing business while the rest of London was asleep. He worked hard, persisting with even the most difficult of traders and eventually getting prices out of them. To those traders who wanted it, and many who didn't, he provided what can only be described as a bespoke service.

Legend had it that he was one of Aggro Bank's first flow traders in London and was one of the best in the business. He'd fallen from grace when he'd refused to agree blindly with one of their Big Swinging Dick partners, which had culminated in him sticking his neck out far enough for them to get a clean shot straight between the eyes, and that was the end of his trading career. Aggro Bank was not a place for mavericks, so he'd tumbled out of their hallowed boardroom and become a broker. Now, years later, he'd chosen to train me as his junior.

I'd become strangely protective of him. Whenever anyone asked how I could tolerate working for 'such a cunt', I always said that he was misunderstood. I felt like I'd discovered a hidden treasure, that I'd somehow cracked the American's code and that maybe he even considered me to be an ally. I was in no doubt that despite being part of a team of ten we were a separate entity. It was the American who had hired me, and it was to him that I was ultimately answerable. I had to believe that he wasn't as much of a monster as everyone said he was, because the alternative was unthinkable.

'Airbags – can you pick up that call? There's ringing coming from somewhere and it's doing my head in.'

'Alright, darling? Where's the Ferg? He's not on Bloomie yet. Lazy fucker. Have him call me as soon as he gets in.'

I'd assumed ever since my first few days on the floor that the Ferg, a simple shortened form of Feargal, was his name – he sometimes called himself Ferg, a few clients referred to him as Ferg and so did some of the guys on the desk – but, of course, it wasn't. As Dory eventually painstakingly explained to me, it was an abbreviation of Feargal Sharkey, which is cockney rhyming slang for 'darkie', but by that point it seemed stranger to start calling him something else than to be using a racist nickname for a mixed-race colleague.

Nicknames constantly presented problems, moral or otherwise. One of the only black brokers on the floor was called Denzel by most people in the market, and I'd also assumed that was his real name – I had no reason to question it. It was only when I wanted to send him a Bloomberg that I realized his name was something else entirely. It was subsequently explained to me that he was nicknamed Denzel because when he started broking everyone thought he looked like Denzel Washington. He was the only black guy on the floor. He didn't really look anything like him, but by then it was too late – Denzel stuck. I never knew whether this was the true story behind the name, or whether it was something far more innocent, but I had very little choice other than to believe what I was told.

Everyone had a nickname. I had no idea what half the floor was actually called; real names were reserved for emails or Bloomberg messages and used grudgingly. Some nicknames were straightforward bits of surnames or shortened first names, but the vast majority were based on physical characteristics, race or rhyming slang. Being given a nickname was a rite of passage; whether racist, sexist, homophobic or just insulting, nicknames were willingly accepted by the recipients and thrown around with little thought as to what was actually being said, or whether it was in violation of some code of conduct in the Company handbook.

Dory got his nickname when he was a junior trader at one of the big US banks. He'd been made to walk around a glass office at the end of the trading floor for days on end pretending to swim – all because a senior salesman had decided one day that he looked like a fish, and swim he must.

Of my various nicknames, Airbags, shortened to 'Bags by certain colleagues, was by far the best, if not the most inspired.

It was first used one slow afternoon when I was being taught how to head a tennis ball, which quickly developed into 'catch the tennis ball between my breasts', which I found far easier.

It was nearly lunchtime. At 11.30 a.m. every day I went out to get lunch for the American and anyone else who put in an order. He ate exactly the same thing every day, and eventually trusted me enough not to feel the need to write it down painstakingly on a Post-it Note or tell me to take the sushi rolls and prepared fruit from the back of the stack to get the freshest. He only wanted a can of Diet Coke if the machine on the floor was broken, and if it was ice cold. For a while I would go through picking up dozens of cans to find the coldest and checking sell-by dates on every single pack of pomegranate seeds and vegetarian sushi rolls to find the freshest. I made an effort. It was never acknowledged, and he barely looked up when I returned from the supermarket, but I kept up the OCD date and temperature checking for months, even when he treated me badly. I was like a beaten wife – downtrodden and bruised but still desperate to get fresh pomegranate.

The seemingly simple task of retrieving breakfast, coffee, lunch and tea for the desk was the downfall of many juniors. A nearby team had employed the younger brother of a French trader who was one of their clients as a favour. Brokers were often expected to provide work experience or jobs for the school- or university-leaving siblings of their best clients, however useless they turned out to be. Luc was heartbreakingly sweet, in that innocent way that only mop-haired French eighteen-year-olds can be, but his failure to differentiate between Marmite and marmalade caused a ruckus every morning and eventually led to him being moved to a less demanding desk of brokers that occupied an insignificant corner at the other end of the floor. No one knew who they were or what they traded – it was the broking equivalent of being banished to Coventry for eternity – but I hoped that they liked marmalade and didn't care if their eggs came poached or scrambled. Nobody ever found out if Luc had any potential because no one cared after his endless stream of breakfast mix-ups. If he couldn't handle breakfast orders, he wouldn't be able to handle bonds, and that was gospel. When he got sent to pick up lunch at the Lahore Kebab House and didn't make it back until four o'clock, having got lost, his career was as good as over. If he hadn't been related to an important client, he would have been humiliated and then fired on the spot.

Good juniors become good brokers. This was a fundamental principle of the City. The best bookies were usually the product of the most aggressive, hierarchical, abusive and loudest desks, and would often have had to endure years of retrieving food and coffee and having phones thrown at them before they were allowed near a client. This behaviour wasn't limited to the guys: Lena had trained her very own junior by hurling a ball at his head with full force every time he got something wrong, in the same way she had been trained by the strange Italian who had rescued her from a career as a physicist.

This was one of the main differences between trading floors at banks and at brokerages: brokers could get away with hurling cricket balls and phones; at banks it was far more controlled after numerous accusations of bullying and dis-crimination had led to long, drawn-out legal battles. It was this bureaucracy and fear of legal action that had also led several of the big US banks to ban their employees from going to strip clubs with clients to conduct 'business meetings'.

The inter-dealer broking industry, however, remained largely exactly how it had always been, despite some of the houses attempting to introduce graduate training schemes and diversity training in an effort to align themselves with the major banks. However, it was widely acknowledged among the brokers at these firms that it was nothing but a charade. As one desk head remarked, 'They'd have to fire the whole fucking floor to stop racist, sexist and abusive banter, and start from scratch, because they ain't got a cat's chance in hell of changing any of us old dirty dogs, whatever fucking courses they make us do. And they know that. HR just wants to look like they're doing the right thing and tick boxes. Cunts.'

There had, of course, been the odd lawsuit taken out by brokers against the firms they worked for. Most famously, a broker accused one of the heads of a big brokerage of constructive dismissal following prolonged bullying and threats of violence and was eventually awarded a million in damages.

A broking floor is arguably the most aggressive, male-dominated environment that anyone could work in. Brokers often have to communicate by shouting to be heard above everyone else. Swearing at each other and smashing things is accepted – not officially, of course, but if a broker smashes a phone, no one notices. It would be unusual not to see outbursts of frustration and anger in an environment where everyone is under immense pressure to make more money than the guy next to them. At the bottom of the food chain anything goes because nobody is looking.

'Oi, Venetia!'

I'd been busy navigating my way through the aisles at Waitrose, when I heard my name. I turned around to see a few of my favourite boys from another desk, who always included me whenever they were getting fish and chips delivered, sitting in the wine bar, waving me over. Putting a wine bar in a supermarket was an inspired decision, and when the market was quiet half of Canary Wharf would stop for a quick glass while pretending to do their lunchtime shopping. The three of them were perched like wise monkeys on stools around a small table where there stood three empty bottles of wine, and some untouched boquerones. They were on their fourth bottle.

'Sit, sit, sit. How's everything, darlin'?'

Avoiding drinking at lunchtime was virtually impossible. The likelihood of bumping into someone heading to the pub in the lift, or being hauled into the bar for a glass of wine while trying to find the American's crispbreads, was high towards the end of the week. Everyone wanted to drink, gossip or slag off someone, and as I sat next to the American, whom everyone loved to recount stories about, I quickly became the perfect drinking partner. As the still relatively new girl, I was also an ideal target for imparting invaluable advice – a favourite pastime of brokers. It was during these impromptu lunchtime drinks that I learned the best techniques for sleeping at the desk – or in the toilet cubicles, if things were really bad – and for handling unreasonable clients, and all about the different kinds of brewed condiments, of which there were many, not just malt vinegar.

'We dunno how you do it. He's an animal. Always picking at his toenails, feet up on the desk, same fucking socks every day. How d'you cope? He's a total nightmare. Why don't you move to a better desk?'

I never really knew how to reply when I was asked questions about the American. I knew that it would be a lot easier to agree and moan about him along with everyone else, but I was always overcome by a sense of loyalty.

'He's all right, honestly. No problems yet. And he never has his feet in my face.'

'Just don't ever trust him, gorgeous, seriously.'

I hurriedly finished off the large glass of sauvignon blanc that had been handed to me as soon as I'd sat down, managed to retrieve his crispbreads and headed back to the desk.

I had been gone for about half an hour; only the American and Dory were on the desk. Everyone else had clearly gone off to the pub or, as it was generally referred to, 'gone down Boots'. There were no new prices; and other than a rambling message from Lena about her electric car, no messages.

The American rarely left the desk during the day, even if there was nothing happening. It was partly out of dedication and partly in the belief, derived from an elevated sense of self-importance, that if he stepped off the desk, the market would grind to a halt. It was also about control: he didn't like anyone else to speak to his clients in case they were given information that he wanted to withhold or that might expose an earlier lie.

He didn't look up when I deposited the Waitrose bag, just let out a single throat-clearing cough without altering his gaze. He was busy, lost in an article on Bloomberg about someone he used to work with. I used to find it strange that he never thanked me for getting his lunch, or bringing him his change, but now, like most of his behaviour, I barely noticed it.

Slowly the rest of the desk began to resurface, armed with everything from whole rotisserie chickens to pie and mash. No one expected the market to pick up. It was a Friday in late January. Half the Street had disappeared off skiing at midday, leaving only their sales teams and trading assistants to field calls. The American was going skiing with Philippe in February, taking some of their clients and their wives, and had promised that next year I'd be able to go, and 'take the young single guys snowboarding'.

Most broking firms took chalets for the entire season, enabling them to fly out as and when, taking whichever clients felt like going. It was a fiercely competitive time of the year, when brokers clamoured to pin down their top clients during the peak weekends, take them to the best resorts, and try to ensure that their weekend was the wildest and most luxurious of all the broker ski trips.

The same rules applied to all the big sporting events of the season, from Ascot and the Cartier Polo to the big rugby and football games. Our corporate entertainment team was able to get tickets to anything, at a price. Throughout the day, emails would be sent around advertising different events and what entertainment packages were on offer – the general rule was simply to find something you wanted to do, then find a client to go along.

Entertaining wasn't as easy as it sounded. Most traders had already eaten at all of London's best restaurants dozens of times, been on countless broker ski trips – some of which had been legendary and some horrific – and flown into Ascot or the Cartier Polo by helicopter, and could no longer be lured. Their free time was precious, and usually spent with their families and friends. As one of the Irish trading mafia once said to me, 'Why on earth would they want to spend it with some cunt that they have to spend all day talking to as it is?'

Getting the Big Swinging Dicks to agree to spend an evening with you, or maybe even a weekend, was therefore a contest in itself, with different brokers competing to secure the best clients for the best events. They had seen and done it all before and had the same jaded reaction, even if you offered a VIP helicopter trip to the Monaco Grand Prix. The younger guys were generally easier to seduce; they had girls to impress, and a day out in a corporate box at Ascot with unlimited pink champagne and their own tipster was a surefire way of getting them laid.

I was still desperately trying to get traders to come out to dinner with me, let alone to Ascot or even gigs at the O2 Arena. Hearing the American talk about ski trips and Wimbledon reminded me of the endless unread Bloomberg messages I'd sent and the constant cycle of arranging dinners only to have them cancelled the day before. I could no longer book tables under my own name.

The American had finished eating and began making his afternoon calls. Even when the market was dead, he rang around periodically, especially after lunch when prices from traders' clients at funds in New York might have filtered through to the Street. If a fund manager suddenly wants X amount of bonds and can't get them directly from whatever sales guys he speaks to at any number of different banks, a trader might in turn put in an order for the bonds, which would eventually make its way through to us in the Street.

'Have you called Ian yet today? Ring him and see if he wants anything worked this afternoon.'

'I called earlier and he said he wasn't working anything in the Street today – too much client stuff.'

'Venetia, don't argue with me. Just ring him. He may not give you a price but you might get some info. You just want him to throw you a bone, you know?'

Striking the correct balance between keeping the American

happy and not annoying the hell out of the few clients I had was difficult. The American's technique of harassing traders until they gave him prices wasn't going to help me build good relationships long term. I didn't want to be the bookie who was nothing but an annoyance that needed to be got rid of as quickly as possible.

I had been focusing my attention on a young guy at a small, permanently bearish European bank, Ian. The American and I had gone for a meeting at their offices with the whole team a few weeks before as a last resort, after it had become impossible to arrange drinks or a dinner. On realizing that he wasn't much older than me, the American decided he was the perfect person for me to cover, while the more senior traders would be looked after by him. Since meeting Ian, the American had come out with a variation on the following every day, usually after I had already rung to harass him for prices: 'Yeah, call him on the outside. See if he'll go for a drink with you. Tell him he'd be doing you a favour, that you need to be getting out with clients. Tell him it'd make you look good in front of me.'

At first I'd thought this would be easy. Convince a young guy fresh off the grad scheme to have dinner or drinks with me? How difficult could it possibly be? But, for some reason, I felt like a sixteen-year-old trying to get a date, having to endure awkward phone calls with some hot sixth-former in the hope that he might agree to hang out after school some day and listen to music.

Ian was painfully shy. Our conversations were strained and usually consisted of me rambling at him for a few minutes while he gave one-word answers and then eventually hung up on me or said he had to go. When he did finally agree to dinner, I knew it would be the most awkward couple of hours of my life. My only hope would be to get him very drunk. As it happened, he kept cancelling, and it wasn't until the end of May that we finally made it out. By then his desk had hired another jub (junior), and he brought him, and a strange German sales guy, along for the ride. They were about an hour late, by which time I was halfway through a bottle of wine and wondering how much longer I could sit alone on a large round table for five in a full restaurant with a queue.

'Have you called him yet? Tell him if he won't give you a price to at least have a drink with you. It's the perfect time to get out with him if the market is quiet.'

I hit his number on my speed dial, knowing that the American wasn't going to let it go until I put in a call. He was crunching on another crispbread, his phone handset propped between his chin and his shoulder. I knew he was listening to my every word.

'Hi, Ian, it's Venetia. How's it going?'

'All right.'

'Great. Yeah. Umm. Well, I was wondering if there's anything that you'd like me to work this afternoon?'

'No thanks.'

'OK. Great. Errrm, also, I was wondering if there was a time we could set up a drink or dinner? Be good to catch up, if you're around?'

'Yeah, sure. Let me get back to you with some dates.'

Click.

It was the sort of conversation that left me sweaty and embarrassed. In reality, Ian was a gawky, shy maths nerd in his early twenties. He was not in the least bit intimidating, there was no chance of him yelling abuse at me, and he was probably as embarrassed as I was by our awkward chats, but in the bizarre parallel universe of trading, he was third in line to Always Bearish Bank's high yield throne and, while not exactly a high baller, was still a baller.

'Venetia?'

Ian. He was actually shouting down the line for me. I was almost too surprised to pick up. I tried my best to sound non-chalant – like traders shouted my name all day every day.

'Yep?'

'Can you show out a couple of Caleos Bs at par and a half?'

'Sure thing. Thanks, Ian.'

'CALEOS Bs OFFERED AT PAR AND A HALF, ACCOUNT 12.'

I bellowed out the price to the rest of the desk, hoping I'd said the right thing, and began typing it onto a Bloomberg message that I'd then send out to my other clients, and the American's if he was in the middle of something more exciting. Wayne let out a yell. 'She's got a price! She's got a fucking price!' – it was clearly still a novelty. For weeks I'd kept saying 'bid' when I meant 'offered', 'buy' when I meant 'sell', 'mine' when I meant 'yours', and 'hitting' offers when I should have been 'lifting'. It was an endless linguistic quagmire that I seemed to be incapable of circumnavigating. The more I said, the more I would fuck up. Never had such small incidental words had so much power.

The American was on hold for someone and, without moving his head, mumbled, 'You won't get anything back – think he's the only guy that even trades that. He'll just be trying to get a level.'

I didn't really know what he meant.

'Yeah, but at least he's showing something, right? It's more of a dialogue than I had with him a week ago.'

I sounded like a desperate, whiney teenager. The American

didn't reply. I was annoyed at his lack of encouragement. He'd been harassing me to get prices out of Ian for days, but when I managed to get something it was instantly dismissed or ignored. I didn't need a high five every time I got a price, but the occasional 'great' or a vaguely positive reaction would have gone a long way. But he was right: getting a price in something that didn't trade and that no one had any interest in was useless. Ian's price wasn't going to start anything, and it certainly wasn't going to finish anything.

I was more dependent on praise than I'd realized. While I'd always liked reading positive comments at the end of essays at school or university, I'd never have thought I'd be craving it so badly in the workplace or be hanging on the American's every word and gesture, looking for some sort of approval.

It was finally four o'clock, which meant two things: someone would be about to send me to get them tea and I only had an hour to get through before I could leave and go to bed. But, of course, I couldn't, because I had Mark's gig to go to – in fucking Shoreditch. I'd barely spoken to him all week and knew that I somehow had to get there, but I couldn't think of anything I'd less like to do than go to a gig in a pub in Shoreditch on a Friday evening. I didn't even like rock music, and while I could tolerate Mark's band because I was in a relationship with him, the support acts would all be horrific. While Mark set up and did sound checks, I'd have to sit and make small talk with his annoying friends, who had all been shipped in from Clapham. I hated Clapham almost as much as I hated Shoreditch. But the sex was great so I dealt with it.

It wasn't until I was safely on the Tube on a Friday evening that I began to unwind. During the week the journey was nothing but a series of sudden moments of panic as I remembered a price that I'd forgotten to update or admin that I hadn't had time to do. But on a Friday, I could enjoy the 45-minute journey home listening to my iPod, crammed against other commuters, safe in the knowledge that I didn't have to get up in the morning.

I was trapped in an endless cycle in which I would be either running away from or towards the nineteenth floor. It was never far from my thoughts, and seemed to lurk behind my right eye like the beginning dark pangs of a migraine attack. I hoped that it would eventually become less menacing, and I could enter the building without my chest tightening and leave without the urge to run like hell. For the time being, the weekend was the only time I got to stand still.

I got home just after 6.30 p.m., peeled off my suit and changed into a chocolate-brown velour tracksuit – one of those ubiquitous Juicy Couture ones. I'd bought it online from Browns during my first year at university when I was living in halls. It had arrived in a Jiffy bag and was, at the time, the most expensive item in my wardrobe, taking pride of place on the free-standing clothing rail I'd had to put up, which periodically keeled over and fell on me in the middle of the night. Every time it fell I let out a scream, thinking that someone had broken in and I was being attacked, but thankfully it was only ever a load of coat hangers and velour smothering me.

The tracksuit was now four years old, had lost its 'J' for Juicy zip pull and had holes in it, but I always immediately changed into it after work because it was still the comfiest thing I owned. I'd once momentarily owned a pair of cashmere tracksuit bottoms, which were arguably comfier, but they'd been eaten alive by moths in the second year of my degree, when I lived in Angel, and I'd never thought to replace them.

I woke up, velour hood pulled tightly around my head, deep under my duvet. My phone was ringing somewhere in the room and for a second I thought it was my alarm and it was 5.45 a.m. again and I needed to get up for work. I fumbled around on my bedside table until I found the phone, and was relieved to see it was still Friday, still only 7.30 and it was Mark calling to see if I was on my way. He'd guessed that I would black out immediately after work.

I felt like shit. Whether I was hungover or not, every time I woke up I wanted to curl up in a ball and die. I kept telling myself that I would be fine as soon as I'd showered, had a coffee and made it out onto the street, and I usually was, but it took all the willpower I possessed not to dive back under the covers and immediately go back to sleep, whether it was 7.30 on a Friday night or 5.45 on a freezing Monday morning. I'd take any opportunity I could to shut my eyes, and even having an amazing boyfriend waiting for me in a pub wasn't always enough to get me out of the velour and out the door.

I answered the call and let out a sleepy moan.

'Baby, you need to get out of bed.'

'How the hell do you know I'm in bed?'

'Come on, it's Friday night. You would've got home an hour ago. There's no chance in hell of you maintaining consciousness for longer than 45 minutes when your suit's come off. And I can hear the duvet rustling. And you've got your sleep voice on. Come on, get up. You can sleep tomorrow.'

'Until two? Promise?'

'As long as you want.'

He was speaking softly, and I could hear the smile in his voice. If I'd had the energy, I'm sure I would've laughed at how well he knew my Friday routine already. Before I started broking, I used to be embarrassed about answering the phone to guys I was dating when I'd just woken up, usually because it would be lunchtime on a Saturday and everyone else would be up doing something exciting and I would be sleeping. I didn't want them to hear sleep in my voice and think I was lazy, so I would always let the call go to voicemail and ring back sounding chirpy and wide awake. I was determined to maintain the illusion of having been up jogging at 8 a.m. and just getting back from brunch with friends. But now that I worked such ridiculous hours, and got up at 5.45 a.m. every day, I slept whenever I could with a clear conscience. When Mark rang and I was asleep (my default mode at the weekend), I never bothered lying about it and he never cared.

I threw on some jeans and some black Manolos and jumped into a cab, with the thought of sleeping on Mark's shoulder until 2 p.m. the next day keeping me going. The prospect of sleep was currently my main source of motivation. Interspersed with 'fuck, fuck, fuck' was now the bargaining rift of 'get through X and you can go to sleep'. I knew that the sooner I got to the pub, saw the band and nodded my head to the music for a while holding a bottle of beer, the sooner I could go back to my velour and back to bed. I chose sleep over most things.

It was, of course, more of a Converse high tops place than a Manolo Blahnik Campari Patent Mary Jane venue. As soon as I pushed my way through the doors, I caught sight of Mark, standing with the drummer and a couple of others by the bar. I kissed him, and as I pressed my face into the side of his neck and felt his arms tighten around me, I hated myself for even considering choosing sleep over the man I was crazy about.

CHAPTER 4

BIG SWINGING DICK JUGGLING

'Venetia, really, he's a fucking wanker.'

Emma was one of the few female traders the desk covered. She had a notoriously bad relationship with the American, but I only realized the extent of her dislike for him when I was sitting opposite her drinking champagne in l'Atelier de Joël Robuchon the following Tuesday.

It was my first client dinner alone. I'd spent most of the day worrying that we would have nothing to talk about, that she'd cancel at the last minute or realize I knew nothing about the market and leave, but much of the conversation had so far centred on the American – a topic that I was used to discussing at length.

Her resentment stemmed from one afternoon a year ago. The American was used to speaking to Emma's boss, Brian, who was then out of the office, and had said, 'I know you can't trade without Brian, but just wanted to let you know that . . .'

She had tried explaining that she was actually the head trader, that Brian was now too senior to trade and spent most of his time in meetings, and that if he wanted to do business it would have to be through her. The American, of course, disregarded her completely; he continued to ask for Brian whenever he called and ignored Emma. She dubbed him a misogynist and never spoke to him again.

She'd agreed to have dinner with me, provided the American didn't come along. We were sitting at the chef's counter at the restaurant, and had made our way through two bottles of wine and most of the menu and were now back on the pink champagne.

'So this is on the American, right? For all those times he refused to speak to me? I honestly think that he doesn't like women. I'm sure he thinks I'm Brian's secretary or desk assistant, which is hilarious given the fact I've been trading longer than most of the guys out there in the market. I just don't get him.'

She knocked back the remainder of her glass of champagne. I'd heard that most female brokers only covered guys, not purely because there were so few female traders, but because generally they got on better with them. Brokers weren't usually girls' girls. They were hired to flirt and entertain in order to bring in more business, and this wasn't a technique that worked so well on other women. But I knew that Emma would be one of my best clients. She was straight-talking and punchy, and exactly the kind of girl I'd be good friends with outside the market.

'I really don't think he's a misogynist. I mean, I sit next to the guy every day; I would know if he was. And the other women in the market have never had a problem as far as I can make out. He's just socially retarded sometimes, and maybe once he'd got it into his head that he had the better relationship with Brian, he pursued it.'

'But he's missed out on so much business. I give long runs of two-way markets to the other bookies every morning, but never to you guys.'

'Would you start if it was just me covering you and you never had to speak to him?'

'Yeah, I mean if I know it's only you profiting and only you that's going to shout down the line for me, then totally. But if I hear his voice, I'm not going to answer. I just refuse to support his business.'

I knew that if I could bring in business from people who previously did none or little with the desk, my stock price would start to go up. This was all brokers ever seemed to worry about: how much they were bringing in monthly and whether they had clients that no one else had a relationship with and were therefore indispensable. I was looking forward to telling the American that from now on Emma wanted to speak only to me, but wasn't sure how to broach the subject without making relations between them even worse.

The bill for dinner was just over £450. I'd recently had to apply for my first credit cards, as putting expenses through on a debit card wasn't an option. The Company had once given out credit cards to brokers but this was phased out after rumours started flying around of their wives using them to pay for sofas, televisions and anything else they wanted. Management decided that it would be better if personal credit cards were used and the money reimbursed a couple of weeks later when receipts had been filed and signed off by desk managers. It was, of course, the perfect way to start racking up air miles and other credit card perks. One broker I knew had paid for two first-class return flights to New York on miles gained as a result of entertaining just one client the previous year.

I doubted whether the slightly perverse novelty of picking up tabs for such large amounts would ever wear off. When I typed in my newly acquired PIN, I felt a rush of adrenalin, and then a bit nauseous when it actually worked and the maître d' asked me how everything had been. Being able to spend over £200 a head on a Tuesday night girls' dinner was the closest I ever got to a pang of something vaguely resembling feminism – especially if what Emma had said about the American's treatment of her was true.

'You know, Venetia, you're wasted doing this. You should come work for me and get into sales trading. We're looking for someone.'

'Sales was always the original plan. I just wanted to cut my teeth first and, believe it or not, I'm enjoying it – really.'

I wasn't sure whether I was doing a very good job of convincing her, or myself, of the thinking behind my City master plan. I knew broking was only ever supposed to be a way into sales, but when I walked onto the floor on my first day, the idea of ever working anywhere else disappeared from my head, despite Lena's constant reminders to see the job as a means to an end. Now, during my first one-on-one client dinner, I was being offered a job. I'd been warned about the likelihood of being propositioned by clients at some point, but I hadn't expected it to be quite like this.

'Well, send over your CV anyway – at least consider it.'

Emma leapt in a cab and I walked home along West Street, drunk and confused, *foie gras* and burgundy sloshing around my system. I wasn't entirely sure what had happened. Had I just agreed to send my CV to a client during our first meeting? I was a traitor.

'Apparently there's a good offer out there somewhere in NTL. Is it Ian?'

'No. He told me he wasn't getting involved in NTL right now.'

'Have you asked him? Make sure you ask him.'

The American had just come off the phone to someone at Aggro Bank. It was 8.30 the next morning. He was coughing and irritated, tapping one of his handsets against the desk. Hearing there was an offer that we didn't have would mean he would obsessively try to find it for the rest of the morning. There were various clients who the American believed gave him all of their business, and whom he could trust with information that was strictly a 'no post' – like trades that had taken place when most of the Street didn't even know there was a market being worked in the bond. But it was usually these traders, those whom he thought he could trust, who traded away from him or would be showing prices in other shops. I knew that the American wouldn't let it go until I put the call in.

'Ian, have you got a sec?'

'Yep?'

'Are you doing anything in NTL? Apparently there's an offer out there away. Can you see it?'

'No.'

I'd thought that after he'd spontaneously given me a price last week he might be more forthcoming, but there seemed to be no way of predicting how a trader was going to respond to you from one minute to the next, let alone week by week.

'Argh. Fuck. Bet it's fucking Emma. Exactly the sort of thing she'd do after a night out with a broker – show prices away. She's told you she wants you to cover her and yet she's not showing you anything?! Yeah, right.' He chuckled to himself.

Emma had been quiet all morning, but there was no way of knowing. I'd shouted down her line a few times, but there had been no answer, and she wasn't picking up my Bloomberg messages. It was clear that however well you got on with someone over dinner, unless they gave you prices the next day it was all fairly meaningless, and the American was quick to remind me of this.

The American never did find that offer, but when he'd confirmed with different clients that nothing had traded, he was happy to let it go. This was why he was successful: given a tiny piece of information, he wouldn't rest until he had got the best market or had traded. He could never be called lazy – obsessive, greedy, paranoid and consumed by the pursuit of trades, but never lazy.

His desire to trade seemed to transcend his need to make money. He was undoubtedly driven by greed, but it was about more than chasing a bonus. He wasn't a man who particularly cared about monetary gain; he didn't drive a sports car, didn't go on excessive holidays and didn't even wear a watch. He wore the same clothes every day, in slightly different colour variations; he didn't really drink; his children were at a mix of private and state schools; and he laughed at the excesses of the other guys on the desk – the Ferraris, the houses in the Caribbean, the annual house extensions and new pool installations. Everything about his lifestyle was modest in comparison.

Whatever it was that motivated him, it provided a longevity that the others lacked. Wayne, Stu and the Ferg would get bored if they weren't making money and would stop chasing it. They needed to be accumulating, and to be within reach of trades in order to keep pursuing, but the American kept going regardless. Even when nothing had traded for days, he was unerringly resilient. Most of the City who knew of him dismissed it as simple greed, but I was convinced that there was an ulterior motive; I just wasn't sure exactly what it was.

Whatever it was, I didn't have time to think about it. Emma had sent through a run of prices out of nowhere and I soon had several markets within a quarter of a point of trading after several of the Ferg's clients countered her bids and offers.

'Are you clear yet?'

The American was waiting to get involved. Broking was ostensibly supposed to work on a first come, first served basis – the first trader to react to a price with a counter offer or bid had control until they had repeated their counter offer or bid, which meant they wanted to stick where they were and not improve any further, and then, finally, they had to agree to let us 'work' the market and let other traders in the Street get involved in the 'picture' before we showed the two-way price to other clients. Whoever started the market off would usually want to be 'kept up' on what was taking place and could step back in at any moment.

Showing something out before it had cleared was the easiest way to fuck yourself or someone else on the desk. Most brokers would let their favourite clients know what was going on using the proviso 'it's not clear yet, BUT . . .' in order to let them get involved quickly when it was a clear market and to find out who cared and who didn't have any interest. Sometimes, when it wasn't entirely clear whether a market was clear or not, the trader who was engaged had disappeared off the desk into a meeting, or just because the broker got impatient, prices were shown out too soon and, before we knew it, we'd have two traders thinking they were entitled to first refusal on what was available. If there was only one trade to be done, someone was going to get pissed off.

'What the fuck is taking so long? Have you got hold of Emma? Call her on the outside.'

'She's not picking . . .'

'CALL HER!'

I finally got the OK to work the markets, and within a few minutes six trades had taken place that more than covered the cost of the previous evening's dinner. I just hoped she'd keep giving me prices when I turned down her job offer.

It had never really been an option. I couldn't leave broking – not when I got to enjoy all the best parts of working on a trading floor without having to worry about risk or positions overnight. Sales would involve having to know vaguely what I was doing, and I wasn't sure whether I was ready to re-engage my brain, which had begun to enjoy lying dormant. I didn't have to read anything; I didn't have to think about the implications of anything; I just had to remember numbers during the day, and in the evenings work on my relationships while eating and drinking in amazing restaurants. Why would I want to give that up to work harder, longer hours? I had the best job in the world – I didn't know why I'd ever consider doing anything else.

The following week, the American was hosting a party in a private room at Nobu Park Lane for our clients. As it was quiet, I had spent most of that afternoon ringing around reminding traders it was happening, and trying to convince those who hadn't replied to swing by. It was the first time I'd spoken to most of them, and it turned out that cold calling traders to ask if they were planning to come to a broker party when they were working was even more awkward than asking for prices in bonds. Most traders went out of their way to avoid having to spend time with their competitors – it was one worse than having to spend time with their brokers; therefore, trying to sell them a Thursday night market cocktail party in early February was virtually impossible. But I had a response to every excuse: if they said they had friends in town, I told them to bring them along; if they were out to dinner, I told them to drop in afterwards – we would be there until at least midnight and would love to see them even for one drink. I didn't care; they could bring their kids, girlfriends, wives or dogs – whatever they wanted – as long as they turned up.

The day of the party finally arrived. When the American and I got to Nobu, after ensuring that everything was prepared and the receptionist knew where to send our guests, we spent the next half-hour in silence, sitting alone around a small table at the side of the large minimalist room, hurriedly knocking back the watermelon martinis the American had pre-ordered. People eventually started arriving, and I was finally able to put faces to the names I'd seen on Bloomberg. Nobody is ever as good-looking or as tall as you imagine them to be.

The American was uncomfortable. He didn't like the room we had hired. It was too big, too white and too quiet. There weren't enough of his favourite spicy tuna rolls going around. He didn't understand why people kept ordering lychee cocktails when we had put vast amounts of watermelon martinis behind the bar, or why the head trader at Kraut Bank had started on £50-a-glass whisky at 7.30 p.m., bypassing the watermelon martinis entirely. He was either attempting to assert his apparent seniority over the rest of the market or trying to punish the American's bar tab – it turned out to be a combination of both. It was the first and last time I would ever see him, and one of the last times he spoke to us.

The Kraut trader believed that he was the biggest guy in the market. Disappointed with the banality of his real name, and the number of other traders with exactly the same name on Bloomie, he'd inserted the initials GM into it, making his middle name Global Markets. In addition to his self-proclaimed status as the biggest of the Big Swinging Dicks, Mr Global Markets also took on the role of Protector of the Street. He decided which banks in the Street were allowed to trade leveraged loans (a 'name give-up' product, meaning the buyer and seller are revealed after the trade in order to close, and pay brokerage separately as opposed to having it included in the price). He subsequently refused to take certain people as counterparties on trades for any number of obscure reasons. These ranged from simply disliking them to believing they weren't running a good enough operation and were too much of a risk to other banks – despite no one else in the market objecting. He was able to enforce this first by instructing his brokers that if he ever came up against these blacklisted banks as counterparties, he would pull their lines. He then decided that this simply wasn't enough, and if he even heard that his brokers were taking prices or doing anything resembling business with anyone he hadn't personally given permission to trade in the Street, he would never speak to them again.

For a while we had followed suit and obeyed GM's instructions, until one afternoon a few weeks after the party when the American was off skiing, and I got a fierce phone call from the head trader at a large US bank.

'Venetia, I'm a bigger fucking dick than King Kraut is. If you don't go to Stupidly Bullish Bank and get me that bid, I will pull your fucking line forever. Is GM really worth losing me over?'

After a brief discussion with Dory, I made the call to Stupidly Bullish and we did the trade on a no post. We all knew it was only a matter of time before King Kraut caught up with it. I broke the news to the American the following morning, who, fortunately, agreed entirely with what we had done.

The problem with Big Swinging Dicks is that there is never just one of them to worry about, and it is impossible to keep them all happy. They are forever locking antlers, and brokers are eternally caught in the middle, trying to limit the damage and make as much money as possible out of them.

We continued to do business quietly with most of the ever-increasing list of banks trying to get into the Street, deciding that GM didn't do enough business with us to warrant playing by his rules and losing other Big Dicks, who by this time had astutely realized that they could use the smaller, less experienced banks to their advantage. But nothing ever stays quiet for long, and a few weeks later GM discovered that we had defied him, and promptly pulled our line after a short sharp chat with the American after hours. We never heard from him again, but we took solace in being the only bookies who weren't working for Kraut Bank. Every bank wants to run the Street, but the American always maintained that the credit market – giant baggy monster that it is – couldn't be controlled by anyone.

Six months later, GM was accepting all of the banks he'd tried to ban as counterparties, but he never gave us our line back and refused to return any of the American's calls. Short term we had probably made money, but long term not seeing his prices would begin to affect us. The American was aware of this, but knew that it was futile wasting energy thinking about it. There were always other megalomaniacs to worry about, and they can only be juggled for so long before you eventually drop one and he has to be written off.

While my relationships with Ian and Emma were slowly improving, and they now both answered more or less immediately when I shouted for them down the squawk box, there were others that seemed to be getting worse.

The American, keen to offload as many of his more time-consuming, slow-moving clients as possible to make room for his beloved punchy Aggro Bank traders, had decided that I should cover a few more of the smaller fish. But the more clients you have, the more likely you are to lose one. It's like walking a pack of dogs: while you're busy trying to untangle two Yorkshire terriers, a Great Dane will come along and flatten you, and you'll spend the rest of the day trying to round them all up. It is easy to pile all of your attention on one trader, ensuring that he is kept informed of every single useless piece of information that happens to come your way, shouting down every crappy price as soon as it comes in at least three times in case he misses it the first and second time, and managing to say good morning, good night and check how his weekend was, while also keeping up with everything else going on around you on the desk.

Throw a couple more Big Swinging Dicks into the equation and it is only a matter of hours before you forget something, be it showing them a price in a name they definitely cared about, or forgetting to work a wide, boring market that they gave you hours ago, only to send it out, get hit and find out it no longer works, or forgetting that they exist entirely, which was easy to do when it came to Ian because he was so quiet.

Brad, however, was impossible to forget. The American had known him for years but found him frustrating, and didn't feel that he was particularly getting the best out of him, so he'd handed him over to me, unknown to Brad, who finally got the message when the American insisted on silently handing the call to me whenever Brad rang in asking for him.

He terrified me from the outset. I'd previously only ever said the words 'hold the line, Brad' before passing him over to the American, relieved that he wasn't my client. Now he was my problem, and called all day, on an outside line, often for no reason at all other than to get an update of live prices, and had a habit of ringing when I'd just got back from the lunch run, or the bathroom, or while I was in the middle of an argument with Philippe over something administrative, when I had no idea what was going on. I would therefore be left frantically flicking through Bloomberg, checking what prices the desk had been sending out over the last five minutes while trying to stall him. He'd usually hang up after 30 seconds. I'd previously relied on the sheets in front of me where I recorded prices. With Brad there wasn't time to trawl through the three pages of names, find the bond or loan and check the price before he'd lose interest and hang up, so I had to make sure that I was permanently abreast of every single market that we were working at any given moment in case he called.

He was also one of the few traders who rang us with prices first thing in the morning. Prices were usually tightened immediately by one of the American banks, but Brad still expected to be treated as if it were his market, despite never improving.

Morning meetings are every broker's pet hate. Traders give a run of prices, and are then unreachable for the next half-hour or longer because the trader is stuck in an office somewhere with his sales team discussing where something should be priced, what needs to be shifted or how they feel about Stupidly Bullish Bank being able to trade in the Street.

I was also beginning to learn that you could never give Brad too much information. 'Colour' would become gospel the second you put the phone down, and within half an hour he would have repeated verbatim your bullshit broker ramblings to one of his clients at some halfwit hedge fund and they would then attempt to act on it only for Brad to find that the market had disappeared entirely.

Every time I saw his number flash up on one of the outside lines I felt nauseous. He had the same gruff tone of voice whatever he was saying, which made trying to work out how he felt, what he was attempting to do – buy, sell or get information – completely impossible. I never knew if he cared until he called in a rage, swearing at me. There was no middle ground – just gruff robotic disinterest or incandescent fury.

This morning, I'd shown him a market in some dogshit retail company's bonds. 'I think there's a chance he might have a tiny bit of room, BUT I really can't be sure, Brad.'

'OK, thanks, Venetia. I'll come back.'

Click.

An hour later Brad called back and told me to go and buy 2 million of the fuckers a quarter of a point lower than where I'd shown him.

'I'll have a go. Let me come back.'

Cue five-second chat with the trader, who can barely remember the offer it was so long ago.

'Sorry, Brad, he's not budging from his last offer. It's been a while and I'm surprised he's even still a seller.'

I waited for Brad's bass American tones to erupt with a slight stutter. I heard him take a quick, pained intake of breath. I knew he didn't get off on yelling at me and found it difficult, like yelling at a child or a dog.

'VENETIA, FOR FUCK'S SAKE, WHAT ARE YOU TRYING TO DO TO ME? I'M, I'M GIVING MY CLIENTS INFORMATION BASED ON WHAT YOU, WHAT YOU, YOU SAID TO ME. YOU SAID HE HAD FUCKING ROOM, AND, AND, AND NOW NOTHING? F-FUCKING HELL.'

He stuttered to a halt and the line went dead. I put the phone down and calmly carried on with what I had been doing as if the conversation had been perfectly civil.

Brad was the only person in the market who would expect old markets to be there hours later. He was slow. Most traders accept that a price is live only for a short period of time and is liable to be pulled at any second. The first time Brad yelled, swore and hung up on me, I was on the verge of tears, gasping for air and about to run screaming from the floor. The second time I attempted to defend myself, which was pointless because he just spoke over me or hung up. The third time I began to realize, after a lengthy discussion with the American, that I had to change how I covered him. I would give him no information other than the bare facts, which is harder than it sounds when your natural impulse as a broker is to please, to tell clients what they want to hear and to run up wagging your tail. I couldn't give up on Brad and hand him over to someone more experienced; I somehow had to build something resembling a relationship with him, and if it meant refusing to give him colour to protect myself, then I would.

Brokers always get the chance to do traders a favour at some point; equally they will always get a chance to shaft a trader when they least expect it. While Brad had been unreasonable and rude on many occasions, I knew that, unlike some clients, he wasn't a bad guy. It was just a matter of time before I'd be able to prove that I wasn't quite as inept as he thought I was, and a couple of weeks later an opportunity presented itself.

He'd been desperately trying to sell 3 million pounds worth of a leveraged loan that there had been no bids in for weeks. One morning a good bid appeared on the horizon and I knew it was the best they'd pay. I had several sellers but felt it was an opportunity perhaps to show Brad I wasn't always trying to shaft him. True to form, he was in his morning meeting, having shown his daily offer at the same level half an hour earlier. A fierce American sales guy was the only person on the desk. His voice was even deeper than Brad's and I wasn't hopeful that I was going to get the trade done. Hauling a trader out of a morning meeting is a last resort. It has the potential to sever relations irreversibly if it turns out to be the wrong call, because they will never take you seriously again, and you'll forever be the bookie who cried wolf.

'Tell Brad I have a par and three-quarters bid in that 3 million sterling of CAA. He was last at 101. I have other sellers but will put him in front. I need to see if he wants to hit it. The buyer won't improve.'

'He's in a meeting.'

'I know. You need to go in and tell him. He'll want to see this bid.'

'I'll see what I can do. That's the best he pays? You checked?'

'Yes. That's his best. Fill or kill.'

The message came flying back to 'hit the fucking bid' as

predicted. Brad called half an hour later when he had got out of his meeting.

'Yeah. Venetia? Yeah. Thanks. You did the right thing. Take an eighth.'

There were now no bids in sight and the CAA was offered at par and a half. Normal brokerage ('bro') on the trade should have been 3 cents – £600 for his side of it. He gave me £3,750, and told me to go and buy myself something pretty. So off I went to Chanel, despite the fact that I would probably never see the money from the trade, as it would all disappear into the pool used to pay our salaries and countless other expenses. I needed several of those sorts of trades every day to have any chance of seeing a bonus. Normal bro on high yield bonds was a sixteenth, and on loans 2 or 3 cents depending on the customer. Distressed – bonds or loans highly likely to default – paid up to a quarter.

I wasn't on a lucrative desk. If we traded bigger volumes, it would be, considering that other products often only paid a cent. We simply didn't do enough to make getting paid a sixteenth each time significant. Some brokers netted at least 150k in bro a month, usually on synthetic products. Cash was dead in the water.

I thought Brad might learn from the experience and start to trust me a little more – maybe even tell me what he was trying to do occasionally – but he never did. We continued to have the same misunderstandings, and I dreaded seeing his number flash up. Our relationship never seemed to improve, and was no different from the very first time we had spoken, but that was his style. He was never going to be the type of client I got wasted in clubs with and had a nickname for. He would always be irrational, impossible-to-manage Brad.

CHAPTER 5

HOSPITALIZATION

I'd somehow made it through to the middle of March. It was the end of a day when everything had fallen apart: Philippe had spent all day yelling at me, Brad had threatened to pull my line twice and, when the American was in a meeting, I'd quoted a senior trader at Aggro Bank a price 50 basis points off where it actually was by reading off a price two lines below where I should have been looking on that day's spreadsheet. The bond was virtually worthless, but I'd told him we had last had a nice wide 70–76 (70 bid, 76 offered) market. Before I'd had a chance to correct my mistake, he'd called me insane, asked me to have the American call him back and then promptly hung up while I was still stuttering and scrambling around with my spreadsheet trying to find the right price. I was lucky that he didn't try to hit me at 70.

It was finally 5 p.m. Everyone was starting to leave, but I still had to update all of the day's prices. I was exhausted, having been out until 4 a.m. with a load of traders from Stupidly

Bullish Bank, and I kept making mistakes as I input the numbers on the spreadsheet in front of me. Every few minutes I was aware of my eyes beginning to fill up with tears, seemingly uncontrollably. The American was the only other person still on the desk. He was waiting for a call from some distressed trader in New York.

'I can't fucking do it.' My head hit the desk, and I began crying. 'I can't carry on. I'm so fucking tired. And this never-ending admin is fucking impossible. It's just not worth it for twenty grand. It's not that I'm not grateful, but . . .' The words came tumbling out among the tears before I had a chance to think about what I was saying.

'Well, what are you saying, Venetia? That you wanna quit?'

The American seemed vaguely irritated, baffled as to what all the fuss was about, and started gathering up his things, having given up on the call. He clearly wanted to go home, and whether I quit or not had very little bearing on anything other than making him late for dinner at the River Café.

'No, I don't want to quit. I'm just fucking exhausted. I need to sleep. And I can't survive on twenty k. And Philippe giving me hassle about some fucking spreadsheet that we don't even use is impossible to take. I'm here either to become a broker or to do piles of admin, but I can't do both well. I'm sorry. It's been a bad few days. I just want to go home. I'm sorry.'

I was slightly hysterical, and aware that every other word I was saying was 'fucking' or 'sorry', but it was too late to start being rational. I knew there was no room for emotion in this environment. I was just tired. I shouldn't have been attempting a conversation about my salary while crying, but I was suddenly unable to stop. I'd always heard people talk of 'nervous exhaustion' and now I was the living embodiment of it.

The problem with a high-pressure environment is that being rational is often difficult; bits of emotion, custard-like, start spilling out over the edges of your otherwise impenetrable façade and, unlike most working environments where you can take yourself off to calm down, as a broker you have to stay in your seat and carry on. Prices are coming in, clients are shouting for you and running off the floor is never an option. Even making it to the safety of the ladies' toilets can be impossible, because as soon as you stand up you're a tear-stained sitting duck waiting for someone to hurl a cricket ball at you. Any sign of tears or the potential for a bout of hysteria will be picked up instantly by one of the two hundred guys around you. They can smell it. So you stay seated. You stare at your screens, piss around under your desk, pretending to tie imaginary shoelaces, reorganize the nearest drawer, take sips of water and wait for it to pass.

Tales of trading-floor breakdowns are legendary. Women who matched the guys around them punch for punch every day for years on end, who never so much as thought about crying, suddenly fall apart and dissolve into hysterical messes until some kind colleague manages to stop gawping, grabs them by the arm and escorts, or carries, them off the floor as they wail uncontrollably and hyperventilate. Most of them are never seen again.

Men lose control in entirely different ways. Someone who has punched a colleague, or a wall, and marched off to the nearest pub mid-afternoon can turn up the following morning at seven and stroll back onto the floor as if nothing has happened. If they had been particularly violent, they might get called into a meeting with the floor manager, but this is just for show and they're sent back to their desks simply having been told not to do it again.

Anger is expected; hysterical, snot-ridden crying is not. It makes everyone feel awkward. So you hold onto it, and pray it doesn't begin to seep out of your pores. Yet here I was crying, only four months into the job. There are some people whom you never want to see you cry, and they are usually the ones you end up in floods of tears in front of at the earliest opportunity. Miraculously, the American said he'd sort out my salary; he understood. And then he left. There was no discussion or argument about it, just acquiescence.

I was relieved that I'd broken down after hours and not in the middle of a busy morning, but I spent the entire journey home embarrassed and furious that I'd lost control when I should have gone home, got some sleep and known it would all be fine the following morning.

Men handle being overtired better than women. They get grumpy, snappish and likely to break things, but they don't start crying. Everything about the job suited the male physiology better, like being on a submarine. I was trying to buck a stereotype when my body simply wasn't built for it: heavy drinking, late nights and long days had turned me into a nervous wreck after a couple of months. The City wasn't sexist; it was fucking exhausting.

The next morning I woke at three, sweating uncontrollably. My lower back, which had been aching dully when I'd gone to bed, was throbbing and it now felt like my kidneys were trying to burst out through my lower vertebrae. My heart was pounding, heavy and urgent. Every gland in my body was swollen. I lay like that until it started to get light, waiting for the painkillers to kick in, but nothing changed.

I knew I had to get to work. After my hysterical rant the previous evening, it was vital that I made it in. Calling in sick was

86

not an option – it would be game over, especially since I'd asked for my salary to be increased. I tried standing, but I couldn't seem to hold my body upright, and I was beginning to have what felt like heart palpitations. My kidneys were calling the shots. There was no way I was going to make it to Canary Wharf. I couldn't die on the Jubilee Line.

I got my keys and my BlackBerry, stumbled pyjama-clad into the corridor and bashed on the door of my new flatmate, Nikki, who had only just moved in. Our conversations had so far been limited to 'Would you like a cup of tea?'.

'Sorry. I think I need to go to A&E. Can you make sure I make it into a cab?'

Calling for an ambulance seemed excessive, as Chelsea and Westminster Hospital was only five minutes away, but as my breathing got more difficult and my heart seemed to be racing even faster, and I was in so much pain that I was unable to speak, it might have been more sensible. In the cab I somehow managed to send an email to the American from my BlackBerry before I lost all ability to function: 'Going to A&E. Sick. Not coming in. Probs explains why was hysterical. Sorry. V.' Somewhere in the back of my mind I was conscious of the need to provide an explanation for my tears the previous evening; apparently even the vast amount of pain I was experiencing wasn't enough to mask the embarrassment.

Everything apparently got progressively worse. I came to and found myself hooked up to a heart monitor, my breasts flopped sideways like discarded water balloons. Various drips and a cannula had found their way into my arm and hand. A doctor was asking me questions I could hear, but they swirled around my overheated brain and failed to compute. My thermostat had given up in the taxi. I seemed to be sweating, shivering and pulsating at the same time, and I was permanently hovering on the brink of passing out.

My back must be broken. My kidneys. My kidneys are shrivelling up. Please save my kidneys. Don't take them. It's my liver. Are you sure it's not my liver?

Nothing made any sense. I think I was glad to see Mark, although I was lucid enough to know that seeing my new boyfriend when I looked like a heroin addict going through withdrawal wasn't an ideal scenario. The last time I'd been hospitalized, with appendicitis, in my first year at university, I'd also just got together with someone. We'd slept together for the first time the previous evening. He'd sat outside waiting to see me after I had been admitted. Post anal exam, I was asked if I wanted to see my boyfriend. It hadn't seemed like the right thing to do, even in my drugged-up stupor, so I'd asked for my gay friend Chris instead, and he'd reported back for me, saving my dignity and keeping the details of the anal examination to himself. On this occasion, I had no choice. I didn't have a doctor's finger up my arse, but I wasn't pretty. I was a thrashing, sweating beast, with breasts akimbo and matted hair. Mark was wonderfully unfazed by the entire ugly episode.

They finally established after endless blood tests that I had come down with a nasty case of pyelonephritis. I had an infection high in my kidneys – so high, in fact, that it had bypassed sending out the usual urinary-tract symptoms and headed straight for heart palpitations, delirium and passing out. I was apparently so run down that my kidneys had welcomed all passing visitors. I knew that I was run down; I hadn't slept or eaten properly for weeks.

As soon as I was hooked up to the icy IV antibiotics, everything got a little less manic. My veins cooled, and my heart finally slowed down. They wanted to keep me in overnight; Mark stayed with me, faithfully carrying around my urine samples while I limped along, dragging my various IV packs behind him, until they moved me to a ward and finally kicked him out at 11 p.m.

The man in the opposite bed was an addict. He'd been in the next cubicle when I was in A&E, and I'd heard his lecture on intravenous drug use as I'd lain there watching my chest rise up and down. We'd both been writhing around in pain simultaneously, and now found ourselves in the same ward. Everyone else around us was elderly and already fast asleep, so it was just me and the heroin addict left to while away the night.

He was slipping in and out of consciousness, groaning and screaming periodically, lying flat out, face down throughout, with the flopped limbs of someone totally incapacitated. I wondered how they had succeeded in silencing his body and not his voice. I lay for hours listening to him. Nurses shuffled through occasionally, giving him more drugs, probably injecting in one of the many perfect tracks he'd already laid out for them. I was half expecting him to give up and die at any moment, but the groaning carried on. I slept uneasily. I kept hearing prices being shouted.

'5/8+ bid.'
'@ 7/8.'
'3/4 bid.'
'Repeat.'

Every time I turned over, I woke up, flinching as the cannula in my hand knocked into something or pulled against the drip, like a fish pulling against a hook through its gill. The hook always wins.

I knew I would be dragged straight back under. Despite having hospitalized myself, and inevitably having to take a week off work to recover, the respite wouldn't last. I had reflected briefly between dreams – I wondered whether my new lifestyle was sustainable, whether after a week off I'd be able to jump back onto the drunken roundabout or whether by now it would be moving too quickly for me, someone else would have taken my place, and my one chance would have passed.

'5/8+ bid.'
'@ 7/8.'
'3/4 bid.'
'Repeat.'

Being ill had always had its benefits in the past: time off school or university for a valid reason was always welcomed. When I found out that I had glandular fever when I was fifteen, I was relieved. I had more or less hated school, and it me. But now I was inconsolable; I hated the thought of anyone else having to speak to my few clients. Emma would be stuck speaking to the American again and he would undo all my work. I kept remembering restaurant reservations that would need cancelling and drinks that would have to be rearranged again. And the thought of having to catch up on a week or two's worth of prices when I had spent so long making sure the spreadsheets were accurate, made me want to somehow drag myself in the next morning, taking the drip with me if necessary.

'*5/8+ bid.*'
'*@ 7/8.*'
'*3/4 bid.*'
'*Repeat.*'

It was 5 a.m. I reached for my BlackBerry and turned off my 5.45 a.m. alarm. The dying heroin addict had returned to his hourly moaning, only now at a lower pitch. Most of the pain in my back had subsided and I was fixated on the tube stuck in my hand, the painful embedding of which had led to purple and yellow bruises surrounding my veins and now spreading up my arm. I always seemed to get the aggressive, sadist nurses, shoving, prodding and generally brimming with rage. I wanted to let out deep, sad groans like the guy opposite. Maybe they'd give me some morphine.

I spent all day waiting for Mark to resurface. I had assumed he would be there as soon as visiting hours started, but there was no sign of him. It wasn't like he had anything to do.

I was moved to another room when the heroin addict started roaming around aggressively. I shared the new room with one other woman, who had gout. I'd always joked about the prospect of getting gout as a result of broking, but to be faced with her giant swollen leg wasn't quite so amusing. I thought of Henry VIII being winched onto his horse when I saw her leg, and wondered if I kept consuming the same quantities of *foie gras*, cheese, various things soaked in butter and endless bottles of wine, I would end up in the same predicament. As I later discovered, gout isn't caused by the excessive eating of rich foods, so I would be fine – fat, but fine.

I had nothing to do but lie there and watch the antibiotics entering my system, like watching sand in an hourglass, while unintelligible nurses bumped slowly around my bed, pulling on my drip and bashing into things. I didn't understand why everything took so long. Even putting two painkillers into a tiny cup took at least ten minutes. Nothing was done with any urgency. It was like being looked after by people in those plastic inflatable sumo wrestler suits. If they moved too quickly, they would probably tumble over, knocking everything in their path flying, so they moved at a pace that was comfortable and caused maximum irritation to the patients around them. After months on a trading floor, an NHS hospital ward was probably the worst place I could possibly have ended up.

When I woke in agony again in the middle of the night and pressed my buzzer, I heard one of the sumo wrestlers ambling along the corridor. She was walking at the sort of pace you would expect from a family navigating its way around Debenhams' soft-furnishing department on a Saturday afternoon, complete with giant pram. I would be dead by now if I'd been having a heart attack.

I had fucking private health insurance. What was the point? It was clearly only of any use if I suddenly needed a hip or knee replacement and didn't want to wait five years, or for an appointment with a top podiatrist when my bunions decided to make their presence felt, which would no doubt happen sooner or later. As I lay in the dark waiting for painkillers, this was of little comfort.

The nurse finally ambled through the door. I explained how I was feeling – that once again I felt as if something were about to burst out of my coccyx. She stared at me in the dark, and I waited for some sort of reaction, but instead she said nothing and walked away at the same pace as before. 'COME BACK!' I wanted to speak to her in the same way that I would be spoken to if I moved at her pace across the trading floor when I retrieved the coffees.

Walking down the street without punching slow-moving people in the back of the head is difficult enough when you leave the floor; being kind to useless waiters is virtually impossible; but watching a nurse waddling away from you when you're in pain is enough to make you wish you were in possession of a firearm.

Someone else eventually came back with a couple of paracetamol. Paracetamol is never what you want to be given when you think your kidneys are failing. You want the strong shit, like morphine, not the standard-issue tablets found lurking in the bottom of every handbag. I took them, not fancying my chances at getting anything else to see me through the night. She checked my drip, and disappeared down the corridor.

I couldn't get back to sleep. The gout woman was snoring. I had nothing to read – only my BlackBerry, which had endless pages of Bloomberg messages containing prices in its inbox. I had forwarded my messages in case I ever missed something while I was out getting the American's lunch, but now the messages tauntingly made me realize how much business I'd missed the previous day.

I was discharged the following morning. I told Mark I would be ready at midday, then spent three hours waiting for my various antibiotics and painkillers to be brought up from the pharmacy and chatting inanely to the gout lady and her husband. I was exhausted and wanted to go home, not chat about how Chelsea had changed over the last ten years with someone whose leg was probably about to fall off. It seemed like the longest three hours of my life. I kept expecting Mark or the drugs to arrive, and every time I heard footsteps outside the corridor I shuffled to the edge of my chair, only to see another savage nurse. I was permanently on the verge of getting up and going to get a cab alone, but I kept convincing myself that Mark would be there in five minutes and that I really shouldn't be travelling alone. The drugs eventually turned up, thrown at me by one of the nurses, along with my discharge letter for my GP, but still there was no sign of Mark and I was unable to escape a monologue on the complications of gout. I don't remember ever having waited so intensely, so desperately for anything. By the time he finally showed up, I was forlorn and irritated. I wasn't even relieved or glad to see him – I had no energy left for good emotions. Once Mark had arrived, late, and we'd made it back to my flat, I just wanted him to leave.

. I felt the same exhausted anger that I'd first experienced when an ex-boyfriend had turned on the *Match of the Day* repeat at 8 a.m. while I was asleep in bed next to him with horrific tonsillitis. I hadn't slept for days, and he'd been away working, promising that he would be there soon to look after me – he was a doctor. When he finally turned up at my flat, I was expecting chicken soup and Lemsip, but he fell asleep immediately, only to wake me up first thing in the morning and blast out football. I didn't even get a cup of tea. I had never felt more alone.

The thought of spending the next week resting, miles away from Canary Wharf and missing out on trading, was far more depressing than I'd anticipated. I hated the timing of it all. The last conversation I'd had with the American was a tearful moan about being exhausted and unable to survive on my 20k salary. It looked as if I couldn't handle the job and I was now sick as a result.

I was restless. Trying to relax and stay in bed after months of surviving on adrenalin alone was impossible. I woke up at 5.45 a.m., even without my alarm, panicked that I was late for work. Adrenalin was as powerful a drug as any Class A, and without it, and my regular doses of espresso, I no longer knew how to function. I sunk into a wide-eyed daytime-TV-fuelled stupor, interrupted only by the Tesco delivery man armed with bottles of water and grapes that I never got around to eating.

When I made it back to work, I knew how long I'd been off only from the dates on the medical certificate I'd been given by my GP after I was discharged from hospital. It could have been months but was a mere ten days, and everything had changed.

A chemical company whose bonds and loans we had traded had posted very bad numbers, and prices had dropped by a couple of points. It had been trading every day and, as I could see from the trade sheets, had been bouncing around all over the place. I was annoyed to see that Ian had been the seller on a load of the trades – the commission would have been mine if I hadn't been hooked up to an IV drip.

Stu had resigned. His desk was empty. He'd apparently said he was retiring, but everyone knew that he would resurface at another shop in three months' time. He had a new house and a Ferrari to pay for, after all.

I found it strange that he had disappeared one day and no one seemed to be particularly bothered. Brokers and traders were forever moving between shops – negotiating better pay packages, joining better teams, throwing tantrums about bonuses, and resigning so they could begin the three months' gardening leave before joining a brand-new desk somewhere else.

Most of the guys I worked with had spent time broking at

most of the other shops in the market at some point and had all known each other for years. There was very little loyalty; people moved to whichever house happened to be offering the most money spread over the shortest period. It was rare for teams to stick together for long, because it was usually impossible for a broking house to lift an entire desk from the competition without a huge legal battle ensuing. Everyone seemed to be permanently in the throes of being 'bid away' and negotiating the price at which they would move, whether they intended to do so or not. It was simple shopping around – that irresistible urge to check the price of something elsewhere even when you've already got what you wanted, taken it home and tried it out.

Headhunters were, of course, fully aware of the fickle nature of traders, and were constantly ringing around to check how happy people were, mention who was hiring, what sort of teams were being put together and what was being paid. Many traders, feeling underappreciated after bonus day or after a particularly bad week, ended up switching banks based solely on the back of a random phone call from some headkunter, as Lena liked to refer to them.

The American had failed to update any of the prices on our spreadsheets, which was no real surprise, as admin had always defeated him. Dory had updated as much as he could, and had also decided to implement a colour-coding system for different industries.

All I knew was that colour printing took twice as long as black and white, which meant more loitering around the photocopier every evening chatting to Giles. His desk, dubbed 'Rajastan 4' by Wayne, stayed later than anyone else's. Nobody really knew what they traded and, like the Turkish desk, they kept themselves separate from the rest of the floor, and got in earlier and stayed later than anyone else. Giles and I had met one night on the Tube; recognizing each other from work, we got talking. He'd been broking for a couple of years, and had fallen into it after university in more or less the same way I had – randomly, through friends. Meeting Giles was a relief. Everything made slightly more sense with him around, and something about him was familiar in an otherwise alien environment.

Most of our desk used the sheets that I religiously updated and printed every day as scrap paper or as placemats to eat on, preferring their own systems for recording prices – much like Philippe's ill-fated CDS data sheets, which the Ferg immediately ripped up or threw at someone, before eventually saying, 'Neesh, I have no idea what this fucking shit means. We barely even trade any CDS. It's a total waste of paper. Don't bother printing me off a copy.'

09:08:10 LENA KLEIN. So did you get the flowers?
09:08:50 VENETIA THOMPSON: Yeah, yesterday.
09:09:05 LENA KLEIN: They asked for your address last week.
09:09:48 LENA KLEIN: Muppets might as well have just waited and given them to you now.
09:10:10 VENETIA THOMPSON: ha. So what have I missed?
09:11:02 LENA KLEIN: fuk all. I've been bored shitless with no one to speak to. But I have adopted a cat.

Lena was always picking up strays. She'd had the cat microchipped and jabbed immediately and was now worrying about getting home early to spend time with her. At least the cat was an upgrade from the last stray, a guy whose English was so limited that when she had attempted to explain to him what she did for a living, he'd smiled and said, 'Your boss must be happy to have such good secretary as you.'

It was a familiar story. Traders and brokers, whether male or female, seemed incapable of having relationships with anyone vaguely their equal, whether intellectually or professionally. It started at the top and worked its way down: the top dog at another firm had picked up his latest wife while in a strip club in Buenos Aires and brought her back with him. She was now clad in Prada and flown into Ascot by helicopter, but she was still a lap-dancer underneath. Strippers, beauticians, waitresses, PR girls and students were all popular choices.

Now I was amusingly a paid-up subscriber to the same strange stereotype by dating a broke musician. It seems that nobody really wants to be challenged when they get home, and having someone who feeds the stray cat and has no idea what you actually do from seven 'til seven every day is every trader's dream. It is therefore no surprise that the Fashion meets Banking networking events were such a success in New York. I'd somehow ended up on the wrong side of the equation, more or less supporting Mark and his dream to be a rock and roll star. However, he had been there to carry my urine samples around the hospital, and let me dribble on his shoulder when I passed out asleep – something a lawyer or doctor would never have been able to make time for because they would be too busy saving lives or working.

The American had seemingly failed to notice I was back, and suddenly looked up, bagel in one hand, surprised to see me sitting beside him again.

'So, you feeling better?'

'Yeah, much better, thanks. Have I missed much? Other than the fact Stu's quit?!'

'No. Bits and pieces. We've sorted out your money. Paperwork should come through in a few days. We need to sort out Stu's accounts – who is going to cover them. Think we're having a desk meeting about it at some point with Leicester.' Leicester was the floor head.

He returned to the *Wall Street Journal* online. The conversation was over. I tried stringing it out a bit, rambling about my time in hospital, but he was immediately focused on something else, coughing occasionally, only wincing when I mentioned the cannula that had bruised my hand.

It was never obvious whether he was listening or not. He had once said, 'I may appear as if I'm not paying attention, but I always am, so never make the mistake of thinking I'm not,' but as yet I hadn't seen much evidence of it. I would frequently have to tell him what prices the Ferg or Wayne had when he wasn't paying attention or had been on the phone. It was hard to decipher where the bagel-chewing, general disinterest ended, and where the shrewd broker with the thickest skin in the market began, and I wasn't sure whether I would ever find out.

CHAPTER 6

THE QUEEN AND THE KUNT

LINO GET A BRA, LINO GET A BRA,
LINO GET A FUCKING BRA

Football and the City are inseparable. Everyone of any importance in our firm was a Spurs fan. There was the odd Chelsea or West Ham supporter, but the vast majority were fiercely Spurs. When I started the job, more shocking to the guys than the fact that I was female, a graduate and not from Essex was that I had never been to a football game and didn't support a team. Going to matches was an integral part of client entertainment. All traders liked football; even the ones who didn't would never turn down the chance to go.

It was no surprise, therefore, when I found myself in the West Stand at Stamford Bridge, about ten rows back, for Liverpool vs. Chelsea, the first leg of the Champions League semi-final, and my first-ever football game. I now understood

100

why most corporate entertainment took place in boxes, far away from the fans likely to launch at you any second for wearing a suit, being American or not knowing any of the words to the songs. We were sitting among the sort of Chelsea supporters who spent the entire match looking for Liverpool fans hiding among their ranks, ready to have them ejected instantly. A couple of Scousers had already been 'outed' a few rows away from where we were sitting and removed by officials. Though I wasn't with Scousers, I was with two men in suits and one in chinos, two of whom were American; none were firm Chelsea supporters, and were therefore equally likely to get thrown out at any given moment. The American had taken to standing and yelling at no one player in particular at impromptu moments. It was slightly like trying to control someone's embarrassing dad at a school disco, but the clients loved it, and sprang to their feet whenever the American did.

I was relieved to get back to the safety of Automat in Mayfair for dinner. I realized that I was probably going to have to learn the rules of football, or find out vaguely what went on, in order to go to more games with clients, because I had nothing to say about it over dinner. I kept hoping that the topic would change, but it kept going back to the match and the remainder of the season. I was totally lost.

After dinner, I went to meet Lena for a drink. She had texted me to say that she was out with The Deviant, a big-drinking, big-swinging CDS trader, and he was on brilliant form. Every time we saw him, we'd sit transfixed and make him tell us the same stories over and over again. They usually involved Zippy, a CDS trader at a different bank, and their 'chalet from hell' skiing weekends with brokers. We would always end up on the floor. I wasn't going to miss another opportunity to hear the stories, and arrived as he was reaching the punchline, 'and the next thing 'e knows, 'e wakes up in the chalet with that fucking cunt's balls being waved in 'is face. He's tryin' to bloody tea-bag 'im, would you fuckin' believe it? And now 'e's being done for assault! Imagine being tea-bagged by your fuckin' client! Of course, when the bookie complained, someone rang up to try and get Zippy to apologise, 'e just says "You can take my job, and all my fucking money, but I will never apologise to that cunt!"'

Rumoured to be because of the tea-bagging incident, Zippy had recently come out of early retirement, having finally 'found himself' during a two-year sabbatical from the market, and realized that, having seen what the world had to offer, and sending frequent group emails to most of the Street detailing the finer points of the retreats he'd attended, he was finally ready to return to credit default swaps. The only physical remnant of his time travelling was a collection of coloured beads that he wore around his neck with various Buddhist charms hanging from them. The emails he sent while travelling continued to circulate, turning up in inboxes all over the Square Mile every few weeks, and being forwarded to the uninitiated. They all began with an insightful quote. The first in the series had begun:

'They lifted up the gold as if they were monkeys, with expressions of joy, as if it put new life into them and lit up their hearts. As if it were certainly something for which they yearn with a great thirst, their bodies fatten on it and they hunger violently for it. They crave gold like hungry swine.'

Indigenous text
Dear all,
It is with great sadness that I am writing to break the news, to

those of you who might not know already, that I have become
disenchanted with the endless pursuit of the Dream (for the time
being) and have decided to take some time out in order to travel,
and hopefully discover more about myself and the world.
Admittedly, there might be nothing to discover, but isn't
discovering that there is nothing to discover a discovery in
itself?

I bid you adieu and hope the markets are kind to you in my
absence.

Ever since the fateful tea-bagging incident during a broker ski
trip, Zippy had been the talk of the Street, seamlessly jumping
from one strange sexual exploit to another. It turned out that
tea-bagging combined with existential ramblings were a winning combination in the City, and Zippy was now something of
a hero – the wrong 'un spiritual voice of the Square Mile. But it
was The Deviant with his perfect impressions who had brought
Zippy alive as a character months before I met the man. Zippy
in person could never be as funny as The Deviant's version.

As well as his impersonations, The Deviant was the master
of executing the stealth c-bomb – when a trader or broker is
nominated and then as many people as possible call him or her
on the outside lines, wait until they're picked up and shout
'cunt' before hanging up immediately. The quieter the market,
the longer the c-bombing would last. Shortly after my first
trade I was c-bombed one afternoon courtesy of The Deviant.
Every call I answered for a good half-hour was someone different shouting, 'Cunt'.

Most people don't even know whom they are ringing, and
are given a number by whoever starts it and told to call immediately. It was a game that nobody ever grew tired of and was

perfect for quiet afternoons. But not everyone saw the funny side. Complaints were made when the market was in the midst of a flurry of activity and someone decided to deploy a c-bomb anyway, blocking all of some unlucky trader's outside lines, making it impossible for his sales team and clients to get hold of him at crucial moments. The trader would then be left to try to explain to his boss or client that the reason he couldn't trade, and vast sums of money were lost, was because all of his lines were blocked by people waiting to call him a cunt.

I got home around midnight to find Mark watching TV in bed. He wanted to hear about the game, but I'd already forgotten who had scored; my brain was full of The Deviant's stories, which weren't funny when I tried to recount them. Everything that was funny or interesting about the City seemed to work only in context. When I got home, nothing translated.

I knew that our relationship was changing. We were running out of things to talk about. He didn't understand my new life; the people I worked with and the stories I told were all of little interest. Our points of reference had completely altered, and the only thing we now had in common was the fact that we shared a bed and occasionally had sex, but I was too exhausted to end things. It was too easy to get home from a night out with clients and climb into bed with him. He never asked anything of me, and always made sure that I heard my alarm and got up, but everything about him seemed slow compared to the rest of my life, which was moving at such an alarming pace. It was like hitting a brick wall every time I opened my front door. I wondered whether this was what happened when a relationship got beyond the initial giddiness; whether most couples lay in bed at night knowing the person lying next to them was no longer the best thing that had happened to them, but simply something that had happened, at some point, and was now as incurable as it was inescapable – like chronic fatigue syndrome.

Calypso. 5.45 a.m. I could hear Mark saying 'baby' every few minutes. I wanted to reach out and hit snooze but I couldn't move my arm. He started saying it louder and groaned as he jabbed me in the shoulder before leaning over me and grabbing my BlackBerry, thrusting it into my hand. This was why I needed him in my life. He made sure I got to work. I would've been fired months ago without him.

I stumbled into the shower trying to remember if there was anything I was supposed to have done before leaving work the night before when we'd rushed out the door to get to the football, but my brain was full of football chants and tales of tea-bagging. I got dressed, leaned over and kissed Mark's snoring lips and headed out the door.

One of the consequences of Stu leaving was that Delusions of Grandeur (DofG) and a few other accounts, along with Stu's collection of vitamins, were now up for grabs. Because no one had anything resembling a relationship with Yank Bank, it was decided that I would try to take over that line.

Yank Bank's huge team never responded to anything. If I shouted prices or sent Bloomberg messages, they remained silent and appeared to be doing all of their business elsewhere. Our line was out – they just hadn't bothered telling us. I quickly became obsessed with trying to get some sort of response from them, and decided that my best hope was to concentrate on individual traders rather than the entire desk. Where better to start than the young Russian guy?

Despite having barely spoken Russian since university, it

fleetingly became my trump card when I started yelling down the line for him and sending Bloomies in Russian. He began not only reading my messages (Bloomberg enables you to see when someone has read a message and when they have replied), but also replying in Russian.

I could barely trade bonds in English, and wasn't sure that attempting to do business in any other language was sensible, so I kept it conversational – what he'd done at the weekend, whether he was busy, and what was trading. For a few weeks I seemed to be making progress, and he gave me a couple of prices in the obscure illiquid names he traded. But then, just as I was starting to build up a relationship, I fucked up.

I shouted down a price, not expecting to hear anything from any of them, only to get hit immediately. Dory instantly thought something was strange, as the hit had come from a trader there who hadn't spoken to us for months, and who would probably only hit something that was too good to be true – and it was. I'd shouted the wrong price, half a point higher than it should have been.

I thought that I was going to throw up. It was my first serious mistake, my first big hook, and it was entirely my fault. I couldn't even blame the trader. It was a straightforward transaction: there had been no conversation, just a price and a reaction. Now I had to go and listen to the tapes to confirm exactly what I'd said.

I'd already admitted full responsibility, somehow stopped myself from bursting into tears and apologized profusely to the desk. I didn't need to hear the tape – I knew I'd fucked up – but Dory sent me up to the voice communications department to make sure, maybe just to give me five minutes off the desk.

I jogged towards the lifts and stabbed at the button

impatiently; the doors finally opened and, after what seemed like hours, I re-emerged a few floors higher into previously unchartered territory. There were dozens of people whom I'd never seen before sitting at desks in various cubicles and glass offices – and plenty of women. It couldn't have been more different to the trading floor. Eventually I found the telecoms cluster, sat down next to the burly communications engineer, who jovially handed me a giant pair of headphones, and waited as he found the exact piece of tape that we needed. I was about to burst into tears at any moment, and was thinking that it was probably better to get it out of the way up here away from the floor if I was going to crack. I tried to focus on what I was hearing. I could hear myself shouting numbers inanely for what seemed like ages, and for a while I thought that maybe it hadn't happened after all, or that it hadn't been recorded. Then I heard a male voice say simply, 'Yours.'

I got back in the lift, feeling sick, still determined not to cry, and went back to my desk and confirmed my mistake to the guys. The trader already knew that there was a problem because I'd sent the wrong price on the trade confirm sheets – half a point lower than he thought he'd hit. Dory had tried to speak to him but he was waiting for me to call.

'Just decide what you're gonna say and stick to it, Neesh. Write it down if you have to. But stick to your bloody story and get it done quickly. The longer you leave it, the worse it'll be. It's just like tearing off a plaster.'

Everyone was pissed off. It was money that the desk really didn't need to be losing. As I found the trader's details on Bloomberg and dialled his outside line, I was as close to shitting myself as I'd ever been. I felt like I was about to pass out. I knew that my only option was to be completely straight with him, to explain that I was new and had fucked up, and to see if he would cancel the trade. Miraculously, he agreed to let it go. I was waiting for him to start yelling at me, but he said that it was fine and to forget about it and buy him dinner some day.

We now needed to speak to the buyer, who was thrilled to have been hit at such a low price and be the proud owner of a couple of million bonds a lot cheaper than anyone else owned them. He, of course, made us wear the trade, refusing to cancel it. So I called the seller back; he made it slightly less painful by knocking an eighth off, which was roughly where it should have traded on a good day.

It could have been worse. We took the hit on the price differential, and Dory fielded the phone call from the guys in Risk before saying, 'Schneesh. This desk has seen far, far worse losses than that, trust me. It's peanuts. Just get on with your job and make the money back.' And then, chuckling, he added, 'It's not like we had anything to lose with that account. They fucking hate us anyway.'

I knew that I had to forget what had happened as quickly as possible and get back on the phones. In broking there is simply no time to become fixated on losses and think about how you could have handled something differently, and it doesn't achieve anything. The only way that a loss can be fixed is by getting enough trades done to cancel it out.

When Dory had said that the desk had seen far worse losses, he hadn't been saying that just to make me feel better. It turned out that Ken and Miles, a guy who no longer worked for the Company, had once lost the desk over 400,000 sterling in the space of a few days several years back, in the height of the high yield bond boom, when everything was far more volatile than it had recently been. Keeping in mind that brokers are never supposed to be exposed to risk, as bonds should go straight in and straight out, this was a fairly impressive loss.

Ken had been long on a load of bonds as a result of a fuck-up on a trade with Miles and a guy at Aggro Bank, and they'd thought that it would be fine, that the price of the bond would bounce back up and they could sell the following day and maybe even make a profit – at the very least they would be back flat. But the price continued to fall, and they couldn't find a bid. It got to Thursday, and the rest of the desk was away – Dory was sick, the Ferg and Wayne were at Ascot and Philippe was on holiday. Ken and Miles were alone on the desk, watching the price plummet and wondering when it would be a good time to tell The Big Boss.

Friday morning, Ken finally strolled into his office, sat down, and said that there was a problem: the desk was long and wrong, and a load of money had been lost – a few hundred grand.

'200,000 dollars? Don't worry about it, these things happen. Just get back to work.'

'No. It's actually 456,000.'

'Dollars?'

'Sterling.'

Ken never really came back from that mistake, and everyone joked that he probably still owed the Company thousands when he finally left to travel the world years later. I never spoke Russian at work again.

Hearing stories of mistakes made by other brokers didn't make the blow any softer. I couldn't believe I'd made such a stupid mistake and for the rest of the day I checked every price three times before saying it out loud. I'd obviously become too relaxed, expecting nothing to happen because the market was quiet and forgetting that quiet markets are often the most dangerous for brokers because someone will always hear your mistake and take full advantage of it.

I wanted the day to be over, so I could get home to see Mark, get some takeaway and go to bed. I was too gun-shy to do anything without checking with the American or Dory first. The American wanted to talk over what I'd done wrong so that it wouldn't happen again, but every time he broached the subject I could feel my eyes filling up and frantically sipped from my bottle of water to avoid making eye contact with him. I knew exactly what I'd done: I'd called out the wrong fucking price. I didn't need to go over it again painstakingly. I needed to forget about it and move on. Luckily, his gardener called and I got a reprieve. I just had to get through the next half-hour without accidentally resigning in a fit of hysteria and I'd be fine by the morning. For the time being, I simply couldn't take any more. I was a nervous wreck again.

At two minutes to five, I stood up, put my suit jacket on and began gathering my things together. The American was straight out the door and, thankfully, didn't attempt any further post-work discourse on my general incompetence. I walked as fast as I could through the mall to the Tube and leapt into a packed carriage, where I stood, head down, quietly sobbing until I got to Green Park and began to calm down.

I reached my stop, relieved to be within a five-minute walk of seeing Mark, but when I was getting off the escalator, one of my Prada shoes got jammed in the step. I lost my balance and suddenly found myself lying face down on the floor, with commuters stepping over me. I'd clearly become one of the ever increasing number of people who have escalator accidents every year, as Ken Livingstone's posters used to inform us. I always used to wonder how accidents happened on escalators, and now I knew.

My spiked heel was jammed in the treads of the escalator, but the body of the shoe was lying at my feet, having been kicked free by someone. The metal heel, now naked, stripped of its leather coating, was sending off sparks and was impossible to pull out. Every time I tried to grab hold of it, someone would reach the top of the escalator and push me out of the way, shaking their head. The escalator finally ground to a halt, and I stood and watched as the Transport for London guard used a hammer to knock the heel free before handing it to me and telling me that it was irresponsible to wear heels that were so thin that they got jammed. I apparently could have broken the escalator. I didn't know what to say to him, and limped away silently.

I hobbled home in my heel-less shoe, got through the door and collapsed into a heaving hysterical wreck on my bedroom floor. It was the sort of irrational PMT-style crying that I knew was ridiculous even as I swiftly filled up with snot and couldn't breathe, yet I couldn't stop. Mark came into my room from the kitchen, where he'd been busy making me a cup of tea, and assumed someone had died. When I'd shown him my shoe, he pulled me up off the floor and got me into bed before lying down beside me and making me go through what had happened in detail until I calmed down. Only when I got to the end of the tale of the day's events did he start giggling. It was the first time we'd laughed properly for weeks. I was suddenly glad he'd moved in after the lease on his flat had expired. We hadn't really planned it, but it seemed one way of being able to spend some time together. I was quickly realizing how easy it was to lose all sense of perspective working in the City, when one bad day and a broken heel could be enough to make you resign or slit your wrists. Having someone to get you through the night was crucial.

I went to work the next day in flat shoes for the first time since I'd started broking. The American wasn't angry about the Yank Bank debacle – just smug. He'd never wanted me to cover that account, and this proved him right: I couldn't focus on that many different products at the same time. He wanted me to focus on Emma, Brad, Ian, Stupidly Bullish Bank and the guys at DofG Bank. I'd answered the line to the latter a couple of times, and had struck up a vague banter-laden relationship with their desk head. He kept shouting down and asking for me, so it was decided that I would attempt to cover their two traders. It all started off well, with a steady stream of two-way markets coming in every morning, and they quickly became my best clients, always having something to do and acting immediately on most of the prices I shouted down.

We arranged a dinner at Nobu Park Lane for Wednesday, and I booked a table at Cuckoo Club for later in the evening. Clubs don't like large groups of guys, especially groups of City boys, and I had therefore lined up Lena to come and join us after her own client dinner. The American and I arrived at Nobu early and headed to the bar, where we sat in silence, the American sipping a Diet Coke while I sloshed back a gin martini, and waited for DofG.

Traders generally sound better than they look. Meeting them destroys the illusion that they are all six-foot muscle-bound rogues, likely to punch the nearest wall at any second. Like celebrities on television, they are generally shorter, skinnier and far less interesting in person. There are always exceptions to this rule, and Christian, the head trader at DofG, was as arrogant and theatrical as he sounded down the line. He was tall and wore a skinny-fitting immaculate suit. His body had all the poise of a young blond German model who had just stumbled out of a Dior Homme advertisement *circa* Hedi Slimane, but his face was that of a forty-something desk head. He was wonderfully camp, like a transvestite on a Soho stage, yet it emerged over dinner that he was married with children, something that I found increasingly difficult to believe as the evening continued and he became more and more of a queen, gesturing wildly with his chopsticks at every opportunity.

The Queen, as I began to think of him, had a penchant for fine wines and, without checking with the American, started off with a £400 bottle of white burgundy, before seamlessly moving to its red equivalent, while the American was busy asking me to order more spicy tuna rolls.

It was the first time I had been out to dinner and felt invisible. When I attempted to interject during a conversation, I was ignored and spoken over. I wasn't sure why I was there; I could have quite easily slid under the table and no one would have noticed. It seemed that all social graces and manners were immediately forgotten during broker dinners, and the more senior the trader, the worse he'd behave. When the waitress asked if anyone wanted dessert or coffee, the question was answered for me. They didn't want anything and, therefore, apparently, neither did I.

We got to the club and were turned away because the American was wearing chinos and moccasin-style boat shoes, which were deemed too casual. There was no sign of Lena, so our group was too male heavy. I would have felt embarrassed that I had failed to get us into the club (seemingly my only task that evening because I sure as hell wasn't there for my insights on the market), if I didn't think that they were all such pricks. So I jumped in a cab and took them to the Baglioni Hotel, where we sat in their Liberace's-coffin-themed bar, drinking our way through their cellar list until it closed.

The Queen had ordered another bottle of wine costing only marginally less than my monthly rent. As it was decanted and passed around, he'd stopped the waiter pouring his junior a glass, offering him only a sip to try. I'd let out an incredulous snort, assuming that he was joking, but he hadn't been. I later discovered that The Queen had pulled a similar stunt at a broker Christmas lunch, and ordered one bottle of particularly fine wine for himself, and passed the undrinkable house wine down the table for the rest of the guests, who included traders from other banks.

The following week, as if the account wasn't difficult enough to cover already, The Queen hired The Kunt, who had been kicking around the market for years, moving from product to product, desk to desk and bank to bank. He was the toxic waste of the Street – impossible to get rid of and likely to destroy anything with which he came into contact.

The Kunt had taken an instant dislike to me when we did our first few trades together. He had bought a large slice of a medical company's loans over the course of one afternoon, but in small amounts at a time because he couldn't decide how much he wanted. I had been told by the seller that the holder had set a minimum transfer amount of 3 million, and had relayed the information to The Kunt, who was initially glad to be warned about this, and put the trade on one ticket as opposed to several smaller ones, which would take longer to clear, until he agreed to a slightly wrong – depending on how you work out averages – blended price. Because the first 2 million had been at a different price to the next 2 million, and then the price had gone up again for the rest, in order to put the whole chunk on one trade he had to work out what the blended average price would be. But instead of working it out for himself, he agreed with the seller's price for the 7-odd million total. A couple of hours later, he came back down the line, convinced that I had fucked him over on the price, embarked upon a ten-minute rant and never spoke to me again.

When the American asked me what had happened, I couldn't even speak. All I managed to say was: 'Just give me a few minutes; hang on a sec,' while pretending that I was sending out prices. I was, in fact, desperately trying not to cry. I knew if I began explaining to the American what The Kunt had said, my voice would crack and it would all be over.

Relations between me and DofG never improved, and a few weeks later I managed to lose the account for good when I fucked up on what should have been a straightforward swap. I mixed up prices on opco with holdco – two different parts of the debt structure – and their third trader decided that I was intentionally lying to him and the swap never even existed, and pulled my line. The American called in a favour and got one of his clients to do the trade the right way around if we covered the difference, but by then DofG were refusing to speak to me.

It was frustrating not being given the chance to put something right when I could have. I'd made a stupid mistake that was a verbal typo: I'd said something quickly and got it back to front. I had known which way around it was supposed to be but had said the reverse; there had been nothing sinister about it. It was always going to happen. I knew as soon as I took over the account that sooner or later the line would be pulled over something totally insignificant. Those guys had started shouting down for me, had asked for me to be assigned to cover them, and then had just waited for me to fuck up.

The irony was that I wasn't experienced enough to shaft the trader intentionally, or to make up a faux swap market. Even if I had wanted to, I couldn't have screwed him over. He knew that, but had taken the opportunity to make an example of me – an early warning shot to his other brokers. The idea that I had intentionally got a swap price the wrong way around, or, as he had yelled at me, 'made up offers that never even existed, did they, you fucking liar', was ridiculous and offensive. I had put a call in to The Queen, hoping that my previous good relationship with him would maybe mean that he would give me a chance to explain what had happened, but he instantly told me that my line was out and hung up.

Their account was impossible to cover. While I was slowly getting used to being accused of deceit, incompetence and generally shit broking by one or all of them on a daily basis, I was relieved when I no longer had to speak to any of the fuckers again and the mantle was passed to someone more experienced. When you spend all day talking shit to each other – traders and anyone else that will listen – it is easy to turn up in Balenciaga at any City event and maintain the same ridiculous façade. The City is built on bullshit.

One of the large US banks was throwing a party for the leveraged finance market in one of the Foreign and Commonwealth Office's banqueting halls, and, like one of the Four Horsemen of the Apocalypse, the American had sent me forth. He had said that he might drop in for a couple of drinks but that I should go ahead without him. The party was comprised of a couple of secondary traders, but was largely made up of the bank's own clients. Various hedge funders and obscure retail banks, who would never be allowed to trade in the Street, were all shuffling around the room, knocking back champagne to the sound of steel drums. It was one of the most surreal situations that I'd ever found myself in.

I knew nothing about leveraged finance, other than what could be deduced from the words 'leveraged' and 'finance', yet I somehow managed to spend the entire evening speaking to fund managers about high yield and distressed debt, and the secondary market (which, as I explained to them, as an inter-dealer broker, I was a small part of).

It was slightly like having a conversation in French when you can only say, 'yes, I agree', 'no, of course', and 'absolutely', and really understand nothing at all. Yet somehow you can gauge from their expressions and gestures whether they are saying something that requires a positive or a negative response and make the appropriate noises. If all else fails, you simply show a little more cleavage and suddenly you are the most interesting person in the room.

I met the competition for the first time – brokers from the two other main shops – who all immediately embarked upon rants about the American, asking how I could work with him, whether he was retiring any time soon, and expressing sympathy that I had to sit next to him when he apparently spent all day with his feet up on the desk picking his toenails. I tried saying that he had never bared his feet around me, but they didn't seem to care.

After an awkward conversation with the PR guy who had organized the party, who was the only person in the room who knew less about leveraged finance than I did, and a quick bash of a steel drum, champagne in one hand, whacking it with the other, I decided it was time to escape. I came away with a handful of business cards and, strangely, a couple of job offers to go and do sales and marketing at funds. By far the most interesting conversations that I had all evening were with a lawyer who was as out of place and confused as I was and, as ever, the cabbie on the way home. 'Pfft. A bank had a party? Arrgh, I dunno, City boys. They're all fucking gits, love. Get out while you can. You look like a nice girl.'

June began with a dinner with three traders from Aggro Bank and the American. We were back in Nobu Park Lane, on the same table that we'd had with DofG a month earlier. The table was clearly jinxed, because the evening was horrific. The traders were all American, all under 5ft 10in and all from the Midwest, which in itself is enough to destroy what could have been an enjoyable evening. There was a severe sense of humour failure in operation, and the conversation naturally centred around all things Yank, moving from US politics to American football, to basketball and back to politics. I could have got up and left at any moment and no one would have noticed, and my one attempt at a joke about New Orleans had gone down particularly badly. I was aware that I was either about to turn into a social hand grenade and unleash a steady stream of inappropriate jokes and keep going, regardless of whether they were speaking over the top of me or not, or totally shut down; the latter was the preferable option.

After the DofG dinner, I got used to the idea of being seen and not heard – not being asked any questions, being spoken over when I attempted to contribute to the conversation and generally being ignored. This was even worse: they were all drinking Diet Coke. Luckily, I had ordered a couple of bottles of wine before anyone had time to realize that I was the only one drinking, and began stoically working my way through them alone, thinking that if I was inebriated the evening would be less painful and I would be less likely to ask them why they assumed that I knew nothing about American politics and were so set on ignoring me.

I caught sight of a bookie I knew from another firm having dinner with his CEO and other senior managers. I'd met him recently at a roof party thrown by a German bank, and we had exchanged the odd message on Bloomberg every few weeks since. He was hot, but I'd spent the entire party reiterating that I had a boyfriend and refusing to give him my number. Now he was in the same restaurant and was my only hope of turning around my horrific evening. I sat, staring longingly at their table – at their many wine glasses and chocolate bento boxes. He looked up and winked. When I saw him head to the loo, I excused myself and caught up with him.

As soon as we were safely out of sight in the corridor, he kissed me warmly on both cheeks and I drunkenly pushed him against the wall giggling, before beginning to tell him about my awful dinner. It was a relief to speak again, to be heard. Having been starved of conversation for the last hour and a half, I thought that I might have lost my voice forever. It was a five-minute reprieve; I'd been resuscitated. As he headed back, he slapped my arse before grabbing my hand and inviting me to join his table instead, where he assured me I would be allowed to speak, I wouldn't have to drink alone, and I could even have a job using my Russian if I wanted it.

'You know, one day I'm gonna have to just chopper in and get you out of that shithole, like the ending of a bad action movie.'

For a second I thought that I could probably get away with it: perhaps not being airlifted out of the restaurant, but at least sitting with them. I doubted that the Americans would even notice I'd gone – they would be too busy struggling to string together an intelligent sentence about the Clintons to care.

He went back to his table and I stumbled down the stairs, and went and hid in the ladies' for another few minutes. I put the toilet seat down and perched, deciding how much longer I could stay there. Being excluded from conversations is worse than being sworn at. I wondered what the fuck I was doing, in the bathroom at Nobu, at dinner with three of the rudest people I had ever met and unable to leave because it was part of my job. Sitting there like some vacuous Barbie listening to three Americans chat inanely about Obama was part of my job. Filling their water glasses and ordering their Diet Coke was part of my fucking job. Being ignored was apparently also part of my job. I was suddenly starting to hate it.

After the dinner with DofG, I thought that it didn't matter. The wine and food had been good, the company bad – it was a trade that I didn't mind making. But as I sat staring at the wall in the toilet cubicle, I began to realize that no amount of jalapeño yellow tail sashimi and Barolo made feeling worthless in my free time even vaguely palatable. I wasn't getting paid enough.

I went back to the table. I'd only been gone a few minutes but they were already on to their decaf coffees. The waiter came and asked if I wanted anything. I wanted to see the menu. I wanted dessert, and then a double espresso, and maybe even some petits fours and an Armagnac – none of which was an option because they were already getting up and putting their coats on. Cunts. I was invisible.

Two of them had already jumped into cabs by the time I made it down the stairs and collected my coat. I said goodbye to the American and began walking down Park Lane. With the best part of two bottles of wine in my system, I wasn't ready to go home; I wanted to go dancing, despite the stilettos and the suit.

The doormen at Bar Salsa weren't used to seeing me this dressed up, or drunk, and seeing their slightly horrified expressions, I was momentarily aware of the need to go home, until I heard the clave bashing away and bolted downstairs onto the dance floor. Bar Salsa had been my second home while I was at university, and I'd spent four nights a week, from 9 p.m. until 2 a.m., dancing there while everyone else was in the UCL Union. As a result, I could still turn up there alone at any time of the night and know enough people to be able to dance salsa solidly until it closed. It was where I'd first met Lena and several other good friends, where I'd met Thomas, who had more parking tickets than anyone I knew and who broke my heart, and where a Brazilian called Paolo had licked both my and Lena's armpits while dancing, which led to a series of events resulting in us both being thrown out of the club. My formative years in London had been spent there, and it was the perfect place to go to forget about my terrible evening. I gravitated towards it like a homing pigeon.

How often I danced salsa had always been in direct correlation to how happy I was. The more depressed I became, the faster I span and the later I stayed out. During my third year at university, when everyone else was in Russia and I was in

London, displaced, having vetoed the idea of spending a year in a country I'd by that point decided I hated and desperately trying to get my Russian to the same standard to rejoin my class and complete my final year that September, my salsa improved dramatically, as did my pool and snooker. As soon as Bar Salsa closed, we would all head to the underground snooker club beneath Centre Point until it became light outside. I became completely nocturnal in my escapism. Now I hardly danced – not because I was particularly happy, but because I no longer had the time nor the energy. I wondered what I was relying on now to stop myself slitting my wrists if it wasn't dancing or snooker – probably coffee and adrenalin.

That night, I danced until they closed and then went home feeling vaguely normal again. Spinning around on the dance floor for a few hours had made me forget all about the traders and the chocolate bento box and remember that it was possible to derive pleasure from something other than dessert and alcohol – I just needed to make time for it.

The next day was marked only by Wayne's resignation, after a seemingly endless morning meeting at the other end of the floor with Leicester. We'd watched as they'd bobbed around in the office and speculated about what was being said. Wayne had been trying to extract himself for months, but because he was the proud owner of countless shares that left him firmly tied to the Company as part of their 'loyalty scheme', he had been unable to leave. He was one of the best bookies on our desk, and at one point had been earning easily a couple of bar [million] a year. But in the time that I had known him, he had become disinterested, finding it increasingly difficult to work with Philippe and the American, coming in late, leaving early, putting in minimum effort and disappearing for weeks at a time.

Once when I had got myself into a mess when the American was away, he was the only one quick enough to know how to get me out of it. He had stood up, come and leaned over my desk, and calmly told me exactly what to say to each of the five buyers and sellers who were calling me at the same time. Within minutes he had ensured that I had maximized the bro I could get out of the trades while simultaneously somehow keeping everyone happy. He was a natural broker, and instinctively knew what to say and how to say it. Now he emerged from Leicester's office, said his goodbyes, and was gathering his things, and I wished that I'd had the chance to learn more from him. He was a giant of the Street.

'Yeah, told them they could fuck off. No pile of shares is worth having to stay in this fucking hellhole for.'

And then he left.

CHAPTER 7

THE GODFATHER

The desk was quickly disappearing. I arrived at work one morning to find that it had vanished, quite literally, and had been moved to the other end of the floor, along with all of our screens, desk tidies and condiments.

Philippe was gone too. He'd moved 'upstairs' to start a new desk doing what he did best: speaking French to clients who traded intricate products and would communicate only in French. I wondered if Wayne would have stayed if he'd known Philippe was leaving. He'd hated him even more than he hated the American, and blamed him entirely for the slowdown in business that the desk had seen over the last year. I'd always got on with him OK, apart from the endless battle with his CDS spreadsheets and his strange French ways; like the American, I had never understood why he was quite so hated. Now he had disappeared and it didn't matter; he would be forgotten immediately, along with his daily *pain au chocolat* and *salade niçoise*.

I didn't like our new position. It was miles away from the

floor-to-ceiling windows that we had previously looked out of, and was sandwiched between the new issues desk and the cluster of itraxx, tranches and bespoke brokers who were overseen by Fabrizio, whom I didn't know and didn't like, although he did wear beautiful suits.

We also now backed onto a new breakaway CDS desk. Although small in number and newly formed, it housed three of the biggest hitters in the market, including The Judge, who was the sort of guy who, wherever he went in London, was treated like royalty by everyone he came into contact with, especially doormen at clubs, who got out of his way as soon as they caught sight of him. Everything about him was severe: he was completely bald, built like a prop forward and barely spoke to anyone unless it was necessary. Only his smile betrayed his otherwise terrifying physique. He was the perfect candidate to cover DofG, who had recently resurfaced, and we willingly handed them over. DofG you fucking get, sell on. The Kunt wouldn't know what had hit him.

The American wasn't concerned about the move, or the departure of Wayne and Stu, but was glad to have even more clients to himself and be nearer the Diet Coke vending machine and the toilet. I sat down; he didn't mention our new location, and just mumbled 'Good morning'.

Fabrizio had hired a new jub, who was put next to me for some reason, and proved to be totally useless from the outset. He never got anyone breakfast or lunch, was usually late and didn't manage to pick up calls for me when I was busy. He instantly got off to a bad start when, after his first night out with us, he didn't stroll in until 11 a.m. Strangely he was never disciplined; it turned out that this was because he belonged to Fabrizio, and only Fabrizio could get rid of him.

It was a very different team from the one that I had originally signed up to be a part of. I didn't know what the hell I was supposed to do with the new useless jub, who didn't seem to want to learn anything and spent the entire day fucking around online. Then, a few days later, in walked The Godfather, and everything shifted once again.

I knew nothing about him, other than he was an old friend of Dory's and a Spurs fan, he'd once been one of the most senior and well-liked guys in the firm, and he was one of the most experienced bookies in the market. He somehow managed to bring the desk together, and within days we were taking it in turns to go on a tea run at 4 p.m., signalled by The Godfather's daily Bloomberg message to the desk, 'tick tock'. Pie and mash would arrive out of nowhere, different brokers would hang around our desk to chat to him, and we suddenly seemed to be back in the game. I began learning a lot about Spurs. Miraculously, the mood continued to improve when we started breaking cake and biscuits together. Even the American seemed to enjoy the 4 p.m. tea run, becoming particularly partial to a ginger snap and, more surprisingly, he also occasionally remembered that it was his turn to retrieve drinks for the desk. He would never really be a team player, but at least it was a start.

The Godfather seemed to bring a benevolent presence to the desk. Having lost most of the dead weight – all the people who didn't really want to be there – the desk reformed and for a while everything seemed like it was going to get better. There was still the small problem of the new jub. He was getting progressively worse – he became more arrogant by the day and didn't do anything I asked him. I'd originally thought that having a junior would make my life easier; he could update prices for me, take calls when the American and I were busy, and get the teas and coffees in. However, he never listened to me, and I spent all day wanting to stab him in the neck with the nearest blunt instrument.

He wasn't just useless; he was also an informer. When he wasn't wasting time shopping online for furniture for his new flat, I caught him sending messages to Fabrizio detailing everything that we were doing, and promptly informed the Ferg and the American, and anyone else who would listen. It turned out that we were caught up in the throes of a senior management power struggle between cash and CDS: we officially reported to Leicester, but Fabrizio wanted us under his control because we were starting to trade more synthetic products, which was his domain. While Leicester liked a drink at lunchtime, and wasn't hugely respected, he was at least vaguely trusted – as much as anyone ever trusted their boss on a trading floor. No one trusted Fabrizio, least of all Dory and The Godfather, and my allegiance lay with them. When it emerged that the jub was reporting to Fabrizio, it only inflamed matters; he was eventually moved away from us after everyone stopped speaking to him, and the Ferg and I took to inviting him into our group Instant Bloomberg chats when we were bored just to bury him, and took it in turns to call him a cunt until he left the chat.

The American didn't seem to care about any of it. He worked for no one, and it therefore made little difference whose group he was theoretically part of. When I had called him into a meeting to tell him that there was an informer in our midst, thinking it was the sort of thing he would relish discovering, he had laughed and told me to focus on my own job and stop worrying about other people. He seemed to oscillate between being ridiculously laid-back about everything going on around him and being restless and paranoid – I wasn't sure which I preferred. When I needed him to be paranoid, and tell the jub to fuck off, he did nothing; when I needed him to back off and let me deal with my clients in my own way, he wouldn't leave me alone. He was completely unreadable, but could always be guaranteed to do the opposite of whatever you expected him to do.

Despite appearances, I knew that it was only a matter of time before the American and Fabrizio locked antlers; they were both arrogant, aggressive and egotistical. However, the American was happy to continue working as he always had done and remaining disinterested in company politics, whereas Fabrizio had his sights set on becoming top dog, or at least number three in the Company, and he would destroy whomever he needed to in the process. For Fabrizio, the American was an inconvenience. He was becoming increasingly involved in synthetic products, as was I, and I knew that soon we would have to make a decision about whose team we were on. Fabrizio wouldn't let us carry on trading potentially very lucrative products without having control over us and seeing us contribute to the P&L of his own group. If there was one thing the American didn't like, it was giving away money.

In the meantime, I had my own problems to worry about. I had to get rid of Mark.

'Darlin', if you don't end it, I'll come round and do it for you. Text me when you've done the deed.'

I knew that The Godfather was right. He'd listened to me moaning about Mark for weeks and found it strange that I was involved with someone so obviously incompatible. I didn't doubt for a second that he would turn up and assist in the break-up if necessary.

There is always collateral damage when you are fighting to hold onto something unsustainable. The flimsy foundations of our relationship had begun to crumble, perhaps even as early as the time spent waiting for him to turn up and take me home after my spell in Chelsea and Westminster Hospital. After months of worrying about how to orchestrate the break-up, my liaison with Mark ended as easily as it had begun. It finally imploded during an argument about money.

Mark's 'friend' had used his debit card and borrowed money without informing him. As ever, Mark owed his half of the rent, and it took him too long to sort out the situation. His casual attitude to money and his ability to live hand to mouth with no desire for anything else was at fundamental odds with my own value system. I couldn't understand why he wouldn't ring the guy, explain the situation and get the money back, or why he was happier to owe his girlfriend money than make a phone call.

I got home on a Friday evening to discover that the situation had still not been rectified; he'd done nothing to get the money back. I looked at him and saw someone I no longer respected, like my very existence was castrating him. I was aware that I had lost the ability to have a rational conversation about the money, but I'd tried rational and it had failed to make any sort of impact.

'You've let your own pride, not wanting to call your fucking so-called friend to get the money he owes you, get in the way of our relationship. I can't deal with this. It's fucking ridiculous. You know what the guys at work said when they found out you owed me money? They were fucking mortified. They'd all rather die than owe money to a girlfriend. And yet you're perfectly fucking happy with it.'

'Baby, just calm down. I was going to sort it out, but I had to do it in my own way, in my own time. It would have got sorted.'

'What makes you think you have time? If I wasn't earning the money I am, we'd have been late paying rent this month and could have been evicted. You rely on the fact that you know I will pick up the bloody pieces. It's my own fucking fault. I've just made this situation too comfortable for you.'

I slammed my fist into the door of the wardrobe. It was the first time I'd ever punched something. It was the sort of conversation that I never envisioned having, and my words sounded alien to me. I'd been forced to take on a role that was unnatural, puffy-eyed and full of rage, and I had to extract myself before the situation deteriorated any further and I started breaking things. I knew that I should have used the fight to end the relationship, but he'd crumbled so quickly and easily, begging for forgiveness when I had started slamming cupboard doors and yelling, that I couldn't do it then.

We got through the weekend uncomfortably, estranged and detached from each other. When I got home late, he was already asleep and I didn't wake him. I went to work on Monday relieved to be getting away from him. I hoped he wouldn't be there when I got home, but I knew that he would be, and we eventually made up because I couldn't ask him to leave.

It is always the seemingly meaningless decisions – the texts sent without thinking, the quiet lies and the unreturned calls – that change the course of relationships irreversibly. That week I had gone to someone's leaving drinks at Corney and Barrow. I was supposed to be meeting Mark later to go to his friends' engagement party; it had been in my diary for months and I'd promised him I'd go. After a few drinks with Giles and the guys, I didn't want to leave. I texted Mark to say that I unexpectedly had to go to meet some clients and I would catch up with him later. He'd gone ahead without me while Giles and I headed to Gaucho for food – choosing the Broadgate branch when the Canary Wharf one was full. Giles jogged up the street to hail a cab while I was saying my goodbyes. As I ran after him, laughing drunkenly and jumping into the back of the taxi, I knew that things with Mark were over. I'd lied, and there was no going back. It wasn't that I was that attracted to Giles, but spending time with him served as a constant reminder that I no longer wanted to be with Mark. Aside from the money issues, I was simply bored, and going home to find him in bed, smiling lovingly at me, made me want to stay out all night.

It took another couple of weeks, many more late steak suppers with Giles, and a final word from The Godfather to end it. It was a Friday night at the end of July. I had been at work late attempting to sort out tickets for the Cartier Polo, which was on Sunday – Giles and I were taking Allen and his girlfriend. I'd left the office fired up and ready to end it at last. There was nothing left to salvage.

It was your classic break-up scene. I told Mark that I needed to be on my own, I was too young to be this committed and it wasn't fair on him, and he needed more than I could possibly give. I rolled out all of the clichéd reasons for ending a relationship that I could before he had a chance to say anything, and thankfully he didn't try to fight me. There was a lot of crying. Mark sat, head in hands, knowing there was nothing he could do or say to change my mind, walked out, hovered in the living room, then finally came back into the bedroom, threw a few things in a bag and left to go and stay with a friend. It all happened in the space of an hour. I found it hard to comprehend the speed with which something could dissolve that had taken months to build. I called Giles in tears, wanting him to come over when he offered; knowing it was a bad idea, I somehow managed to say no.

That weekend marked the final separation of two worlds. Mark was the last remaining part of my old life, pre-broking. Now he was gone and I was worrying about what shoes to wear for a day at Guards Polo Club with an Aggro Bank trader and a colleague I'd nearly kissed on numerous occasions. Sliding doors. With Mark gone, I knew that there would be no one to notice what time I was getting home or whether I managed to make it out of my suit and into bed, or at 5 a.m. to turn off the static snowstorm noise, which would soon become the soundtrack to my drunken sleep.

Sunday morning, Giles arrived at 10.30 dressed in a white linen suit and ready for a day of polo. We picked up Allen and his girlfriend, and the four of us sped off across the countryside to enjoy a quintessentially British day out. I'd spent most of the last 24 hours crying, but now, laughing with Giles in the back of the Addison Lee people carrier, it all seemed irrelevant. I no longer found myself drawing comparisons between Mark and Giles, or looking at Allen and his girlfriend's relationship and wishing that I, too, was dating an Aggro Bank trader, instead of a struggling singer in a rock band. I was relieved. Mark had been the only thing stopping me from slipping fully into City life, and I was now free to enjoy all that it had to offer without worrying about there being 6ft 2in of dead weight waiting for me in bed at home. The only trace of Mark was the patch of grease left on the wall on his side of the bed, where his head had rested as he'd lain in bed for most of the day, while I'd fought my hangovers at work.

It had nothing to do with Giles really. My landscape had altered irrevocably and Mark was simply no longer a part of it. I was spending all day and several evenings a week with men whose masculinity was so potent in all aspects of their lives that I could barely be around Mark without feeling nauseous. I had fallen out of love with him and suddenly found everything about him slightly repulsive – the way he smelled, even the patch of neck I used to fall asleep with my face pushed into, as if I wanted somehow to inhabit the same space. Everything had begun to smell and taste stale. I would lie next to him, feeling inescapably full. We hadn't had sex for months; every time he had initiated it, I had been unable to think of anything other than the nagging desire to run to the bathroom and throw up. It was the closest I had ever come to bulimia.

Being out in the sunshine, in the middle of Windsor, I finally stopped feeling sick. We met up with Lena and sat on the grass, flirting, drinking champagne and covering our faces in mustard and mayonnaise as we all bit into Argentine steak and chorizo baguettes. Allen and Cecelia were perfect company – positive and open in that American way that instantly relaxes everyone in the vicinity. Without Giles I would have been worried about whether they were having a good time, if they needed more to eat or drink, or whether they needed suncream, but his presence made client entertaining easier. I finally had an ally – someone to share the weight of the champagne buckets with, who would help me get everyone safely back to London at 2 a.m. I hadn't realized quite how lonely the job could be at times, and having Giles around made everything more bearable.

Even he couldn't find our car as we traipsed through Windsor Park in the dark at 1 a.m. though. Cecelia was starting a new job first thing in the morning, and Allen, as the youngest trader on the desk, would need to be in at 6.30 a.m., yet miraculously everyone was in surprisingly good spirits, fuelled with vodka Red Bulls and champagne. It wasn't an option to buy anything by the glass in our particular area of the tent, so we had ended up getting through at least six bottles of vodka, which seemed excessive as the four of us staggered around drunkenly in the dark, narrowly dodging oncoming traffic, with only intermittent headlights to light our way.

I was slightly regretting the brief chat that I'd had with the traders from DofG, who were still refusing to answer my various attempts at getting the line back. I had caught sight of The Queen holding court at a table in the Chinawhite tent, and had sidled up to them with Cecelia to inform them that I was there with Aggro Bank. I was only a few shots of tequila away from adding a 'so fuck you'.

The Queen had introduced me to his wife, who was petite, blonde and sweet, and, finally, to The Kunt, my nemesis.

'Hi, it's nice to meet you.'

He was looking at me blankly, like someone who has no recollection of ever calling me a cunt. He had no idea who I was. He was shorter than I had expected, and younger, but just as arrogant, and simply said, 'Yes, I think I vaguely remember having spoken to you a couple of times.'

I hadn't been sure what was *de rigueur* at social events when it came to estranged clients – whether I was supposed to make polite conversation as if I still spoke to him on an hourly basis, or to act as if I barely knew who he was too, or whether it would be a good opportunity to remind him of the horrific way he had spoken to me on numerous occasions and then ask for my line back. I really didn't want it back. It was the one line that I still dreaded hearing anything out of, and I was finding it increasingly difficult to maintain anything resembling professionalism, and hide my disdain for them from other clients. I wasn't alone: The Kunt had upset most of the market at one time or another, and he was one of the few reasonably active traders in the Street whom no one wanted to speak to. I excused myself after a few minutes, grabbed Cecelia, who had been busy chatting away with The Queen's wife, and headed back to the bar.

Lena hadn't been drinking, having driven down separately. She'd rip-corded her way out of the ensuing carnage hours ago, and would probably be the only one to make it in by 7 a.m. Her inability to handle alcohol, ever since a particularly drunken incident while at Cambridge University, when she found herself standing on the riverbank in nothing but a strapless bra at 6 a.m. as the rowing team cruised past, meant that she was one of the few traders in the market who didn't drink. She was therefore indispensable on nights out, and could always be relied upon to bundle me into a cab before I wreaked havoc. And now, as we walked through the grass, seemingly for miles, I longed to see her and her useless electric car come crawling over the horizon.

I passed out on Giles' shoulder the second we fumbled our way into the back of the car. I woke up somewhere near South Kensington. Everyone was quietly drifting in and out of sleep, and there was barely any traffic around. It was that strange time between Sunday night and Monday morning when the streets and roads are empty and London is finally sleeping. I was glad to have my head on someone's shoulder – someone who also had to be at his desk in less than four hours. Exhaustion loves company.

It is always unwise to start the week on three hours' sleep. It's really only something that can be done after Wednesday, yet Giles was out again that evening with clients. He'd seemingly developed the ability to function on no more than four hours' sleep a night, and was always at his desk before 7 a.m., knocking back milk thistle tablets and Berocca. I was still a beginner, and Monday morning was painful. The American was asking far too many questions about Allen, with whom he was particularly keen that I form a good relationship, as he knew that Allen would soon be one of the most active traders in the Street.

When the American decided that someone was important, he didn't care how much was spent on them in expenses. He didn't even mind if I was late in if I'd been out with one of the big hitters, as when the market was quiet my time was often better spent getting drunk with them in clubs. When I had resurfaced from my stint in hospital, he'd asked me to go along to an Aggro Bank dinner, saying that if I needed to take the next morning off to recover, it was fine. When I had tried to explain that taking it easy after being in hospital didn't really mean going on a heavy night out with someone else's clients, even if I did take the next day off, he had just coughed. I'd wondered whether he was going to attempt to force me to go to Scalini's.

Trying to put my health first was difficult. There is nothing healthy about broking; the hours, the lack of sleep, the drinking and the eating are all conducive to nothing but a general state of constant ill health. I always lied to my GP when he asked how many units of alcohol I was consuming weekly, mainly because I genuinely couldn't remember. I knew that I was probably teetering on the brink of alcoholism.

The main fallout from my break-up with Mark was that I was drinking and eating more – there was no point going home to cook when I could go to Gaucho and have a steak with Giles. On average, when I wasn't out with clients, I was probably drinking at least a bottle of wine a day, often accompanied by a martini or an Armagnac, and eating the sorts of food that are nothing but a fast track to heart disease five nights a week. That amount of *foie gras* and raw meat isn't good for anyone, even if it is washed down with antioxidant-rich Barolo.

Most conversations with my mother contained a slot on the health of my liver, during which she would repeatedly divulge the contents of a recent documentary she'd seen on liver damage in young women. I didn't want to think about the irreversible damage I was causing or add up the number of units I was drinking. I knew that there was a lot of wine, a lot of gin and a lot of coffee, but there wasn't much I could do about it other than quit.

The only way of getting through the day was by downing hourly espressos, and the only way of getting through a tedious or wildly out of control dinner was by drinking vast amounts of whatever alcohol I felt like. All I could do was hope that milk thistle actually worked. Weeks went by when I seemed to be simply topping up the levels of alcohol in my system and never managed to sober up completely. My body seemed to get used to being permanently inebriated; my liver would occasionally ache, but I would dismiss it as a bit of back pain.

I surrounded myself with people who were of the same monstrous make-up – other brokers, traders and salesmen. I knew that I had strayed too far, that I struggled to communicate with old friends on the rare occasions I managed to meet up with them. I cared about money: the pursuit of it, the lifestyle it bought me, and how it felt to be earning it. This shift in priorities was impossible to hide from the people who had known me longest. Mags, one of my few remaining school friends, told me over supper a few weeks after my break-up with Mark that she was worried about me. She could see I was fully buying into my new City life, and flinched every time I snapped at the waiters and ranted about needing a man who earned more than I did.

'But V, this just isn't you. What happened to wanting to be a writer? This is all so sudden. I haven't seen you for a while, but I didn't expect this much to have changed.'

'Well, maybe I didn't know before what I wanted to do, and now I've found it. I'm happier than I've ever been. Really. OK, so I'm permanently exhausted, but it's an awesome fucking job. If you spent a day on the trading floor you'd understand. And I'm only going to do it for, like, a few years – five tops – and then, sure, I'll get out, and maybe then I'll write. It's just clearly so far removed from what you do that it's incomprehensible that someone might actually enjoy working in the City.'

I was irritated that she didn't understand. She was one of my oldest friends and I didn't get why it was so difficult for her to offer me a bit of support.

'Oh, for fuck's sake, where the fuck is my food? Why does it take them so long here?'

She ignored my outburst, returning to our previous topic of conversation. 'It's not that. It's the way you're talking about it. Nobu, Chanel, different wines you've been drinking, the polo, Ascot – it's all madness. And what the hell happened to Mark? I thought he was great.'

'It just didn't work out, you fucking know that. We were going in different directions.'

'What? You were going to Nobu and he was going to the pub? That's hardly his fault, V.'

'Oh, come on, fuck off.'

'Can you stop swearing constantly? People are staring.'

'Are you taking the piss? It's just the way I speak. OK, I get it. You hate my job; you hate the swearing. Is there anything left about me that you actually like?!'

'You just never used to swear this much. V, I love you, but let's talk about something else. You want a career in the City now. I don't understand it whatsoever, so let's leave it there.'

The rest of the evening passed uncomfortably. I had, of course, dismissed her concerns instantly, like an addict confronted by a family member. I told myself that she didn't understand. She worked for a charity and would never approve of my lifestyle, so it was pointless trying to explain it to her; maybe she had never really known me at all. If I was in denial, it was denial in the shape of Chanel handbags and endless bottles of Barolo. It was my soul to sell. The solution was to surround myself with people who saw nothing reprehensible in my new lifestyle, in a place where I was safe from the scrutiny of old friends.

I was nothing but stucco clinging to a house of cards. My relative success as a broker had not arisen from anything tangible, such as an in-depth knowledge of the financial markets. It was glorified painting by numbers. I had spent hours discussing the high yield bond and leveraged finance at functions without having a basic understanding of economics. I had cajoled traders into buying or selling financial instruments without knowing what the numbers I was giving them really meant. It was an act – nothing but a role I had adopted – full of sound and fury, signifying fuck all.

CHAPTER 8

HELP, I'VE LOST MY DISCO BISCUITS

'Excuse me, would you mind limiting your use of the F and the C words? I am trying to have a quiet dinner with my wife and you are disturbing us.'

The couple sitting at the next table had stopped eating and were looking at us with a mixture of disgust and irritation. They had the faces of people whose evening had been ruined by a rowdy City trader – my companion for the evening – disturbing the gentle, inoffensive sounds of a nice Mayfair restaurant.

By Mo's fifth trip to the gents, before we had even finished our starters, every other word had turned into 'fuck', 'fucking' or 'cunt'. The more coke he snorted, the worse his language got and the more indecipherable his intense rants became. I had given up trying to get any information from him regarding how I rated compared to his other brokers, where he saw the market going over the next few weeks or what kind of volumes were trading when he had begun responding to any attempt at conversation with an existential rant about the pointlessness of brokers, the market, high yield, trading and the City in general. He'd managed to consume the best part of three bottles of Barolo on his own, on top of the two bottles of champagne we had got through at the bar. The request for less swearing had fallen on coked-up, drunken ears, and it therefore continued regardless.

I'd spent the last few weeks of summer trying to pin Mo down and set a date for dinner; he had cancelled three times and, despite occasionally giving me a smattering of prices in obscure bonds, was proving to be totally elusive. No one else on the desk had ever gone out with him or built up anything resembling a relationship, so when he had finally walked through the swing doors into the restaurant I knew that I had to maximize the few hours that I would have his attention. Now here I was, sitting opposite him at dinner, listening to him slur that he was only at the shovel to try to counteract the effects of the alcohol. I ordered another bottle of wine and downed the remainder of my martini.

A gin martini was always my first drink of the evening when meeting new clients. A hefty slosh of nearly neat ice-cold gin was stabilizing on an empty stomach. I never chose anything easy drinking; with straight spirits it was far easier to control how much I drank. Zuma's famed pink mojitos had snuck up on me in my first month, during a night out with too many bookies and not enough clients, with all the pinky innocuous power of a Calpol highball. By the time we sat down to eat – six bookies (one from a different shop altogether but a friend of the Ferg's) to one client – the manager had already had a word about the Ferg, who was staggering, mojito in hand, around the robata grill harassing some girls. He briefly returned to the table only to begin hurling handfuls of soft-shell crab at his client. The five of us then spent the rest of the meal attempting to keep him in his seat.

I ordered another martini: Miller's Westbourne Strength. 15:1. Vermouth made me nervous. I could never ask for a dry martini or Manhattan, as they were inevitably never dry enough and would therefore have to be sent back. Sending drinks back was irritating for all involved, so I had taken to providing a helpful ratio to aid whichever schmuck was unlucky enough to find that they were behind the stick.

'Yeah, I know him. Got his sights set on the top prize, had he? Pffft. He always used to turn up at clubs and beg one of us for a few lines. He would have done anything for some bugle but would never score his own 'cos he was always too scared of someone finding out. Snivelling wreck. Don't trust him. He's a cunt. Now a sly cunt in an expensive suit, but still a cunt.'

I'd mentioned The Kunt and Mo had immediately inter-jected. The City never forgets, and it doesn't like reinvention. Once a cunt begging for coke, always a cunt begging for coke.

Some time around 10 p.m. Mo wanted to go dancing. This thought struck him as he stood up and turned to embark on yet another pilgrimage to the gents. He yelled over his shoulder while narrowly avoiding an incoming tray of food. Twenty minutes later, Mo had yet to return to the table. The maître d' slid up to me, 'Madam, I am sorry to have to ask you, but could you please control your friend? He is harassing some of our diners over at the bar and one of them has just complained.'

Short of somehow finding a stun gun filled with horse tran-quillizer and a retractable dog lead, I was fucked. I could see his head bobbing around the other side of the oyster bar, arms occasionally flailing expressively. It was a strange scene. I realized that I was powerless. Trying to control a drunken marauding forty-something with a coke problem was not within my remit. I could only hope that he had forgotten about going dancing and I'd be able to bundle him into a cab with the help of the doorman and get home.

The parameters of acceptable behaviour in Mayfair restaurants are narrow. Eyes begin to roll, complaints are made and quiet dinners are all too easily ruined. Anyone standing up, swearing or laughing excessively, or absent from their table for a prolonged period, is immediately noticed by someone, usually the maître d' or section manager, and then the questions start:

'Should we wait for Sir before serving the main courses?'

'Will Sir be returning?'

'Will Sir be having dessert?'

'Is Sir going to be long? Should we keep his dessert warm?'

I never knew how to answer, only that somewhere along the line it had stopped being embarrassing and I no longer felt the need to apologize for my endless stream of rowdy dinner companions, be they clients or colleagues. A drunken coke addict is always preferable to a Diet Coke-drinking WASP.

'There's someone fucking breastfeeding over there in the middle of the restaurant. What's more offensive: my swearing or that fat old bird with her tit flopped out on the table? Some of us are trying to eat. Cunts.'

Mo had apparently been warned about his language again and returned to the relative safety of our table. 'Nope. That's it. I can't stomach this fucking panna cotta now. It's all over. There's nothing for it. We have to leave. As your client, I'm telling you we need to leave. We have to get out of this place.

Suckling everywhere. Suckling. Fucking suckling. Suckling pig.' His eyes were wild. He was frantically twisting his napkin and humming, occasionally muttering the word 'suckling'.

I'd had enough gin by now to be suitably anaesthetized. I paid the bill and we made it as far as the cloakroom without any further incidents, apart from Mo's parting words to the maître d': 'There's a suckling pig in a dress over there, and I'm not allowed to say cunt!' The good news was that he was steadier on his feet, and the shovel had indeed appeared to have sobered him up a bit. The bad news was that he was now fixated on dancing and I was a staggering drunk in four-inch Manolos.

Mo was on the phone. He wanted to go and join a couple of his friends at their club. He mentioned the name, and I'd never heard of it, so we jumped in a cab. Luckily the driver knew the place. As we sped along through Mayfair, Mo slid around the back seat, squashing me against the window every time we turned. It was like being with an overgrown child on a fairground ride.

Eventually we pulled up in Soho, amid neon lights, hotdog stands and hookers, and it emerged that his urge to go dancing was actually an urge to be lap-danced – of course. I didn't really have time to process the information, and just followed Mo up to the entrance, where the doorman eyed us suspiciously. Mo gallantly paid my entrance; I would have been touched if I hadn't been so busy navigating the pitch-black staircase down to the cloakroom. My ankle gave way on the final step, and I discovered that, while upright, I could pass myself off as only a bit tipsy, but attempting to get back up off the clammy carpet of a strip club in stilettos revealed the true damage wreaked by eight gin martinis and the restaurant's entire selection of Venetian wines. Mo may have been a coke fiend, but at that moment he was steadier on his feet than I was. As he hauled me off the floor, I was grateful for his fleeting moment of sobriety.

The club was too quiet. There must have been at least fifteen butt-naked girls hovering by the bar, too bored to speak to each other. A few turned and looked at us expectantly, like dogs needing re-homing, as we walked in and joined Mo's hedge fund buddies, who had already selected a couple of girls, Candy and Lola, to join their table. It turned out that they were regulars.

Other than a lone middle-aged guy at the other end of the room, we were the only people in the club. Mo's friends, Charlie and Jeremy, were the kind of ubiquitous public school boys I might have known at university and who were to be found lurking in every investment bank, hedge fund and private equity shop in the City and, as it turned out, in Soho's more questionable establishments.

After the guys had been assured by Mo that 'she's fine, she's my bookie; they've seen it all before', we exchanged pleasantries as if we were in a Fulham pub on a Sunday afternoon. For a few minutes, while I was shown a photo of one of the guys' kids, it was almost possible to forget that there were two naked girls in our midst and that I couldn't really move my ankle, which had begun to swell.

Women behave strangely in strip clubs. They overcompensate, pretending to be interested in the life story of one of the girls – what she is studying, where she is from, whether she enjoys the job. I was never particularly interested, but I asked all the appropriate questions anyway. It gave me something to do other than drink from one of half a dozen bottles of horrific white wine that had somehow made it to our table. Strip clubs are not known for their wine lists.

'Doesn't it just make you want to snort vast amounts of shovel off her tits?'

Mo was whispering so closely that I could feel his nose, dog wet, against my ear every time he put emphasis on a particular word. His hand was on my leg, more in order to support himself as he leaned rather than out of any attempt at seduction. He was far too interested in the bare nipples in front of him.

I wasn't really sure whether a reply was needed, and instead popped a couple of Tramadol that I found lurking in the bottom of my handbag, left over from a migraine bonanza a few weeks ago. On seeing me taking pills, Mo proffered some Ketamine with a wink. When I shook my head, he pulled out a couple of Temazepam, 'mazzies, my fave of the pams, muscle relaxants, perfect for ankles – unless, of course, you're pregnant. I remember someone telling me that once. Or maybe it was something else.' I declined and he looked briefly hurt before shrugging and knocking back a bit of everything with a slug of pinot grigio, before wincing dramatically. I wasn't sure how he managed to maintain consciousness with such a bizarre cocktail of drugs cruising through his system, but he was clearly indestructible. Everything then got a little blurred, and I remember being strangely incapacitated, unable to lift my arms while getting lap-danced, which was probably down to the Tramadol. Throughout the dance, I attempted to hold down a conversation with Mo, my head permanently swivelled towards him. If someone buys you a lap-dance, it's rude to turn it down, but you don't have to look directly at it.

Everything about the club was slightly sticky: the table, the booths, the carpet, the girls' lipgloss, which had somehow spread around their chins, the clunky glasses, which were the same shape and weight as those at Cipriani but with an added film of murky filth. The girls were plastered in a mixture of fake tan, moisturizer and talc, soft focused, slipping inoffensively around the room, their bodies blurred around the edges, occasionally stopping to gyrate against stools, handrails and each other. After we had all had our fair share of lap-dances, and somehow seen off the last of the dubious pinot grigio, we staggered out into the shining lights of Soho. The guys were keen to go to some dive bar around the corner, off Rupert Street, but as we navigated the stairs down to the basement, past the signs for 'models' written in fluorescent highlighter on A4 paper, I doubted whether a nightcap would be on offer.

There was some sort of dimly lit reception area, where a few guys were already waiting: one was wearing the remainder of his suit, eyes shut, head in his hands, BlackBerry resting on his knee; another was a young guy wearing a leather bomber jacket and jeans, speaking on his phone in an unidentifiable language. A copy of some porn magazine was lying between his feet, and he was flicking through the pages as he spoke. No one looked up as we staggered through the door. A bottle of Evian at one side of the room was the only available liquid. It sat next to a CD player blasting out Duran Duran. I wouldn't be able to get a martini here. It had the same air of frustrated boredom as a doctor's waiting room. A girl appeared from behind a chipboard door and spoke to Charlie. Her accent was heavily Eastern European, but she could have been from anywhere. I said goodbye to Mo and made my way back up the stairs.

I got home just after 5 a.m. – according to my doorman when

I crashed back out on my way to work. I made the executive decision to take an hour and a half's sleep rather than none at all, but when my alarm sounded, I felt like I was in a coma, which was probably the cocktail of Tramadol and gin. Miraculously, my ankle didn't appear to be broken after all and, other than being a slightly strange yellow colour, felt good to go. I reached for my BlackBerry and saw a text from Mo, sent at 6 a.m.:

'Veneeshhh. Last night was a total no post. Keep it that way. I'm fucked.'

When the American asked me an hour later how my evening with Mo had been, I took a deep breath, tried to sound as coherent as I could, despite the fact that my tongue felt like it was blocking my airway, and told him what he wanted to hear: we had had a quiet dinner, Mo did most of his business with FHP, another broking house, but he would get involved in any markets I sent him if he could. He wouldn't give us starts, as he liked to give runs to his mate at FHP, but he would get involved. Mo thought the market would pick up over the next couple of weeks, more CDS than cash would be trading over the next six months and FHP were the best positioned, because their screen was better than ours and he felt safer with them.

'Great, nothing we didn't already know, but it's good you got out with him. Keep working at it. You never know when someone's suddenly going to become lucrative.'

The nearest Mo had come to any of that was, in a brief moment of lucidity, his approval of Irina, one of our screen girls who had been deployed to try to get him and his team to use our trading platform, her arse and what he wanted to do to it. He thought the screen itself was useless, but had told me that if we kept sending her round to see him he might consider using it.

Many products were now trading on electronic platforms, where the trader can log on and input prices, then remove them whenever he wants, or set a timer so the price automatically expires. Our competitors had far better screens; they had made the move to electronic platforms before we did, and we were having to catch up, with a dedicated team of beautiful sales girls, bearing muffins and coffees, who could be sent out to teach our traders how to use the screen. So far the girls and the muffins had proved more popular than the screen itself, and very few clients wanted to have it installed when they already had three others to look at, let alone input prices on it. In the long term, electronic platforms would theoretically mean the end of voice broking. When they had first emerged into the market, there had been a lot of noise about loss of jobs and machines taking over, but ultimately some traders would always prefer speaking to someone rather than using a screen.

I could see the Ferg's wry smile from the other side of the desk. He'd taken one look at me and known instantly that it hadn't been a quiet dinner. It was 7.30 a.m. Mo's status on Bloomberg was still red. I doubted he would make it in before 10. While I was desperate to IB Lena and fill her in immediately, I knew a no post was a no post when it involved strippers, whores, prescription drugs, senior traders and fund managers, so I kept my word, because at that moment it was all I really had. While I felt bad about bullshitting the American, I wasn't exactly lying; I was protecting my client, which is, after all, the first rule of broking.

Another text came in from Mo: 'Neesh, did I give you a bag of MDMA to look after last night? Can't fucking find it.'

'No, sorry. Where are you? Are you coming in this morning?'

'When I find the sodding disco biscuits, love.'

I was glad that he was still alive at least. I found out a week later through raucous guttural laughter over a drink on our second outing – seen as a particularly good sign by the American – that Mo was late in because, despite having failed entirely to make it home, he'd miraculously remembered that he had a chiropodist appointment at 10 a.m. He had turned up to it still fucked, only to be escorted out of the building when he had taken off the wrong sock and, on thinking his verruca had miraculously disappeared, got a little overexcited. He was now short a chiropodist and long a verruca, which was still exactly where it had always been – on the other foot. It wasn't exactly market talk, but it was something.

The events of that first evening were never mentioned again, but Mo gave me a steady stream of prices. Whenever I bumped into him at parties, there seemed to be some sense of recognition that we had experienced something ugly together, and he always attempted to thrust whatever medication he was currently sampling into my hand. I once found a pot of Adderall in my handbag, and can only assume that it was a gift from Mo. No one else I knew was quite such a fan of random prescription drugs.

After an evening like that there seemed to be very little need to meet up for regular broker dinners. He told me he couldn't really be arsed; he didn't really like being wined and dined. If I wanted to spend time with him, it would have to be at either a casino or a strip club, as those were his chosen forms of entertainment on the rare occasions that he was able to escape from work and his wife – either way he wasn't that bothered. He soon disappeared into a more senior role, too senior really to trade, but I'd still get the occasional message in response to the endless stream of prices I continued to send him.

Charity Day, taking place on the anniversary of 9/11, was the one day of the year when traders were expected to do as much business with us as possible – to ring us with endless runs of prices, to pay double or triple bro on everything and to trade anything that they could through us, because all the money made goes straight to various charities.

Dozens of television, political and sporting personalities mill around the floor, and traders get the chance to buy or sell to their celebrity of choice. We are all made to wear rugby shirts emblazoned with charity logos or fancy dress. But 2007's Charity Day was taking place in the midst of the credit crunch and it was doubtful that anyone would be feeling particularly charitable. For most brokers it was their favourite day of the year. Nobody really does any work because business falls into their lap, pizzas pile up everywhere and they get to sit next to footballers and page three girls and have their photo taken with Alex Ferguson. But it was still 9/11, and no amount of sporting legends and giant breasts could dull the resonance of that.

I understood the theory behind Charity Day – trying to turn something horrific into something good that raised millions worldwide for different charities, and somehow attempt to erase the damage – but 2001 couldn't be forgotten. The brokers who had been in the London office listening down their wires that were still open to the New York desks as the planes hit would never forget. They'd never forgive the traders who called the following day expecting the trades to be done and for trades to stand despite the fact that the bookie handling the buyer in New York was killed in the middle of the trade and it was impossible to know if he'd sent a confirm out first. And it was unlikely that the desk heads who had sent young bookies off to trade in New York the previous week would ever stop blaming themselves for their deaths. But 9/11 was now called Charity Day and everyone joined in the fun and games as if it were the best day of the working year, and tried to ignore the few guys who sat in silence with their heads in their hands until they could finally leave at 5 p.m. and try to forget about it for another year.

A few days later we saw the first run on a bank in 150 years, when Northern Rock made an emergency call to the Bank of England to ask for a few billion to save them from going under, after it emerged that they were unable to raise any further funds because other banks had stopped lending to them. There was a time when this news wouldn't have affected prices on high yield bonds or loans in the credit market, and only stocks would have tanked. But because hedge funds, pension funds and banks now trade such a wide spectrum of products – often, in the case of funds, unregulated – everything is automatically exposed. There is no way of isolating a problem because everyone is tied together and hanging from the same rope; some are just nearer to the bottom than others.

We sat and waited. Crossover (the high yield index) was jumping all over the place, gapping wider, unexpectedly tightening and then blowing back out. Cash was eerily quiet. Nobody wanted to show any bids and most traders were sitting back and waiting for someone else to make the first move. Then a few funds started selling off, needing to lighten their books, and suddenly the Street was flooded. My first Bloomberg message of the day read simply 'strap in'.

It was chaos. Stuff looked cheap, but no one knew where the bottom was, and everyone was wary of posting low trades and bringing the value down further. It was the sort of market in which you couldn't afford to get hooked because you risked wiping out your entire desk if something dropped three quarters of its worth inexplicably. Everyone was staring at their screens and trying not to make any sudden movements in case the ceiling caved in. It was totally unprecedented. Food sat untouched on desks, having been delivered hours ago and ignored. There were sudden flurries of screaming, shouting activity on different desks across the floor, but no one wanted to turn around and look. We were all too busy watching the red lights flashing wildly on our Bloomberg terminals as stocks dived. All of sudden September was about more than Charity Day.

CHAPTER 9

WHEN IN DOUBT, GO FLAT

'Yes, we'll have twelve crack babies and a bottle of Dom.'

Despite various banks and funds having gone under, the show had to go on and there was still entertaining to be done. It was like any other Thursday – another client, another tray of undrinkable shots and another bottle of champagne being brought over to our table by a scantily clad Eastern European waitress. The evening had started with a civilized dinner at Daphne's in South Kensington, where I'd spent most of the main course rubbing my new gold Louboutins against Giles' ankles, like a cricket, while discussing the supposed impending credit crunch with Cecelia and Allen. We must have looked like two young couples on a perfect double date.

A couple of hours later, we were stumbling down the stairs into Boujis, and being led to a discreet table hidden safely away in a corner far from the dance floor. Before we had even taken our coats off, Giles, who kept being called Mr Goldstein by the manager for some reason, had ordered several rounds of shots, and a tray of small fluorescent orange frothy glasses immediately appeared, along with a bottle of champagne.

'Why does he keep calling you Mr Goldstein?'

'I have no fucking idea. He obviously thinks I'm someone far more important than I am.'

The drunker we got, the more difficult it was becoming to hide from Cecelia and Allen the fact that we were on the verge of dating. I was aware that I kept instinctively reaching for Giles' hand, and had to stop myself and remember that I was out with a client – a client who had become a friend but a client nevertheless.

After the third tray of crack babies and the fourth bottle of Dom, most of which was poured straight from the bottle into my mouth as I lay stretched out on the seats, everything became sideways: my view of the dance floor, my view of the street – the pavement a little close for comfort. I woke up in bed, slumped against the wall, still wearing my suit jacket but otherwise naked, with no recollection of getting home. I'd pushed all of my pillows onto the floor, apparently choosing the comfort of the cold wall over goose feathers. I also couldn't move my neck. It must be how babies feel who can't hold their heads up. I could hear the calypso alarm, but couldn't work out where it was coming from. At least I hadn't lost my BlackBerry.

Everything appeared to be surprisingly in order. The contents of my handbag were scattered, but present and correct; my shoes had been taken off before I'd fallen into bed; and I'd somehow managed to remove half of my eye make-up. Then I slid the door of the bathroom open and saw the fluorescent orange passion fruit remains of the crack babies splattered up the wall, and remembered that I had been rather ill. I just hoped that I hadn't thrown up on Giles.

I couldn't see what I was doing in the dark and took the only pills that I could find in the bottom of my bag. I clambered into the shower – the next stage in the now familiar routine of attempting to make it into work on time following a night out. The nights seemed to be getting bigger, drunker and later, and the hangovers more difficult to shift, but the 5.45 a.m. alarm never changed. That was the problem. The amount of sleep I was getting was slowly decreasing, as were the details of the evening that I could remember, which was probably for the best. Amnesia was my only saviour. If I couldn't remember it, it didn't happen. And it was his fault for ordering the shots.

I was feeling strangely unsteady, exhausted and ready to go back to bed immediately. It turned out, on closer examination of the packet, that I had taken two strong anti-seasickness tablets which, combined with the alcohol still flooding my system, might as well have been Rohypnol. Fuck. This couldn't keep happening. I had to start keeping track of the drugs.

'So you know I practically had to carry you out of the cab and get you into your flat? You were all over the place. But so was Cecelia, so it's fine. Fucking lightweights. And why do you look like you've just popped a valium?'

The message popped up on my screen. It was from Giles, who apparently had been at his desk since 6.30 a.m. and looked surprisingly well.

'Lightweights? What the hell were you thinking, ordering endless shots? When was that ever a good idea? And it's the seasickness pills. Don't ask.'

I was sure I would have remembered being carried, but apparently Giles had been the one who had removed my shoes and got me into bed. If it had been anyone else, I probably would have been embarrassed.

156

'Did you see me naked?'

'It was hard not to. You immediately took all your clothes off as if I wasn't even there, including two pairs of pants – one was apparently to keep your tights from falling down, which was the only thing you managed to say with any coherence – and then you promptly passed out. So I sat you upright in case you choked, put your jacket around you and left. Glad you're alive and fully clothed this morning, you moron.'

Stripping with total disregard for whoever else might be in the room is always the mark of a good evening.

> '9 and three quarters offer in 3 prosie opco. I'm still a seller of ineos b/c but only got a short 2 mill, and where is BAA these days?'
> 'X is gapping wider. Fucking choppy out there, kids.'
> 'Pull my bid in Thames Water.'

I didn't have much time to think about the implications of Giles seeing me naked as I was suddenly inundated with offers. There was panic in the air. The Street was spooked. I was still heavily under the influence of seasickness pills and alcohol and fairly incapacitated. The message to flatten overinflated books had apparently gone out in a few of the larger banks. The news was filtering down through the upper echelons and the minnows too were selling off the little bits of bulge that they had tentatively accumulated over the last few months. Even Stupidly Bullish Bank were offered in everything. When in doubt, go flat.

I knew that DofG were long in everything. They'd been buying up paper at an alarming rate in an effort to try to make themselves the biggest in the Street, and couldn't possibly hang onto it that much longer at the levels they owned it. They still weren't speaking to me, though, having pulled my line, and were probably doing all their business elsewhere.

Of course there are always traders willing to pick up stuff cheaply. A couple of banks were happy to show low bids, only to get whacked immediately by the likes of Aggro Bank, and find themselves the proud owners of paper that they owned five points higher a week ago. They believed that it gave them a lower average price – a theory that I never particularly saw the logic to, because ultimately all they had was more of a loan or bond that everyone else was trying to get rid of. It didn't matter that it was cheap; no one wanted it. They had to hope that when it went from high yield to distressed, as these unwanted instruments tended to, they would be blessed with a new customer base – the distressed market.

Some stuff is too fucked even for the distressed guys, such as the chunk of a German hardware company's bank loans that we had sold at 86, which were single-figure 9 bid a week later. The guy who had bought it at 86 wasn't happy, as the loan was now so distressed that even the specialist hedge funds had no interest. Worse than the tanking price was the fact that the buyer was now convinced the seller had been privy to information that the company was dead in the water before selling – information he could only have had access to if he'd ventured to the other side of the Chinese Wall within his bank. It was quickly turning into a compliance issue and, as usual, we were caught in the middle. The buyer kept calling to speak to the American, who was busy on the other line and kept shaking his head and giving me an elaborate 'I'll call him back' hand movement. Dealing with an angry trader who was about to be the proud owner of shares in the now defunct hardware company, as well as dealing with my own clients and the horrific hangover, was becoming more than I could handle.

'FOR FUCK'S SAKE, DORY, CAN YOU JUST SHUT THE FUCK UP FOR ONCE?'

An argument had erupted between Dory and the American. I had been too busy pulling my bids to hear how, but the American was on his feet, arms flailing and spouting fairly nonsensical abuse at Dory. Within seconds Dory was also on his feet, and The Godfather had stuck out his arm, while continuing to read the paper, in an effort to stop them from getting any closer. The rest of the floor were goading them on, and I expected to hear the familiar playground chant of 'fight, fight, fight' emerge from somewhere. Everyone immediately got excited if there was any hope of the American getting thumped. The sterling desk started playing his theme tune, Leo Sayer's 'You Make Me Feel Like Dancing', on full volume over the open wire. The resemblance was uncanny.

There was a sudden crash. The American had picked up his Bloomberg keyboard and hurled it at Dory, but because it was still connected to his screens by a thick cable, it had come flying back towards him, the keys bouncing across the desk, and only the spacebar making it anywhere near Dory. He then grabbed his coat, slammed his chair against the desk and stormed off the floor, dragging his rucksack behind him. This wouldn't have mattered had it been a less busy day, but I suddenly found myself having to handle both the American's and my own clients, and explaining that he had been taken ill and had to leave when they asked where he was.

The phone rang.

'Yeah, Venetia? Ring the helpdesk and make sure that I have a new keyboard in the morning.'

He hung up.

'Was that him? Fucking prick.'

The American had made the request in exactly the same voice he used when he asked for a cup of tea, and sounded completely nonplussed about the entire incident. I wasn't sure whether Dory was more annoyed about having a keyboard thrown at him, the American leaving for the day, or the American having the nerve to ring and ask me to sort out his keyboard as if it had malfunctioned and gone bouncing across the desk all by itself.

Whenever there was an incident involving the American, the Ferg and Wayne would quickly spread it around the market that he had died or been rushed to hospital. I'd heard the same legendary stories told through bouts of hysterical laughter by so many different brokers. There was the time the Ferg famously lost it with him one afternoon and tried to choke him before he was eventually pulled off; Bloomberg messages went flying around that the Ferg had put him in A&E. Then there was the time that Wayne got the American in a headlock, pulled him off his chair and pinned him to the floor under the desk, his legs waggling in the air.

It was apparently only ever a matter of time before the American would do something that would cause someone to flip – even the calm, easygoing brokers like the Ferg were likely to be pushed to breaking point at any moment because the American frequently refused to play by the rules. The American's view was that it was better to get stuff done and keep it as simple as possible. If he was dealing with only his own clients, he could remain in control at all times. The second there were any variables, in the form of someone else's clients getting involved in his perfect picture, he started to panic.

It wasn't long before Giles saw me naked again. This time I was sober, and he was wasted. After a week of frantic kissing in various alleys throughout the City, and drunken suggestions about getting a hotel room, I finally opened my front door on Friday evening, and he was immediately on me. It was like being rugby tackled by an eager badger. He had been at a club with some clients and another guy from his desk, but was later than he'd intended because they'd been locked in the manager's office when his idiot colleague had forgotten his credit card PIN number and couldn't pay the bill. Giles had finally escaped and left his colleague at the club trying to find another card, so here he was, falling through the door at 2 a.m. There was all of the same removal of clothing, crashing around and passing out that there had been last time, when he'd put me to bed after our night at Boujis, but this time there was the added bonus of a couple of ineffective, forgettable thrusts somewhere between the fumbling and staggering.

I knew that it was over before it even began. Expectations had been too great. We had spent far too long flirting and getting drunk together, and now our relationship was doomed. It was an alliance that worked perfectly on the trading floor and in clubs and restaurants with clients, but it didn't seem to function outside those parameters.

We weren't really the same people away from work, and stripped of our suits and our shared City lifestyles, we didn't have much to base a relationship on. I had probably realized that when I had taken Giles to Ronnie Scott's to see a set by Avishai Cohen. In our own clothes, without clients, miles away from the

City and Canary Wharf in a Soho jazz club, we were strangers, and he was asleep within minutes. He was short in purple corduroy trousers and strange alternative shoes. I was blow dried and tall in patent Manolo Blahniks. He liked Indie rock bands and music festivals, and could easily have been wearing one of those black cord necklaces with a trinket from travelling attached to it; I liked Chanel and obscure Israeli double bassists, and had been to a festival once when I was sixteen.

We'd sat in the cab, awkwardly perched for the first time since we'd known each other. I wasn't drunkenly slumped on his shoulder or leaning against him with one hand on his arm; we were holding hands like teenagers in the cinema. We quickly fell into our comfortable default mode of discussing various people at work, and moaning about the American, Fabrizio and our clients, because we didn't really have much else to say to each other. Neither of us would ever have admitted it though, so we carried on regardless, and saw it through to its natural conclusion, which was lying awkwardly in the dark wondering what it was that we were doing.

I tried lying on his shoulder, but it was the wrong shape. He kissed my forehead, saying that it was Saturday, and he wanted to go for breakfast at The Wolseley. For a second I thought that brunch might save us – if we got out of bed and into a restaurant, had poached eggs and some lapsang souchong, it would all be fine and we would be back on track for commencing our perfect relationship. But it all felt wrong: his shoulder, the kiss, the sex. I knew that in the morning I would just want him to go. It was over, but I wasn't sure how to tell him.

I'd forgotten to turn my alarm off, and it sounded at 5.45 a.m. I woke up, reached over the sleeping body beside me, and fumbled around to find my BlackBerry, but I hit snooze accidentally and it went off again ten minutes later. Giles didn't move.

It felt strangely unnatural to be sober, but I still felt sick. I got out of bed and padded around my flat, disgruntled, wanting my bed back. I was dreading having to disentangle myself from him, having to explain that I didn't want to go for brunch, that I wanted him to leave and I just wanted to be friends. I had been the one who had pushed for a relationship, who had said that I didn't want to get involved unless we were going to give it a proper go, whatever that meant. I wasn't sure how I had managed to get it quite so wrong. I made a cup of tea, pushed myself up onto the kitchen surface and waited.

I didn't really like sharing my bed with anyone. It was probably as a result of having once sat alone in the corridor outside my room at UCL's halls of residence at 4 a.m. with nothing but some medic's forgotten textbook for comfort, all because my single bed had been taken hostage by a French guy I had been dating who had slept over. It had seemed like a good idea at the time, until he managed to push me out and I retreated to the corridor. The experience had left me extremely protective of my sleeping space. Even Mark had once complained when we first started dating that I had tried pushing him out of bed throughout the night. Giles never really stood a chance.

I methodically emptied the dishwasher and made another cup of tea. It was the first time in months that I felt like cleaning. 7.30 a.m. I crept back into my bedroom and lay down in the dark, watching the shadows on the ceiling. Giles was face down, snoring. There is nothing worse than having an unwanted body beside you in bed, taking up space and making unfamiliar sounds. I woke up to find his right arm lying across my chest, heavy and clammy. I tried sitting up but he pulled me back towards him.

I needed to get up.

I had stuff to do.

I didn't have time for brunch.

I kept repeating those three sentences in a variety of ways and voices. I was beginning to have some sort of panic attack. He was asking me too many questions, sleepily, forgetfully, and I was getting increasingly irritated, but trying to sound kind. My mother always told me to be kind. I'm not sure whether she had these circumstances in mind, but it seemed as good a time as any to try to be nice.

Be kind. I knew that brunch would last only a couple of hours and would provide a far less abrupt ending to the last twenty-four, but the more he tried to convince me to spend the morning with him, the more I wanted to bolt out of the building and down the street as fast as possible. And I knew that it was only going to get worse. Luckily he seemed to realise that I was in no mood for eggs, made an excuse and left.

I wasn't sure whether there were rules in place about fucking co-workers, but there should have been and I should have taken heed. Rules are there for good reasons: in this case, to prevent months of awkwardness, passive-aggressive Bloomberg messages and furious outbursts getting in the way of work.

In the course of one weekend I had gone from wanting to spend all my time with Giles to being repulsed, irritated, frustrated and generally irked by his every movement. Even his facial expressions across the floor now made me want to slap him. When I heard his voice shouting prices, I flinched. I hated the way he walked. I had, of course, said nothing to him about how I was feeling, opting instead for being non-responsive, passive-aggressive and avoiding him whenever possible. I wondered whether this was how guys felt when they slept with girls and lost interest immediately afterwards.

As the weeks went by, my frustration and anger began to filter into our working relationship. I had finally explained that I didn't want to take things any further between us, and for a while we managed to go back to being friends, but I started attacking him, ripping pieces off whenever I got the opportunity.

The situation got progressively worse when I began covering Fitz, a new client who traded one of Giles' products as well as mine. Because Fitz wanted to trade everything through me, I was forced to interact with Giles and the other guys on his desk regularly. We'd never previously had to work together, just entertain together, and I didn't like the way Giles did things.

His desk was reliant on screen-based broking, very rarely having to do much by voice, and everything about Giles' broking technique was contrary to what had been instilled in me by the American. He never seemed to make calls. When I got markets for him from Fitz, who thought our screen was useless and therefore didn't want to have his prices put up on it, Giles would struggle to get me a counter. If he got a tighter market on the back of it, he wouldn't show me the better side to see if Fitz wanted to improve and just went ahead and worked it, often without even shouting out the market. It was slack and careless.

14:29:46 GILES SMITH: anyway are we still ok working 94.75/95.25?

14:29:50 VENETIA THOMPSON: kunt off

14:30:08 GILES SMITH: we would know the answer if it was on screen

14:30:20 VENETIA THOMPSON: no we would know the

answer if you got a counter. I am not refreshing until you morons come back with something. He's given us a start, am not going to harass him every five seconds when we don't even have anything to show him. And for the last fuking time he doesn't want to use the screen. The screen is sh1t.

14:33:23 VENETIA THOMPSON: surely u can broke it by saying 'i was this, do u care in that context' etc

14:33:36 VENETIA THOMPSON: am not going to be checking him evry 5 mins when have fuk all reason to

14:33:48 GILES SMITH: ok superstar

14:34:11 VENETIA THOMPSON: why is the credit swaption desk, or whatever the fuck you are, asking me so many inane questions today

14:34:54 GILES SMITH: you get stressed and aggressive for no reason

14:35:32 VENETIA THOMPSON: hahaha no i get irritated when i get asked stupid things

14:36:26 VENETIA THOMPSON: and when u cant remember who is the 1st offer between u etc like this morning

14:36:56 VENETIA THOMPSON: it's not live on the screen so it doesnt need to be refreshed every 5 mins

14:37:04 VENETIA THOMPSON: surely u can broke around that

14:37:16 VENETIA THOMPSON: without having to commit a market as live

14:37:37 GILES SMITH: ok, you are right as ever

14:37:43 GILES SMITH: you should just remind me

14:37:54 GILES SMITH: i forget at times

14:38:12 VENETIA THOMPSON: yeah, forget how to voice broke?

14.39:20 GILES SMITH: you really are not right but i
  understand that you don't know as you are not
  involved in these sort of products

14:45:14 VENETIA THOMPSON: and u are so involved u
  cant even get a counter to a market i have given u, i
  dont even trade this shit, I have one guy with an interest
  and I have got a market out of him which is more than
  you guys have and all you lot can do is annoy me with
  ur stupid questions. Like working with halfwits.

I had copied and pasted the entire conversation to Lena who,
while siding with me from a broking point of view, remarked
that she never wanted to be on the receiving end of my wrath.

I wasn't sure why I was so angry. I was far more aggressive
both on and off the phones than I used to be, but I had increased
responsibilities and tougher clients to look after. I had to be
aggressive to get the job done. I didn't enjoy spending all day
snapping at Giles, but I couldn't stop. It had got to the point
where it was the only way that I could communicate with him,
and I hated it, but I had totally lost the ability to be nice.

15.24:40 LENA KLEIN: just hedged self on 16m bonds,
  client wanted bid after all, lost 4 ticks on 20m bund.

15:25:01 LENA KLEIN: for nothing

15:26:20 VENETIA THOMPSON: fuck. Any chance it'll go
  unnoticed? Our sh1t is all over the place, stuff that was
  trading in the high 90s a few months ago now sub 90.
  Nuts. Can't Markham help you out?

15.26.50 LENA KLEIN: nah, he's not in today. Sod's law.
  Nothing he could have done anyway really. Kill me
  now.

Lena and I now spent most of our time thinking up ways of getting out of our respective jobs. We were both as miserable as each other, but she had the added bonus of trading positions that were losing her hundreds of thousands with no end to the downturn in sight. We longed for the simplicity of a nine-to-five retail job, preferably working in a cheese or wine shop, but making coffee in Starbucks was becoming increasingly appealing – something we wouldn't spend all night thinking about and we wouldn't wake up at 5.45 a.m. dreading.

I missed the fish restaurant where I'd worked as a waitress during my second year at university. I turned up, raced around for six or seven hours, got fed oysters every time I ran through the kitchen, then sat and drank a glass of whatever wine was open when we closed before going home to bed. There was nothing complicated about it – you didn't get called a cunt, and you didn't spend all day worrying about whether some Yank trader would ever speak to you again.

The problem with trading was that every time you made plans to fold, started looking for jobs in cheese shops and even sending off applications, you would have a good day and months of misery would instantly be deleted from memory. You lived for those elusive good days: when it was 4.30 p.m. before you finally remembered to eat or got the chance to go to the toilet; when you're on your feet all day, yelling out fresh prices the second you put the phone down and lining up your next trade. If this is then followed by a perfect night out, eating and drinking in one of London's finest restaurants, it is easy to forget all about the minimum wage and making coffee for a living, because you spend all night thinking that you have the best job in the world.

CHAPTER 10

SASHIMI REVISITED

Nobu Berkeley was the scene of my first-ever client dinner, in January 2007, when I was asked by a broker on another desk to join him and his two clients. The evening had marked my first encounter with Cristal champagne, wagyu beef, the chocolate bento box and a very old bottle of Amarone. The restaurant was a favourite broker haunt; that night I'd spied four other groups of guys from our firm, two of whom weren't with clients.

We had all ended up in Chinawhite, which at that time was a club that no one really went to any more, but was always rammed with brokers on a Thursday. I'd spent most of the evening sprawled across their giant cushions, clutching a bottle of Grey Goose and wondering how I was going to stand up after vast amounts of sake, red wine, champagne and now vodka. Inexplicably, I'd somehow got home by midnight, having sensibly changed into flat shoes by the cloakroom and jumped into a cab. It was one of the only times I ever made it out of a club before 2 a.m., or had the good sense to switch footwear.

Now, nine months later, I was back in the same restaurant on a Wednesday evening, along with the American, the Ferg and a load of traders from Big Bad Bank, working our way through the entire menu. A bottle of Château Rothschild 2005 appeared in front of the Ferg, and I watched as it was decanted and passed around. The American was blissfully unaware of the £600 bottle of wine at the other end of the long table, and was deeply ensconced in conversation with another Yank while stuffing spicy tuna rolls into his mouth. They were the only two people having anything resembling a civilized conversation about the market amid shouts of 'GET ME A BRASS!' and the endless impressions of the American going on a few feet away from him.

I used to be surprised at the speed with which a group of men in their thirties and forties could regress to behaving like children on a school trip in the middle of a restaurant, but now it was familiar territory. As soon as the first drink was knocked over, the dinner would descend into chaos: blindfolded games of 'guess the sashimi' would be played, endless shots of sake would be knocked back, and seemingly endless amounts of food would appear. All you could do was hope that everyone remained seated and nobody was thrown out. But there was nothing anyone could do about the shrimp tempura that was currently swimming around at the bottom of the decanter. We'd just have to wait until it ended up in someone's glass and they won the prize.

Dinner eventually ground to a halt, but the drinking continued at Cuckoo Club. We'd lost the Ferg, who I later discovered had taken a detour en route, and gone to meet a good friend of his who was a bookie at another firm. The friend had been enjoying quiet post-dinner drinks at the Savoy until the Ferg burst through the door, and apparently asked the bartender for a Twix and an *Evening Standard* before falling over a bar stool and being asked to leave. He eventually caught up with us around midnight, and after a brief stint attempting to breakdance, finally calmed down and stayed slumped in the corner of our booth for the rest of the evening, swigging from a bottle of Grey Goose in one hand and a can of Red Bull in the other.

The American had gone home quietly hours ago, but everyone else was still going strong on the dance floor. I left just after 1 a.m. As I stumbled out of the club onto Swallow Street, I walked straight into Mo, who seemed to be waiting for a car to arrive. He was with Jeremy. They were both fucked. When Mo asked if I wanted to join them for a drink, I figured it would be rude not to and jumped in the back of Jeremy's blacked-out Range Rover when it crawled around the corner. It turned out that Jeremy was leaving his fund and heading to another one in Geneva the following week for double the money. It was his last night out with Mo and they'd been visiting all of their old haunts.

Mo had no particular reason to go home, as his wife had left him after deciding that he had a coke problem that he wasn't prepared to do anything about. He was already fucking some 25-year-old sales girl and didn't seem too bothered about his marriage evaporating into thin air. 'She goes like a fucking train. Dunno why I ever thought I was the marrying kind.'

As we sped along through Mayfair, he sat next to me, one elbow propped on the armrest, snorting several lines off a copy of *Country Life* that Jeremy produced from his briefcase. 'Can you not wait 'til we get back to mine? We're two minutes away, you cunt. Don't fucking get it all over the floor. I need to get this beast to Switzerland next week and it ain't going anywhere if it's covered in remnants of bugle. I don't want Bruno licking it up off the floor.' I hoped Bruno was a dog.

Mo lifted his head. He started saying repeatedly that he was about to be made redundant, that the credit market was finished and so was he. 'The only thing left to do is get fucked, Neesh. Seriously. You should get the fuck out of the market while you still can. This bitch is going down in a couple of months, and not in a good way, trust me – just you wait.' Everyone was always convinced that the credit market was finished when they were fucked. Yes, we had been seeing sudden sell-offs, and a few banks had auctioned off vast chunks of their portfolios, but the market still felt strong.

We finally pulled up outside Jeremy's Knightsbridge crash pad. There were flat screens in every room, including the guest bathroom, but other than that it was barely inhabited. The fridge was empty apart from half a pint of milk and six bottles of champagne – a mixture of Cristal and Dom Pérignon. He handed me three glasses. Mo manically flicked through various SKY channels, finally settling on News 24, which he quickly became transfixed by. We sat in silence drinking until I realized it was 3 a.m. and I should go home. Jeremy hurled me the key to his Bentley GT. 'Just drive yourself back and I'll come and pick it up tomorrow. Far more fun than Addison Lee, and the idea of you driving it turns me on.'

I hadn't driven for about five years. I'd passed my test in Devon and then immediately gone back to university in London and hadn't driven since, but with enough alcohol in my system to convince me that I could drive a tank, I picked up

the keys and thanked him before rushing out the door. I found
the car parked around the corner, and walked up to it slowly,
like I was approaching a nervous horse from behind. As I
reached the driver's side, it suddenly unlocked automatically
and I slid in. I thought that if I sat in it for a while I might
remember how to drive, but I couldn't see the ignition, and the
key in my hand didn't seem to have anything keylike to insert
anywhere. It was, however, extremely comfortable and for a
few minutes I leaned back with my eyes shut and contemplated spending the night there.

I'd never driven in London, and wasn't convinced that sitting alone behind the wheel of a huge car that I probably
wasn't insured to drive was the best time to attempt it, so I got
out and took the keys back to Jeremy, who called me a cab. It
was perhaps one of my few good decisions that month. I
wasn't sure that being drunk in charge of a Bentley was really
something I'd be able to come back from.

'So what the fuck happened to you last night? When did you
leave?'

It was 7.15 the following morning and I'd just logged onto
Bloomberg when someone started shouting down the line. It
was one of the traders I'd left in Cuckoo Club when I'd made
a break for freedom before running into Mo.

'Two-ish? I was wasted. Had to get out of there. What happened after I left?'

'Well, put it this way: I haven't been home, can't find my car
or house keys and have no phone. Great night. Don't expect to
see the Ferg before lunchtime. We stuck him in a cab bound for
Southend but have no idea if he actually made it.'

The morning disappeared. Nothing had traded; the same

offers sat on their own, no bids in sight, and everyone went off to lunch. By 2 p.m. things suddenly started to pick up, but I was beginning to feel sick – that pure, impossible to ignore feeling of nausea that I knew was heading in only one direction. My stomach began cramping, and I was starting to sweat profusely. But the phone kept ringing, prices started coming in every few seconds, and before long I had a handful of bonds and loans that were about to trade. The American's clients were quiet, and I had the buyers and sellers on everything. I couldn't leave the desk, particularly as the American had no idea what was going on, having just spent twenty minutes in the toilets with a copy of the *Sun*.

I was about to sell 5 million of a random chemical company's bank loans when I began to retch uncontrollably. I managed to swallow before calmly saying, 'Dude, sorry, I'm going to throw up. I'll call you back.' I threw the handset down and ran towards the toilets, my shoulders raised, desperately trying to fight whatever hell was rising up out of my stomach. I threw up as I reached the cubicle, then ran back to the desk and completed the trade. I expected to start feeling better after that, but soon I was regularly running to the toilets to the accompanying shouts of 'There she goes again! She's gonna fucking blow! Steady as she goes!'

Stuff was trading every few minutes, and I couldn't hand over to anyone else as no one knew my markets. Over an hour had gone by. I'd thrown up every ten minutes, and blown several tiny blood vessels around my eyes. The Godfather was trying to get me to go home, but not only was I incapable of sitting in a car for an hour without hurling the whole way home, but I was also in the middle of one of my busiest afternoons of trading ever – so I stayed put, and waited for it to pass.

174

By 5 p.m. my hair was matted, I was shaking uncontrollably and my eyes were completely bloodshot. I had never been so violently ill for such a prolonged period, even during a serious bout of seasickness while crossing the Bay of Naples on a hydrofoil.

17:02:45 GILES SMITH: you ok? You look horrific. Go home.
17:03:30 VENETIA THOMPSON: can't. still hurling every half-hour and I'd rather be here than stuck on the Tube or in the back of a cab. Sure it'll stop sooner or later. It has to, right? No one can be this sick for this long. Must have been that sole. Nobody else ate it and I knew it tasted odd.
17:03:50 GILES SMITH: well if you need me to take you home later just say. You don't look well.

Somewhere between shagging, fighting and hating each other, Giles and I had found our way back to being friends again. I knew that I had fucked up. I should never have treated him the way I did, and the fact that I was unable to control how I was behaving towards him concerned me. I hadn't been that cruel to someone for a very long time – if ever. I wasn't sure whether the job was bringing out sides to me that I didn't like, or whether I had just handled the entire situation badly. I didn't want to get to the point where I was blaming the long hours and the lifestyle for behaving badly towards others. Giles was one of my best friends, but I doubted whether we would ever regain the closeness we used to have.

The American had remained quiet all afternoon, ignoring the carnage unfolding from my side of the desk, until he checked the bill from the previous evening and noticed the

Rothschild wine sitting halfway down the receipt. He attempted to find out who had ordered it, and why he had never tasted it, but I was too busy dashing backwards and forwards to the ladies' to see the inquisition unfold. I knew that he would never find out who was responsible. I knew who had ordered it, as did the Ferg, but I knew that I couldn't say anything, however much allegiance I felt towards the American. He left without saying goodbye. I then found myself alone on the desk, praying the phones would stop ringing and I would somehow get home.

The Head of Entertainment and Events brought me over a supply of Crème de la Mer gift bags left over from Ladies' Day at Ascot to use as sick bags. We had given all of the female traders and various wives and girlfriends of traders Crème de la Mer handcream and lipbalm as gifts. It was the first time that the Company had decided that the corporate box would be reserved solely for ladies on Ladies' Day.

I'd originally invited several female traders the desk spoke to, but as the time got nearer, they'd all dropped out apart from Emma. She ended up being the only trader there that day; everyone else on the coach was either the wife of someone in senior management or the girlfriend of one of the Company's top clients. We were given our own personal tipster, and didn't have to leave the comfort of our own box, complete with endless pink champagne and gourmet food, once during the day.

I never expected to be revisiting those gift bags in quite this way, but when I finally made it into a taxi they were indispensable. I was sick all the way through the Limehouse tunnel, stopping briefly as we crawled along the Embankment, before recommencing at Hyde Park Corner. The cab driver was politely trying to ignore me, but I expected to be asked to step out of the cab at any moment, and avoided catching his eye in the rearview mirror. The cab was prepaid, so the driver really had no incentive to make sure I made it home, yet he kept driving regardless of the groans and splattering coming from the back seat.

By the time we got back to Chelsea, I could barely get out of the cab. I hadn't eaten since breakfast, had clearly expended all available energy on trading and retching, and now couldn't move my legs. My entire body seemed to have been hijacked by toxins. The cabbie helped me out, offering me his arm, and got me through my front door. He'd joked that it was normally something he found himself doing at 3 a.m., not early evening, but I didn't have the energy to explain that I was totally sober, just ill.

For the first time in months, I called in sick at 7 the following morning, knowing that I would need a full three-day weekend in bed to recover. My mother wanted me to come home to Devon. She was worried that I wasn't taking care of myself, which was true, but there wasn't much that I could do about it. There wasn't really anywhere to run to any more – not since the divorce. Home didn't have the same healing powers it once had. So I promised her I would go to the doctor if I wasn't feeling any better within the next few hours, got into bed, arming myself with several sick buckets and a bottle of water, and rode it out.

At 9.30 the following Monday evening, I was sitting precariously at the bar in the Sanderson Hotel, where I'd been since 8 p.m., waiting alone for a trader from NYC, The Insomniac, who was in town for one night only. We called him The Insomniac because he somehow managed to trade through all time zones.

I had no idea when he slept – he seemingly responded to Bloombergs throughout the night. The only time we couldn't reach him was during his commute from home to office, when he would inevitably disappear under the Hudson at some point. As I hadn't met him before, I figured it was worth trying to grab a drink with him before he headed back to the States, but he'd already texted several times to say that he was running late, and another text had just come through to say how sorry he was, but he would be another half-hour. It wasn't the time that was the problem, but the fact that I had been up since 5.30 a.m. and drinking cocktails since 8 p.m. It was unlikely I would be able to stay vaguely sober, or even awake, for longer than ten minutes. I wasn't going to make a great first impression. I looked like a drunk, desperate hooker propping up the bar; I'd long since given up all attempts at conversing with the cute Colombian bartender. It is impossible to drink alone in a hotel bar without resembling a prostitute. There was nothing that could be done about that, but I could at least try to stay alert and sober up.

I was once a regular at the Sanderson's Long Bar. When I lived on Newman Street, I could make it from my living room to one of their bar stools in less than three minutes. It had been the scene of various dates, disasters and encounters over the years, and to be back here waiting for a client seemed strange. As I turned to look towards the door to see if there was any sign of Josh, The Insomniac, I caught sight of a familiar bald head standing at the end of the bar: Richard. I wasn't sure if he'd seen me, but I kept my head down, slid off my stool and bolted towards the toilets in case. I wasn't sure what exactly I was going to do once I reached the safety of the ladies' room. I couldn't hide there all night; I had to meet a client. But it was

Richard: Richard, whom I had been dating for a while, and who had then disappeared never to be seen or heard from again; Richard, the fucking Lone Ranger. Now here he was, standing in the exact same spot that he'd stared at me from a couple of years ago when we'd first met. I rang Lena.

'Richard's here. At the fucking Sanderson.'

'What? Who's Richard?'

'You know, Richard – looks like Vin Diesel mixed with Billy Zane. I dunno. The guy I was dating who Lone Rangered me inexplicably. We thought he'd died. You know, Richard. For fuck's sake, I'm hiding in the toilet. What am I going to do? I'm alone in the bar, drunk.'

'Just go out there and sit down and see if he sees you, and if he does, be civilized. It was him that disappeared, not you, so why does it matter? Just calm down, V, you sound fucked. Have some water.'

I decided to walk back to my bar stool while keeping Lena on the line. Having my phone pressed to my ear as a prop made me feel less conspicuous, but as I turned the corner to go down the last flight of lime-green walled stairs I somehow slipped and slid the whole way down. Both my shoes came off and I dropped my BlackBerry, which was miraculously still connected.

'Hello? V? What's going on? Hello?'

I scrambled around for my shoes and my BlackBerry.

'Just fucking wiped out down a whole flight of stairs. This is why I should have stayed in the toilets. One glimpse of the man and I can't even stay upright. Can you come down here?'

'No, don't be ridiculous. Just get back up and go to the bar. You deal with intimidating men all the time. How is this any different? Suck it up.'

I hauled myself up off the floor and rounded the corner, back in full view of the bar. At least my fall had been completely out of sight. Pushing myself back up onto my stool, I ordered a double espresso and a bottle of fizzy water to try to dilute the last hour and a half's worth of drinks, and called Giles, who was out with clients nearby. I needed back-up.

As I hung up, a martini appeared. 'From the gentleman at the end of the bar.'

Fuck it. I took a sip.

'Thank him for me.'

I was trying to strike a balance between politeness and self-preservation. I could never turn down a perfect martini, but I had to avoid making eye contact with him or I would undoubtedly be back on the floor. Richard was so far keeping his distance, but he was still inescapable. Even the martini ever so slightly stank of him, and packed all the same punch.

'What happened to you? You look wasted! Have you been sitting here drinking alone for the last few hours?'

Giles was leaning against the bar next to me. Thank God. I finally calmed down, knowing that Richard would never approach if there was another guy with me.

'So if you're calling me in a drunken panic, we must be friends again.'

'We never weren't friends. I just couldn't work out how to act around you. But, of course, we're friends again.'

'I'm glad. Maybe you'll be marginally less psychotic towards me now. I never knew you could be such a bitch.'

'Ha. I know. I've said I'm sorry. But you were pretty damn smug and annoying for a while back there.'

'Well, can we just make sure it doesn't happen again, please? Anyway – what's new? You think Josh is actually coming tonight? You need to eat something, by the way; you're off your tits.'

We ordered a club sandwich.

'Yeah, he'll be here. He got stuck at dinner or whatever. Nothing's new. Still mediating between the American and the rest of the desk; he's still driving everyone insane. That's the thing about this job: nothing ever really changes.'

Josh eventually turned up, stayed for one drink and disappeared off to his room complaining about jetlag. Other than now knowing that he was far shorter than I'd imagined, and that he was planning to retire soon, I'd failed to discover anything vaguely helpful, and was back to being drunk in a hotel bar. But at least Giles was sitting beside me and Richard had gone. We ploughed our way through another couple of rounds, out of habit, and caught up on everything we had missed when we hadn't been speaking. I eventually made it home just before midnight, irritated that I was wasted yet again and it was only Monday evening.

CHAPTER 11

BROKER BULIMIA

It was slowly becoming increasingly difficult to drag myself out of bed each morning. I got up in the dark, walked to the Tube in the dark and got home in the dark. The only time I saw daylight was if I made it out of the building at lunchtime.

In early November I met the boys from Stupidly Bullish for lunch at Coq d'Argent. A banker had once thrown himself off the roof there, and it was something of a City landmark. Ever since we had spent a Thursday afternoon in April downing Krug on the terrace at Corney and Barrow, they'd been one of my favourite accounts. We now spoke around ten times a day. Marco, their main trader, gave me prices in everything he had, and very rarely traded away. Months later we were out again, and Dale, his boss, had decided to join us. We had made our way through a few bottles of wine, all chosen by Dale and all under 50 quid – a far cry from the £600 bottle of Barolo ordered by DofG's desk head. When Dale returned to the office, Marco and I carried on drinking, finishing the red and going back to pink champagne and then on to various brandies.

I made it back to Canary Wharf at 4.45 p.m., and walked straight into Fabrizio in the lift. He was the worst person I could possibly have seen in this state. He began asking me convoluted questions about a new product we were starting to trade. The pain above my right temple had spread behind my tear duct and I was barely able to see out of my right eye. There were dark patches obscuring my view of Fabrizio's swarthy face, and it had taken my full concentration to avoid sliding down the wall. I knew that white wine and any more than a couple of glasses of champagne gave me migraines, yet I seemed to forget this detail every time a glass was handed to me. I needed to wear some sort of identity badge telling people not to give me champagne – or more than a glass of white wine – under any circumstances.

I can't remember anything I said in response to Fabrizio's inquisition, only that I failed to get out of the lift on the right floor and leaned against all the buttons, making the lift stop every few seconds, and that he had asked if I was feeling OK.

He finally got out of the lift, but I didn't want to risk him seeing me staggering across the floor, so I carried on going up, took the fire exit staircase down a level and quietly tried to get back to my desk unnoticed.

'TAKE IT OFF!'

'GET ME A BRASSSSS!'

'NICE OF YOU TO JOIN US, BIRD!'

'FERG, FEEERRRRRRRG! FERGGG!'

'YOU'RE 'AVIN' A FUCKING LAUGH, AIRBAGS! WHERE THE FUCK 'AVE YOU BEEN?'

There was a photocopier repairman walking along behind

me, so the various howls and shouts coming from across the floor were doubled. He scurried along past me as I veered off towards my desk and the abuse continued. He was black, and the standard response to anyone black or mixed race appearing on the *Sky News* screen, or walking around our floor, was to shout, 'Look, it's the Ferg' at them as loudly as possible.

'You know we're meeting Jack at 6.00 p.m. at Zuma, right?'

The American. I had, of course, totally forgotten. Jack was a new trader at a small European bank and we had arranged a drink weeks ago to introduce ourselves properly.

'You're gonna have to go on ahead. I have some stuff to sort out here first. I'll be there by sevenish. You might as well get out of here now.'

I got back in the lift and made it to Boots, where I bought some Migraleve and Co-codamol. I was fumbling around in my handbag for a good five minutes before I managed to find my credit card, and feeling increasingly ill. It was, of course, too late; if I didn't take pills at the first sign of a migraine attack, I would be vomiting violently within the hour, in addition to being unable to see properly or balance. The fact that I was also drunk wasn't particularly helpful.

On the Tube I shut my eyes, hiding from the various flashing lights and drifting dark blobs that were obscuring my vision. Maybe I was going blind. I was also feeling increasingly nauseous and sweating profusely. When the doors opened at London Bridge, I dived out onto the platform, convinced that I was going to throw up. I leaned against the wall for five minutes, trying to ride out the nausea, which eventually passed, and I hobbled back onto the next train.

When I arrived at Zuma, it was 5.45 p.m. I had 15 minutes

to attempt to get some of the alcohol out of my system, get over my migraine, and somehow regain a normal level of consciousness. I caught sight of myself in the mirror and I resembled someone who has just had a minor stroke. I ordered two large bottles of water to sober up, a double espresso to counteract the fatigue, and ice, which I wrapped in a napkin and held against my eye socket, and sat and waited, taking deep breaths while keeping my other eye half shut.

The woman at the next table leaned over and asked me if I was feeling OK. This wasn't a good sign; I could more or less get away with feeling horrific, but if I also looked ill there was no way I would be able to pull off a client meeting alone. I got rid of the ice, which had only smudged my eye make-up further and not numbed the pain in the slightest. I'd probably also given myself chilblains.

'Venetia?'

He was, of course, slightly early. I got up to shake his hand. I was light-headed, sick, and I was still sweating uncontrollably. We sat down and discussed his move from New York to London and his family. Another bottle of water arrived. He ordered a mojito, and I joined him – at this stage it wasn't as if alcohol could make the situation any worse. I was drunk, about to hurl and in the throes of a migraine. Rum was a welcome addition to the cocktail of painkiller, red and white wine already sloshing around in my stomach.

The drinks arrived, and I managed a further few minutes of inane chat about his children and made vague references to the market. He was speaking about his background in M&A (mergers and acquisitions) and how he'd realized that he simply wasn't suited to it when I felt myself retch. Luckily he was looking the other way, distracted by a waiter laying out a large plate of sushi at the next table who had knocked over some glasses and splashed sake up his leg.

I somehow managed to excuse myself, grabbed my handbag and walked as casually as I could to the ladies', engaged in a battle of wills with my stomach. The only thought running through my mind was that I couldn't possibly throw up on the floor in Zuma. I spent what felt like the next twenty minutes being violently ill. By the end I was kneeling on the floor in the cubicle, as I was struggling to stay upright and my stomach muscles could no longer hold me over the toilet. Fucking champagne. Fucking migraine. My eyes were bloodshot, and my mascara had left trails down both cheeks. I scraped my hair back into a ponytail and quickly attempted to resuscitate what was left of my make-up – more eyeliner, more mascara, more blush.

When I got back to the table the American had arrived; I had never been so glad to see him in all the time I'd known him. 'Venetia, we were just looking at getting some food – can you order some spicy tuna rolls and anything else you feel like?' He thrust a menu at me, and returned to his conversation with Jack; my vomiting had apparently gone completely unnoticed. It was a simple task that I was used to carrying out, but I could barely focus on the words in front of me. There are few worse things than being made to navigate a menu of raw fish when you've just been violently ill. Every organ in my body was either shaking or shrivelling up with disgust at the thought of raw eel and deep-fried soft-shell crab.

I managed to order by pointing at the safest options, then sat back and attempted to tune in to the American's soliloquy on his role as inter-dealer broker to the stars of the Street; how he liked to work in a bespoke manner; and how he was able to access information that other brokers couldn't. His voice was having the same effect on my senses that the thought of raw eel had. I was staring at the green muddled mint and sugar at the bottom of my mojito, wondering if I was going to throw up again and realizing that perhaps drinking more rum hadn't been such a great idea after all. My migraine had at least subsided and I had somehow slightly sobered up; it only made everything more difficult to tolerate.

The food began arriving and, after a few tentative moments, I felt something familiar – a hunger pang. Against all odds, I appeared to be having a second wind. It was broker's bulimia. Get rid of a lunch of *foie gras*, steak and a chocolate bombe, and carry on afresh. The rock shrimp tempura tasted better than it ever had done and I was suddenly speaking about the distressed debt market with renewed excitement.

'Just hurled guts up in Zuma and now back on it in size. How's that for hardcore?x'

I texted Giles, knowing that he would be amused. I was vaguely aware, somewhere deep in the back of my mind, that this wasn't something to be proud of, and most of my friends would be appalled that I was wearing my vomit as a badge of honour, which at that moment only made it more fulfilling.

I was glad to get home to an empty flat. I climbed into the shower, basking in post-migraine, post-sickness warmth, remnants of analgesics, champagne and rum still swirling around my central nervous system. It was a lesser version of that safe, morphine-induced sleep after an operation. There might be tubes hanging out of you all over the place, but you've had a shot of morphine in the arse and know you will soon be slip-sliding away into a deep, cocooned sleep where nothing can hurt you any more. Thank you, nurse.

'So, I think it went really well with Jack. He's a nice guy. And he's smart.'

It was the following morning. The American was in good spirits following our apparently successful evening with his latest project, Jack. He was now talking about arranging another dinner. Part of me was keen to drop in that I had spent a portion of the evening throwing up lunch and had zero recollection of anything Jack and I had spoken about before he had arrived. I just hoped it hadn't been anything inappropriate and I'd managed to stay vaguely on the topic of distressed debt.

> *'RM apparently just went up at 92.5 away, we got any sellers?'*
> *'Nah, only at 94 and he hasn't got any room.'*
> *'Where's the bid? Do we even have a fucking bid?'*
> *'I've just got a 90 bid. Fuck, it just traded away at 93.'*
> *'Where the fuck is the seller?'*

The bond and the loan were going up all over the place. There had been news out. Good numbers had been posted, but without a seller there was nothing we could do but watch it trade at different shops. When prices start moving quickly, traders usually try to show their offer or bid only in one shop to avoid getting hit or lifted at the same time by two different bookies, unless they have a larger amount for sale and can afford to lose 2 million followed by another 2, or even a six pack (three lots of 2 million).

> *'I'm about to get hit at 91. Account ten is whacking it back down.'*

'GOING DOWN AT 1, LEFT 89 BID ON THE FOLLOW.'
'FUCK, GETTING HIT AGAIN. DOWN AT 89. TAKES MY
BUYER OUT.'

One of the Big Swinging Dicks had apparently got bored. The high lift at 92.5 hadn't gone down well, and he'd shifted at least 4 million, hitting once at 91, then down again at 89, as well as selling more away from us, pushing the price down further. There was a split opinion on exactly how good the company's numbers had been, and whether it even mattered in this market. Some traders were negative on certain names, disliking them whatever the news was, and if they had a big enough book, could manipulate the market by selling the bonds or loans low and trying to decrease their value in the Street.

Because of the total lack of transparency, traders get paranoid easily. If low trades happen inexplicably, they often assume someone has access to information they don't and can start panic selling. This is particularly rife in the leveraged loan market, which is private. Only holders of the loans have access to information and no one can really be sure what's going on.

The only thing left to do when the market is disintegrating is party, so the American decided it was time for another event at Nobu, but this time he allowed the rest of our desk to invite their clients too. Despite being unhappy with the private room we had used last time, he opted to book it again when he quickly realized his other option was to have it at Mint Leaf, which didn't have quite the same cachet; besides, he liked Nobu's spicy tuna rolls.

Even in the absence of Kraut, who were still refusing to answer any of our calls, and DofG, who although they had been showing prices to The Judge were avoiding socializing with us, there was a good turnout, including some of the more elusive traders, who dropped by for a drink. Everyone was far drunker than they had been at the last party, and nobody was mentioning work. There was no need: everyone was losing money. No one knew if and when prices would stop tanking and who would get tinned in January. It was the last supper. We were probably all damned.

I'd somehow ended up in Trader Vic's in the basement of the Hilton Park Lane with a motley crew: Emma; her boss, Brian; one of the guys from Giles' desk, Shaun; and a random sales guy who had appeared from nowhere. We were drinking out of a giant treasure chest filled with something that tasted like alcoholic cherryade using foot-long straws. I had no idea where the rest of my desk had gone, or why Emma's boss was drunker than anyone else, or where the straw skirt and coconut shells had come from. Nobody knew the sales guy, but everyone was so drunk it didn't seem to matter, and the more cherryade I slurped, the more attractive he became.

It's always the clients you least expect who turn into marauding drunks at the first opportunity, and Brian was proving my theory perfectly. He suddenly fixated on the idea of going to a club and had begun yelling, in a polite middle-aged way, 'Come on, Venetia, you're my broker; you're supposed to have the keys to this city. Please take me out. Take me to every club you know. I want to dance and I want to get fucked before we all disappear in a puff of smoke.'

Emma was trying to calm him down and get him to go home, as she had set her sights on Shaun, and having Brian in tow was cramping her style. I wanted to get out of there altogether before I ended up caught in a warped foursome. I put

Brian in a cab, left Emma and Shaun face down in a treasure chest, jumped in a cab myself and called the Salsero, one of my favourite dancing partners.

'Where are you?'

'Just leaving Bar Salsa. Why?'

'You wanna grab a drink? I'm just round the corner.'

We arranged to meet at Freedom Bar in Soho. It was open late, and I knew with him it made very little difference where we drank. I was already sitting at the bar knocking back rum when he arrived, wrapped up in endless layers of wool and a huge duffel coat. He didn't like the cold and was shivering as he pulled me off the bar stool and put my arms around his neck in one swift movement. He ordered a Jack Daniels straight up, and we stood leaning into each other, drinking in silence. He had never been much of a conversationalist, I'm sure partly due to his limited grasp of the English language. I sometimes wondered if he was more intelligent in Portuguese, but on the dance floor it was totally irrelevant. After an evening spent discussing leveraged loans, it was a welcome change.

We ended up back at his place in Clapton, which was possibly the furthest east I had ever been, bar the odd trip to Stratford when I was dating an army officer with a house there. I had every intention of jumping him as soon as we got through the door, immediately stripping down to nothing but my tights and bra, but as soon as I was vaguely horizontal, the effects of the 5.45 a.m. alarm in combination with the vast amount of alcohol I'd consumed in the last few hours took immediate hold and I must have passed out, because the next thing I heard was the dreaded calypso alarm.

I rolled over. He was still asleep, wearing a white T-shirt and boxer shorts, and I was still in my tights and bra. I'd come all the way to sodding Clapton for a completely innocent sleep-over. At least I was already in East London, although I had no idea where I was or where the nearest Tube station was. Creeping out of bed, I got dressed as quickly and quietly as possible before leaning down and kissing him goodbye. He was still half asleep and I didn't want to wake him to get direc-tions. I finally worked out how to open the front door and emerged into the darkness with no idea which direction to head in. I needed to find a street sign and then I'd be able to use the Google Maps application on my BlackBerry, which had pre-viously only ever sent me round in circles or taken me the longest possible route, but it was my only option. Clapton. Did Clapton even have a Tube station? Fuck, fuck, fuck. This was exactly why it was unwise to venture outside Zone One during the week.

After twenty minutes of walking down a street I thought was vaguely in the direction of Hackney, I gave up, found a house number and the street name and called Addison Lee. It wasn't until I was safely sitting in the warmth of one of their VW Sharans that I realized how crumpled my suit was and that I had a mammoth ladder in my tights. I tried to repair the damage to my make-up and unclog my eyelashes, but there wasn't a lot I could do without make-up remover. My lashes had bunched together into one solid clump and half my eyeliner was spread across my cheek. I couldn't pos-sibly walk into the office like this, but there was nothing open at this time in the morning and I couldn't make it home and still get to work in time. All I could do was pray that I hadn't accidentally put waterproof mascara on the previous day, and attempt to wash it off and start again when I got to the office.

It was 6.30 a.m. when I pulled up outside the building. When I walked onto the floor it was still fairly empty, and luckily there was no one on our desk. I managed to get to the bathroom, grabbing my spare pair of tights and a bottle of foundation out of my drawer en route, without anyone I knew seeing me. Having to do a walk of shame in last night's make-up, laddered tights and crumpled suit across a packed trading floor would have been a step too far, even for me.

07:18:32 VENETIA THOMPSON: thank fuk you're here – haven't been home. Oops.

07:20:56 LENA KLEIN: Ha! Good work – who'd you bone?

07:21:30 VENETIA THOMPSON: No one in the end. Ended up in fuking Clapton – total washout. Managed to pass out unconscious within five minutes of getting back to his. Poor show.

07:30:23 LENA KLEIN: haha brilliant. You do know we're out with Markham tonight, yeah? He's been wanting to meet the famous Airbags for a long time, you better not flake.

07:35:30: VENETIA THOMPSON: yeah yeah, I'll be fine, might need to somehow go home first and repair my face though. It ain't pretty.

Scalini's with Markham was an invitation I could never turn down. I'd wanted to meet him properly ever since Lena had first mentioned his superhuman broking powers. Dinner with a broker from a rival firm was usually unheard of but, as I was Lena's best friend, I usually got invited along as her date – she hated the late nights and endless alcohol consumption, and I could therefore operate as her second; drinking all the wine she spared, and eating the offal she couldn't stomach. I was a broking black hole, happily consuming anything in my path.

Markham was everything I'd expected – he arrived with four guys from his team flanking him, and it was immediately apparent who ran the desk. He liked Lena – months of terror every time he called down the line for her had finally morphed into a broker-trader relationship where she was able to freely banter with him without worrying about angering Markham or taking it too far. It was, however, clearly a relationship reserved for his favourite clients. I was an outsider – an interloper from another firm who, although fun to spend the evening with, he would always be wary of. Whenever I caught his eye I was reminded of this – there was no straying outside of the parameters he had somehow installed. I was captivated.

It wasn't long before we were the last remaining table in the restaurant, along with a large group of Italians, and we had somehow ended up taking it in turns to sing carols across the room in our respective languages. Intermittently, one of the guys would make a small smoky lantern by rolling up an amaretti biscuit paper and setting fire to one end and we would all sit, mesmerized, as it floated across the room. Remnants of ash would inevitably get down my cleavage, at which point one of the guys would lean over and attempt to brush it away, 'in case I caught fire,' and we'd all descend into hysterics.

I went to bed dreaming of one day working with Markham, covered in smudges of ash.

CHAPTER 12

THE DESCENT

Sanza speme vivemo in disio[1]

It was the end of November. Matt, a broker from another desk, had booked lunch at Petrus for his favourite clients, who were in town from Frankfurt for the weekend. He had extended an invitation to me when someone had dropped out and there was suddenly a space. It was a quiet Thursday and the American happily let me go. We left the office at 11.30 a.m., and took a cab to the Berkeley Hotel. I knew that Matt intended to make a day of it when we started on pink vintage Krug at midday in the bar, and were halfway through our second bottle before the second of his German clients arrived.

There are quick lunches, when you arrange to meet at 1 p.m., knowing that everyone has to go back to work in the afternoon

1 'Without hope we live in desire.' Dante, *The Inferno*, 4.42

and there is therefore a limit on what can be consumed in an hour and a half. And then there are the times when your clients have flown in to do a course, or for a couple of meetings in their London office, and have their afternoon and evening free; they are in transit. These lunches are perfect opportunities for all-afternoon eight-course tasting menus and endless bottles of wine, as they have nowhere to go other than their miserable hotels. You can more or less hold them hostage for as long as you want. This was one of those rare occasions, and Petrus at the Berkeley was the perfect place for it.

'Just bring whatever you would recommend, as long as they're all less than 500 quid, mate, and I'd like a glass of Château d'Yquem with my *foie gras*. Boys? Neesh? Who wants a glass with me? It's fucking delicious.'

Starting on £100 a glass dessert wine was punchy, and something only Matt could have pulled off. One of the Germans promptly ordered a bottle of Brunello that was marginally north of 600, asking Matt if he minded, which, of course, he didn't.

What followed was five hours of the restaurant's finest food and wine. Periodically the guys would excuse themselves between courses to go and smoke, and I would be left alone on a large round table, surrounded by bottles, staring out blankly at the other diners. Even a year of entertaining clients at London's best restaurants hadn't fully prepared me for that day.

We eventually moved into the bar, where Matt promptly sent over a bottle of Dom Pérignon to two girls, one of whom turned out to be the wife of a broker at our firm. It seems that in London's top restaurants and hotel bars you are never further than a few feet from a broker or a broker's wife.

The smoking ban had led to all sorts of problems. Cigars, along with fine wine, coke and whisky, were a central part of the City lunch or dinner, but it was becoming increasingly difficult to find somewhere to sit your client, order them a cigar and have a much-needed rest while they lit up. Fortunately, the cigar terrace at the Lanesborough Hotel was nearby, and they served the same year of Croft Port that we had been drinking in Petrus. We lay back, fading into plumes of Romeo y Julieta smoke, but the calm was promptly ruined by Matt deciding that the 1965 port 'didn't taste right' and sending it back. After seven hours of drinking and smoking, I wasn't sure how he could taste anything; it was now all Ribena to me.

By this time it was 7.30 p.m. At some point I knew I would have to get home, change and get across London to Marketex's Christmas party at Shoreditch House, where around ninish I was supposed to be meeting Lena, who had got me on the list as her sales girl when she had sent in her RSVP. I managed to extract myself, leaving the Germans, one of whom was comatose on a sofa under an outside heater, and Matt enjoying another round of cigars and yet another bottle of port, and jumped in a cab.

Staggering around my bedroom, fighting with tights, Louboutin shoes and various pieces of clothing, I felt sick, stank of cigars and could barely stand. I knew that the Addison Lee car journey was going to be painful. I wound down the window, hanging my head out like an Afghan hound, and shut my eyes as the car navigated its way through the City's streets. It was like being on a waltzer at a fairground, and I couldn't work out whether I felt worse with my eyes open or shut. The driver kept trying to speak to me, but I could barely hear him and was incapable of replying.

We made it all the way to London Wall before I needed to stop the cab to throw up. I don't know what I shouted, but it was clearly abrupt enough to make the driver pull over. He looked mystified that I was in that much of a state so early in the evening, and I mumbled something about food poisoning by way of explanation. I was vaguely aware of people walking past as I sat propped sideways, leaning forward out of the car, with my head hanging between my knees, one hand holding my hair back in a ponytail as I tried to avoid throwing up on my £350 shoes. After a few minutes, I swung my legs back into the car and we carried on across the City while I attempted to reapply my make-up – a ritual that I always seemed to be performing in the back of cabs, Azazel sitting quietly on my shoulder.

I arrived at the club feeling marginally better, having rid myself of most of lunch, and managed to check in my coat and get my wristband on, with the help of the doorman, relatively unscathed. They were checking ID on reception to ensure we were on the guest list, and I was hoping that they didn't also need proof of where we worked, as brokers from rival firms aren't generally welcomed at Christmas parties. Luckily, my driving licence sufficed and I got in the lift with a load of Marketex brokers, who assumed that I was a client and began asking me which bank I worked for. Pretending to be part of Lena's sales team was always going to be difficult enough sober, but in this state it was tricky to remember who and what I was supposed to be. One of the bookies helpfully told me that I didn't 'look too good' and asked if I was feeling OK before I had time to answer where I worked. I replied that I had just come from a long lunch, and they all nodded in sympathy and left me alone. 'Client lunch' seems to be the universal City code for 'I feel like shit, please don't ask me any difficult questions.'

I was convinced that once I had found some water, a chair and Lena, who wasn't picking up her phone, it would all be fine. Navigating the wooden slats on the roof required intense focus, and by the time I made it over to the bar, my legs were about to buckle. Everyone was far too sober, and having very civilized conversations in clusters of two or three. There was no way of hiding a 5ft 9in (6ft in the stupid heels) blonde drunkenly flailing around on the slats. I was relieved to reach the relative safety of the bar, where I could at least steady myself. I ordered a martini and a glass of water, then downed the water and held the martini as a prop. I couldn't walk around empty-handed, as that would automatically cause someone, probably a Marketex broker, to come up and ask me if I would like a drink, and I wasn't ready to have that conversation.

I couldn't see Lena anywhere. After a few brief tedious conversations with random emerging-market traders, and having sloshed most of my gin down my shirt and the rest down the back of someone's cocktail dress, I realized I wasn't capable of small talk, and sought cover before I ran into any of my clients. I ditched the martini glass and took myself off to the ladies', where I locked myself in a cubicle with a bottle of water to buy myself some time and try to sober up. It was a self-imposed time out. I could hear a load of inane girly bathroom chat going on about lipgloss, boys and plans for the Christmas break. They were Marketex screen girls. I just hoped that they didn't all need to use the toilet, as there were only three and I was holding one hostage. I half expected someone's head to pop up over the partition wall.

'Where the fuck are you? I'm fucking covered in gin, drunk, probably about to hurl again, totally fucked and totally on my own at this fucking party.' I'd finally got hold of Lena, who was still miles away and hadn't left her dinner. I was speaking in a drunken stage whisper.

'Sorry. Running late. Why are you whispering? Where are you? You're awesome at this shit, and you're always going to market parties alone; you'll be fine. Just get back out there and I'll be there in half an hour.'

'In the ladies'. Not this drunk this early in the evening, and not at a rival firm's Christmas bash posing as your sales girl. Just hurry the fuck up before someone thinks I've passed out and breaks the loo door down.'

It wouldn't have been a problem if it were later in the evening, when everyone would be drunk, staggering around and generally behaving badly. I knew the safest option was to stay put for a bit. The cubicle was a wonderful cocoon, and I leaned my head against the partition before slowly sliding backwards. The next thing I knew, my BlackBerry was vibrating in my lap. I bolted upright, having fallen asleep, stomach muscles strained, head balanced on the cistern, mouth dry. It was Lena. Over an hour had gone by.

'I'm here. Where are you? Fitz said he saw you heading for the bogs but hadn't seen you since. Quick, some fucking moron is seeing how many lengths he can swim underwater for a hundred bucks, and is about to get in the pool.'

Bookie parties were always social quagmires, but this one was particularly spectacular. The entire market, all getting drunk together, with the added bonus of a swimming pool, a skittles alley, a chocolate fountain, too many concrete staircases and an open bar, was asking for trouble.

I emerged from the safety of the ladies' room and spotted Lena by the bar. Walking towards her, I felt far less precarious than I had earlier, and managed to walk at a normal speed.

Standing a few feet away from her were three traders, all of whom either one or both of us had dated in the past. She had recently been seeing someone else, who was at the other end of the room, and although she had decided that she was no longer interested, after an unfortunate incident when he had danced naked to 50 Cent, she hadn't had a chance to tell him.

'Oh fuck. Hugh's heading over. You reckon we can just push him in the pool? At least he can't swing his cock around to gangsta rap in public. Urgh.'

It was a shame, because, like a lot of guys in the market, he'd originally had potential. He was funny, clever, a successful trader at a big European bank, but without the arrogance we had come to expect, and seemed to be totally enamoured of Lena. In one foul press of the play button on his ghetto blaster, he had unwittingly terminated the relationship.

Nobody can pull off dancing naked to 50 Cent. It had been the worst attempt at seduction I had ever heard about. Lena, as much of a gadget and technology lover as she was a music lover, had described the shock as twofold: first she had been hit by the emergence of the ugly CD player with tape deck, and secondly by the vision of him beginning to thrust flaccidly into thin air, mouthing the lyrics to 50 Cent's latest album. She had fled the building immediately.

It was a City phenomenon: men who spent their days making and losing ridiculous amounts of money, and who were seemingly infallible – able to cope when the FTSE shat itself, or when companies went up in smoke – were unable to function in a relationship. Clearly all their energy was so deeply intertwined in the buying and selling of bonds and CDS that there was quite simply nothing left for other pursuits. Even the most aggressive, testosterone-fuelled traders could quickly dissolve into nothing more than limp husks, lying naked and awkward in the dark, apologizing profusely, the second they were away from the safety of the trading floor.

I moved down to the floor below, clutching the wall as I climbed down the stairs. I came around the corner and walked straight into three of the traders I covered, who were all, thankfully, drunker than I was and propping each other up. They said that they were on their way to the pool and carried on past me upstairs. I hoped that none of them drowned or I'd be short a client in the morning.

I stood hovering by the chocolate fountain, attempting to speak Russian to a Ukrainian emerging-markets trader I had apparently spoken to earlier in the evening, until I lost my balance, covering my forearm in chocolate, then excused myself before promptly collapsing onto a sofa. Mo, whom I'd spotted when I'd arrived, but had scurried past, had been staggering around the dance floor for the last hour. He came and joined me, arm around my waist, whispering drunkenly that I was his favourite broker, before quickly remarking that he'd never date a female broker because he didn't think that spending so much time around guys was healthy.

I was drunk, but not drunk enough to forget what he had said. Fitz had once said the same thing, but I had dismissed it instantly as nonsense. I couldn't possibly be destined for a life of solitude just because I was a broker. But hearing it again made me question my femininity – whether it had changed over the course of the year and whether I had now morphed into some sort of monster. I didn't want to end up like the Incredible Hulk. My forearm had remnants of chocolate clinging to the blonde hairs, which suddenly seemed strangely long, making me wonder if I should get them waxed, and I had a client lying across my lap with his arms around my neck. It probably wasn't the best time to be contemplating whether the job had somehow soiled me.

'Neesh, got any bugle? There's a distinct shortage. We're in fucking Shoreditch, for fuck's sake. My dealer's on his way, but his Mrs is having a shit fit. Fuck knows how long he'll be. And fuck knows where everyone's gone. Probably whoring.'

I felt a hand on my shoulder, and recognized the gravelly voice speaking into my ear in a stage whisper, but I couldn't move my neck to turn around and face him because of the vice grip Mo had me in. It was Gonzo, one the biggest producers in the market, whom I'd run into on several nights out. He walked off before I could say anything. I was glad that Mo hadn't heard the word 'bugle' and gone into a frenzy.

The sofa had seemingly taken us both captive, and every time I attempted to stand up, Mo clung to my hips, pulling me back down. I was too drunk to fight him, and the sofa was too soft to be of any help. He eventually disappeared onto the dance floor, spinning around until he came to an abrupt halt and sat in a leftover plate of miniature sausage rolls.

Toby – a mutual friend of me and Lena, who happened to trade at Aggro Bank – was hovering by the bar, all beige chinos and pastel shirt, wielding a gin and tonic and engaged in conversation with a girl. We'd exchanged a few brief words earlier in the evening but we hadn't spoken properly since his efforts to get me a job in sales at his bank, priming me beautifully for interviews. The prep had finally culminated in a series of interviews, the most memorable of which was the hour I spent being grilled on bond maths by his colleague, which had only confirmed my total lack of numerical ability. I had turned into a stroppy teenager being quizzed by a maths teacher on something that, however the question was phrased, I wouldn't be able to grasp. School memories of daily humiliation as I struggled with long division and equations came hurtling back, and all the previous good impressions and groundwork that I had laid down in interviews with senior sales guys was destroyed as I became a defensive wreck, head down, slumped in my chair hiding behind my cream highlights. I nearly walked out, it was so painful.

Toby wasn't my type physically – he was wide, moved and looked like a tank, or perhaps a rhino – yet that night I was strangely attracted to him, having previously never considered the idea. He dropped down onto the sofa beside me. I was glad to see a familiar, vaguely sober face. Lena had disappeared with Hugh; she'd decided it would be easier to break things off outside where she could easily jump in a cab and escape.

I didn't really want to go home. It was 3 a.m. and now fairly pointless. By the time I got back, it would be 4, giving me an hour's sleep at best. I'd reached that point in the evening where pulling an all-nighter seemed like the most sensible option. And Toby was the perfect companion. He was less drunk than me, lived near me, and would hopefully therefore ensure I got home. He was more interesting than the Ukrainian trader now loitering alone by the bar. Toby wasn't really a client, so he was fair game, and I was one martini away from finding him the most attractive tank in the world.

Before long we were dancing in our seats to Blackstreet, the sofa conveniently having swallowed both of us, rendering any further movement impossible. There were a number of Aggro Bank, Yank Bank and Big Bad Bank's credit traders still *in situ*, dancing en masse to 'No Diggity'. All of them had to be at work in four hours, and had clearly collectively vetoed sleep. The chocolate fountain was drying up, games of skittles were becoming increasingly treacherous, and the bar was still open. Everyone had, at least, been moved off the roof away from the pool. I never did find out who won the underwater swim challenge, but there were several decidedly damp traders slumped asleep in armchairs a few feet away. Only the troop of masseuses, who had been on hand at the beginning of the evening to ease the aches and pains of the City's finest before the serious drinking could begin, had fled the building.

'So are you glad you stayed put? You know, looking at you now, I think you have far more fun broking than you ever would have doing sales.'

Toby was right. It seemed ridiculous that only a few months ago I had been desperate to get out of broking when now I couldn't imagine leaving, and I was more embedded in it than ever. It was one of those nights when I felt like I did the best job in the world. I didn't know how I was going to get through the next day at work, and I could barely string a sentence together, yet I knew that I had never really been happier than I was at that moment on that sofa drunkenly flirting with Toby, picking bits of chocolate off my forearm.

It was obviously time for another gin and tonic. Toby went to the bar. I scrambled around in my handbag and quickly checked my eye make-up, which was predictably blurred and clogged post taxi reapplication, toilet nap and the last five hours of drunken antics. My eyes were bloodshot, and there were tiny red spots around my sockets where blood vessels had clearly exploded when I'd thrown up earlier. It was dark. Toby would never notice, and I knew that I'd never make it all the way to the ladies' without falling over, so I stayed where I was and put the mirror away.

I don't know what time we left. Marketex had laid on a fleet of Addison Lee cars to take everyone home, and we somehow navigated our way from the door into the back of one, armed with goodie bags and the remainder of another couple of G&Ts for the road. While rummaging through the bags and eating the chocolates we'd been given, Toby and I chatted about meeting up over the weekend – a friend of his was having a birthday party, and it had sounded like he'd invited me, but when I got home it was impossible to recall the conversation. I would have to wait to see if he sent me a Bloomie later.

I managed to shower and change, and made it into work just before 7 a.m. I knew that anyone who had been at the party wouldn't be in for another few hours. When one of my clients finally groaned down the line at 9.30 a.m., it was to inform me, deadpan, that he was too drunk to trade and had been banned from putting any bids out there by his desk head and I should speak to his boss if I needed to do anything. Two of the other guys he worked with still hadn't shown up, and couldn't be reached. Toby still wasn't in; neither was Lena nor the hapless 50 Cent thruster.

A few stories started trickling in. One of Yank Bank's biggest hitters was caught altruistically sharing his six-pack of beer with some tramps at 4 a.m. outside an all-night store – he had apparently been caught in the act by a car-load of bookies who happened to drive past and see him on their way back from a bit of whoring nearby. They had of course immediately stopped their car and hurled a load of abuse at him, and the debate was now over who was more of a 'wrong 'un': the trader for insisting on sharing his beer with a couple of tramps, or the brokers going home to their wives after a trip to a brothel.

One party had single-handedly brought much of the credit market to a standstill that morning, in a sort of reverse of Charity Day. Traders were either AWOL, banned from showing prices, or had surfaced only to be sent home to sleep it off. Most of the Marketex brokers weren't online, knowing that their clients would be late in and there was therefore no point in showing up until lunchtime.

Our own firm had vetoed the idea of having any more Christmas parties, knowing the carnage it caused the following day, and had instead opted to throw smaller individual desk parties, spreading the load throughout the run up to Christmas, figuring that individual desks and their clients couldn't possibly cause as much damage as one party for the entire credit market. But an email had gone round about the Back Office Christmas party, stating that all brokers were strictly banned, which had caused a certain amount of annoyance. Apparently the Back Office could be trusted to behave, but the Front Office couldn't, which was probably fairly accurate.

I used to speak to Back Office hourly, while trying to sort out unsettled or mismatched trades. There had been a plan at one point to send me off for two weeks to work with them and learn how bonds came in and went out again, as a sort of rotation in the style of a grad scheme, but it had never taken place, and the job of sorting out trades had been passed on to someone else.

Back Office probably deserved their own Christmas party without the interference of a few hundred rioting bookies. They spent all day trying to sort out our administrative errors, trying to explain to irate brokers that a trade didn't match up because a seller was coming in with 3 million bonds and the buyer for 2 million at the wrong price. They were hung up on frequently, made to speak to juniors who didn't understand anything they were saying, and were left on hold for hours.

Like retrieving food, having to deal with Back Office queries was a rite of passage for every junior broker. I had once yelled at Philippe that there was no point in me taking their calls, because I didn't understand what they were saying and therefore couldn't be expected to be of any use to them. But after a few months I had begun to understand what they needed and was finally able to speak to the right trade assistants at the banks to get the problem sorted. It was luckily now someone else's problem.

A Bloomie popped up in my inbox from Toby: 'Good to see you last night. Feel horrific. Let me know if you still feel like coming with tomorrow night.'

I had had the good sense to turn my messages off forward when I'd realized there was a fairly high likelihood that Toby would be contacting me. I didn't want our plans for Saturday night flashing in front of the American as he stuffed his face with pomegranate seeds. I wasn't sure whether it was a date or not, or whether I was even attracted to him, but I figured spending a Saturday evening together could do no harm. And at least he was nothing like Mark or Giles.

I messaged JP, another trader I'd met:

08:15:05 VENETIA THOMPSON: hahaha
08:15:20 VENETIA THOMPSON: sorry that was meant to be 'lovely to meet u, sorry I headbutted u' not just 'hahaha'
08:16:39 JP ANDREWS: no probs . . . how are you? you were the cute blonde wasn't you :)

08:16:54 VENETIA THOMPSON: hahah one of 2 cute blondes . . . me and the lovely lena.

08:17:08 VENETIA THOMPSON: only got an hr of sleep. feel dreadful.

08:18:10 JP ANDREWS: of course . . . can't forget her. i'm about the same, feel terrible and have to go to Budapest tonight for the weekend for a desk xmas party . . . hardcore ha ha

08:18:45 VENETIA THOMPSON: wtf! How you going to survive that? You go away for a whole weekend for an xmas party? That's crazy.

08:19:22 JP ANDREWS: ha ha more worried bout getting thro 2day. market shatting itself again and I ain't been to bed.

The night after a big market party, there was always a certain amount of banter with anyone you might have shared a few words with over the course of the evening. With Toby there was an ulterior motive, but in JP's case, Lena and I had accosted him by the bar and, in one drunken swoop, partly caused by my Louboutin getting caught in a rug, I'd head-butted him. I'd since discovered that he was one of another desk's biggest clients and I felt a bit of damage limitation might be due in the form of a bit of IB chat. I didn't want to make a habit out of headbutting other brokers' clients at events.

It was a long, slow day. Everyone in the market was fighting the ramifications of a sleepless night and an open bar, and no one was in the mood to trade, or even chat.

Lena had finally made it in, but after a quick rundown of our respective evenings, had shut our chat window and headed off to the machine that served the banking version of Douglas

Adams' 'almost, but not quite, entirely unlike tea' liquid, and had undoubtedly gone off to the ladies' for a nap on her way back.

09:15:34 LENA KLEIN: uuurgh. Hugh is IBing me. Wants to go out at the weekend. Kunting hell.

09:16:02 VENETIA THOMPSON: Ha. Well, it's your own fault for reigniting things last night. Could make it a double date on Saturday?

09:17:10 LENA KLEIN: It's fine, have told him I won't be in London. And why the hell did you say yes when Toby asked you out btw? WTF? You know he's basically a client right? It can only end in disaster.

09:17:55 VENETIA THOMPSON: Yeah. I dunno. Seemed like a good idea at the time. He's nice, right? But re. Hugh, you do know that at this rate you're gonna have to emigrate to get rid of him. Just end it. Tell him you're not interested.

09:18:02 LENA KLEIN: I know. But I don't want to make things awkward. I'd rather just keep making up excuses not to see him until he gets the message.

09:18:15 VENETIA THOMPSON: Ahh the head-in-sand-denial technique, always the way forward. Shut your eyes and hope he can't see you. That'll make him go away.

09:18:45 LENA KLEIN: I just don't want him slagging me off to the entire market. I'd rather he loses interest naturally than tell him I don't want to see him again.

09:19:23 VENETIA THOMPSON: someone has to tell him that there's nothing sexy about gyrating around flaccidly to 50 cent. Think of it as your karmic duty. You'll spare his future girlfriends.

Saturday night I found myself outside a bar in Shoreditch, being handed a pair of devils' horns and a mask by Toby. It was apparently a seven sins theme – not entirely inappropriate given the excess of the previous week. We had escaped phase one of the evening, which was his friend's birthday drinks in a basement bar just off the High Street, and were heading to someone's house party. I still wasn't sure whether I was particularly attracted to him, and knew that to risk getting involved with a pseudo client, I'd have to be at least fairly certain of wanting to jump him at any given moment. I needed to check the Company's compliance handbook for the party line on dating clients, but in the meantime I donned the horns and took his arm.

The party was rammed. I was wearing the sort of shoes that made standing in confined crowded spaces particularly difficult. It required perfect balance; there was no room for error. If I'd suddenly needed to use one leg like a tripod to avoid falling over, there was nowhere to place it strategically at the right supportive angle without spiking someone else's foot. So I stood, feet together, like a skittle waiting to be hit, and hoped someone would eventually pass me a drink so I could maintain my current position.

We must have kissed around midnight, on the makeshift slightly tilted dance floor, faux cobwebs dangling from the low ceiling, horrific house music blasting out of giant speakers, and being knocked into every few seconds by Lust, a blur of red, staggering sideways at high speed. It was an awkward lust-lacking kiss, or rather he was awkward and I wasn't drunk enough not to notice.

A bad kiss sets a precedent. If there was ever any question about whether I was attracted to him, it really should have

211

been answered there and then. But he was smart, successful and funny – and on Bloomberg, which was more or less now the only medium through which I could successfully communicate, or flirt. So we carried on swaying to the music, kissing. He dropped me home and I gave back the horns.

I woke up at 2 p.m. to find twenty missed calls and ten new voicemail messages. My phone had been on silent and I'd switched my alarm off the night before, so there was really no way of reaching me. All the messages were from David, one of my best friends. I'd meant to meet him for brunch at 11 a.m. in Notting Hill.

'V, it's me. I'm on Westbourne Grove; hope you're nearby. Call me when you get this.'

'V, me again. It's now 11.30. I hope you haven't lost your phone or something and are just asleep. Call me.'

'Well, it's now 11.45 and you're not here. I'm hungry so I'm going to eat. Hope you get this.'

'It's 12.30. I'm going home. Guess I'll speak to you later – when you fucking wake up.'

Fuck. I'd completely forgotten to set my alarm, and without it there was no chance that I'd regain consciousness before lunchtime. We'd been trying to meet up for weeks but I'd kept cancelling, and this was the second time that I'd stood him up because I was in a sleep coma. When he'd sat through brunch alone last weekend at Automat, I'd promised him that it would never happen again, but a week later, here I was lying in bed while he was roaming the streets of W11 alone. I wasn't sure that our friendship would survive another abandoned eggs Benedict.

I'd become the sort of unreliable, unreachable, chronically late and forgetful friend everyone eventually gives up on and stops calling. Even if I did manage to set my alarm, my body would somehow override it and I would instinctively turn it off and immediately return to sleep. I was a weekend narcoleptic with a trail of missed coffees, brunches, lunches, hair appointments and dinners scattered behind me.

My GP had told me to try exercising more often – that my energy levels would improve if I could improve my fitness. But the few times I'd attempted to go to the gym after work had resulted in me passing out on the Tube home and ending up in Stanmore.

Short of somehow getting my hands on an amphetamine prescription, I wasn't sure how to regain control of my free time or if I was ever going to see my friends again. I'd have to add chronic fatigue to my list of ailments and hope it would eventually go away and I didn't become a reclusive narcoleptic alcoholic with liver failure. I now understood why the City was rife with coke addicts: not because of some hedonistic culture of excess, but because everyone was desperately battling sleep addiction. Without cocaine, nobody would be awake long enough to trade anything.

CHAPTER 13

CDOs COME TO TOWN

December was nothing but a long list of parties strung together by the occasional cautious trade. There was endless speculation about when we would start to see the full effects of the subprime crisis take hold. Every day there would be fresh rumours and Bloomberg articles sent around about expected hedge fund redemptions and foreclosures.

The American was bearish, but everyone else was under the impression it was something that would pass – crisis was far too strong a word. No one really knew what subprime mortgages were, or why they were having an effect on our previously endlessly buoyant market, in which prices never went down by more than a quarter of a point and were generally always rising.

However, when many high yield bonds and leveraged loans have been trading for a prolonged period at 102 – or, in some cases, 104 – that were issued at par (100), bears get nervous, and the American was no exception. When financial instruments are being bought and sold at levels that are miles above their true worth, a fallout is often imminent. The bubble has to burst sooner or later; prices cannot keep rising limitlessly. What goes up must come down.

We had all become complacent, used to seeing 100 handles. Hardly anything was trading sub par, even some of the riskier slices of debt. There simply wasn't enough paper to go around. Everyone was making money, and everything continued to go up, so investors and, in turn, traders, began looking for the more volatile, riskier products with higher yields. They began eagerly vacuuming up PIK and mezzanine debt, fairly risky instruments of the debt structure, often without knowing any-thing about the companies or exactly what comprised the various tranches i.e. what percentages of the different parts of the debt structure were contained in their package. But they didn't seem to care, they just wanted to own as much as they could of everything that was available: the higher the yield, the better. Horse manure could have been packaged into a mezz loan and someone would still want to buy it.

It was this same insatiable desire for higher yielding, riskier products that led a load of bankers on the other side of the Chinese Wall, somewhere in structured finance, to come up with the idea of CDOs (collateralized debt obligations), which for a while suited everyone. Poor Americans got to buy houses; hedge fund managers, other bankers and pension fund man-agers got an appealing high interest rate in exchange for shouldering the inherent risk of these new loans, which would ultimately culminate in bigger bonuses and richer funds. Of course, by this point nobody knew who owned what, or how many of these CDOs were lurking on the books of banks.

There was nothing fit about the credit market; it was overindulged, overinflated and bulging at the seams. When the penniless Americans woke up to find that their one-time too-good-to-be-true introductory mortgage rates had suddenly shot up, they began defaulting on payments, and the market was too fat to get back up.

We were only starting to see the effects of the subprime disaster. Since the summer, with endless rumours and the occasional company going up in smoke, trading had begun to slow down. There were fewer bids out there, everything was starting to tank, and suddenly everyone cared where crossover was trading. When there was a flurry of activity, it was unexpected and it was easy to get caught on the wrong side, as prices were frequently jumping around by a couple of points. The American would be silent for most of the day, apart from the occasional shout of 'X is going wider, watch your bids'. It was an endless refrain, and one that everyone ignored. The index brokers were the only people worth listening to when it came to crossover, but the American liked hearing the sound of his own voice boom across the eerily quiet floor, and maybe it reminded some of the more relaxed brokers to treat any old bids as subject (no longer necessarily 'live').

It wasn't long before I met Toby again, this time for a civilized Sunday brunch, which turned into an afternoon on his sofa in Chelsea, swiftly followed by a trip to Maroush for a shish kebab at ninish and then a sleepover.

I should have bailed when I saw the CD collection. He was another ghetto blaster-owning trader, and despite having an iPod, had failed to sort out any sort of sound system. He explained, 'I'm never at home, so there's not really any point.' But when you have a woman in your large single bed, and the only musical accompaniment is the greatest hits of Kate Bush,

Bryan Adams or an inexplicable Cape Verdean holiday homes CD-ROM, there is surely suddenly, urgently, a point.

The sex was as awkward as that first kiss – compounded by the Bryan Adams soundtrack. It added further fuel to my theory that while most high-flying City traders seemed to expend all their available energy on the trading floor, yelling at brokers or their sales team, taking home their millions, they have all the sexual potency of fumbling fifteen-year-olds when the lights are out. The better the trader, the worse the sex. What you need is someone who does nothing but lose money, or a research analyst who doesn't spend all day on his feet shouting.

I contemplated leaving. It was Sunday evening, we both had to be at our respective desks at 7 a.m. and I couldn't lie in the dark listening to Bryan belt out 'I'm ready to love you' any longer. It was making me nauseous. But I was too exhausted to get dressed and go find a cab, so I stayed put and hit eject, finally drifting off to sleep in the early hours of the morning.

Later we shared a cab – he dropped me home to change and haul myself to Canary Wharf while he continued on his way to the City. It was Monday. I shouldn't have had any reason to feel horrific and sleep deprived. Jumping into the shower and stumbling around my room in the dark trying to find something resembling a suit was normally something I left for the end of the week. Attempting it at 6 a.m. on a Monday was unwise and only worth doing in extenuating circumstances, such as after a fabulous Sunday spent at the Cartier Polo, not after bad sex and Bryan Adams. Luckily Toby was off on holiday at the end of the week, so I just had a few days of Bloomberg chat to get through. Then Christmas would come and go and we could hopefully forget all about it and return to being friends.

I immediately checked that my messages weren't on forward to the American; post-coital Bloombergs were never
something you would want your boss to be reading. At around
8.30, Brad's number flashed up on the outside line.

'Venetia?'

'Brad?'

There was a long pause. I could hear him breathing. I was
sure he had called me. I wasn't sure whether I was supposed
to think of something to say in the event that I had accidentally
hit dial.

'Yeah, Venetia, what are we doing?'

Excellent– another bout of amnesia from one of the Street's
most senior traders. If he never remembered what prices he
gave me, I could easily make them up, tighten everything by a
quarter of a point and he would never know.

I wondered how he managed to function on a day-to-day
basis if he couldn't remember what prices he'd shown me, or
why he'd called. I hoped that he didn't speak to his clients in
the same chaotic way.

*'FOR FUCK'S SAKE, YOU FUCKING IDIOT. WHAT THE
HELL? HOW MANY TIMES HAVE I TOLD YOU ABOUT
THIS? YOU SHOULD KNOW WHERE THE BASIS IS. WHY
THE FUCK ARE YOU ASKING ME AGAIN? JUST GET THE
FUCK AWAY FROM ME.'*

I thought for a second that he was somehow reading my
mind, but then realized he was yelling at a sales guy mid
phone call and hadn't bothered to use his silencer or put me on
hold. I wasn't sure whether to hang up and leave him to it, or
whether he would come back down the line.

*'STOP TALKING!! JUST STOP TALKING BULLSHIT . . .
WHO THE FUCK ARE YOU!?'*

'Sorry, Venetia. What are you working for me?'

I was at least relieved that for once someone else had managed to annoy him more than I had. I read out the various offers that he had shown me that morning, but before I could finish he had hung up and the line went dead.

As well as marking the run-up to Christmas, and a constant stream of parties, December was also bonus season. Every broker and trader is always aware of how much they are up or down on a daily basis, the total amount that they have brought in over the last bonus period and therefore how much they are theoretically entitled to receive on bonus day. Each individual is called into a meeting and given their number – the amount of money they have brought in less their own salary and other random deductions. This figure should theoretically match their own number but never does. Then the negotiations begin.

December 2007 was different. Activity had ground to a halt. Despite profitable months earlier in the year and the odd manic few days, it was unlikely that anyone would be receiving a bonus on our desk. I was still hopeful; I had made money in a downturn and figured that this would be rewarded.

I was called in and informed by Leicester, the floor head, that I would be receiving a couple of grand, half of which would be paid in shares, as a goodwill gesture to 'pay for Christmas', I was the only broker on the desk to be receiving a bonus and I shouldn't mention it to anyone else because shares are rarely given out. I wasn't sure whether he genuinely expected me to be grateful, scurry off and sit smugly at my desk knowing that I was the only one receiving a payout, or whether he was taking the piss. Nobody wanted shares in the Company. They could barely give them away. There was no logical explanation for this pathetic offering other than he obviously thought that I was a complete moron who would buy his bullshit.

Discretion is always encouraged because it allows firms to get away with paying their brokers and traders less. The only thing more annoying – and even more likely to result in walk-outs – than being shafted on a bonus is discovering that some tosser who crawls in at 7.30 a.m., sits reading the paper all day and leaves at 4.55 p.m. is getting a bigger bonus than you are.

Two grand was a long way off what I believed I was entitled to after the evening I'd spent painstakingly working out exactly how much I had brought in, but I was also aware that by the time the American's ridiculous salary – rumoured to be in the region of 250–300k basic (thanks to someone in Back Office leaking info) – was covered there would be very little left in the bonus pool.

I quickly realized that all the effort I'd put in, the money I'd made while fighting food poisoning, the late nights spent attempting to win back clients that the American had lost and regularly staying far later than anyone else on the desk had been completely pointless. If I'd known that I was going to be paid my basic salary plus a token gesture, I'd have put in minimum effort – happily gone home at 5 p.m. every day, left clients to their own devices beyond 11 p.m. and strolled in at 7.30 a.m. like the majority of the desk did. It was simple incentive economics: the job didn't make sense without there being sizeable remuneration packages on offer.

I left Leicester's glass office and returned to the desk, picked up my bag and strolled out. It was 11.30 a.m. I headed straight to the nearest bar, where I ordered a martini, downed it, cried for a few minutes, then tried to work out what could be done now that I'd realized I was really doing the job only for the money after all. It wasn't the adrenalin that was addictive; it was the fucking money. Adrenalin is just a by-product of money making. I began laughing so hysterically at my new realization that the barman asked if everything was OK.

After my third load of gin, everything seemed a little less bleak. The lunchtime drinkers had begun arriving. So far I'd avoided bumping into anyone I knew, which was fortunate because it was barely midday and I was drunk – not in the cheeky-glass-of-wine-in-Waitrose way, but properly drunk with mascara running down both cheeks, as I saw when I caught sight of myself in the mirror behind the rows of spirits.

The American probably thought that I'd gone to retrieve his lunch. I decided, in a wave of drunken irrationality, that I hated him, the job and Leicester and they could all go to hell. I didn't want to go back to work but I knew that I would have to, and the sooner I did the less an explanation would be required. The gin had at least ensured that I was relaxed enough not to do anything sudden – like resign. When you're on the brink of incandescent, irreversible rage, you don't want a vodka Red Bull because you will hit someone; you want half a pint of ice-cold gin with a barely decipherable hint of vermouth.

I walked back through the mall feeling perfectly content, and stopped for a Krispy Kreme doughnut and some Itsu sushi. Everything in Canary Wharf seemed better through inebriated eyes – no less ridiculous, but somehow its edges were softer. I retrieved the American's lunch, suddenly worried that if I came back empty-handed my drunkenness would be more apparent, and that if I handed him food he would be less likely to ask where I had been for the last hour and a half. I ambled around Waitrose, picking up random items and returning them to their shelves, reading the backs of bottles of food supplements and a few gossip magazines before finally reaching the blue boxes of crispbreads, the vegetarian sushi rolls and the pomegranate seeds.

Of course I walked onto the wrong side of the floor, and instead of walking back through the double doors, nonchalantly walked all the way around, past the furiously noisy swaps desk, where no one ever seemed to sit down for long, stumbling only a couple of times as I banged the Waitrose bag against various people's chairs. I was thinking only two things: that it was great being drunk and that I should be drunk in the office more often. I was indestructible – provided I could stay upright and make it back to the safety of my desk.

The American hadn't moved. I deposited the bag on top of the pile of scrap A4 paper on his left that he never wrote anything down on, and sat down. He mumbled something that could have been thanks or just clearing his throat, and continued reading the *Wall Street Journal* online. I said I'd got stuck at the bank, but I don't think he heard me. Dory raised his eyebrows and mouthed, 'Are you OK?' across the desk. I nodded, flashing a quick smile and sat down.

I knew that being drunk on the desk was wrong, but it was the lesser of two evils. It was either that or resign dramatically. It wasn't as if I were the only one drunk in charge of a Bloomberg terminal. At any one time handfuls of brokers were drunk in the afternoon, either as a result of a long client lunch or because they had disappeared to the pub at lunchtime. I knew of at least a dozen bookies who drank a bottle of wine every day at lunchtime. It mostly went unnoticed, but occasionally keys to Ferraris had to be wrestled away from drunken owners at 5 p.m. or alcohol-fuelled fights were started.

I got through the rest of the afternoon unscathed and left just before 5 p.m. I was supposed to be meeting the Yank that night for drinks and needed to get home and change. He was an old friend who I'd briefly dated, in town from New York for a few days and staying at the Sanderson, where we had first met a couple of years ago. I wanted to get as fucked as possible. The Sanderson was the perfect place to do it, and he was the perfect drinking partner.

He was sitting at the end of the bar, BlackBerry in one hand, Japanese whisky in the other, open-necked white shirt, slightly unkempt hair, the perfect amount of stubble and a hint of a tan – instantly recognizable, even with my rapidly deteriorating eyesight. He immediately looked straight at me as I came clattering through the foyer and ordered me a martini as I sat down.

'Now what did I say about getting into the market? Thought I warned you off!' His accent was broad New York.

'Yeah, and I thought you were getting out of the market? What happened to moving upstate and opening a restaurant?'

'I got married again. And divorced again. Women are expensive. Or rather maintaining women is expensive. Did you know highlights cost at least $200 a time? I thought she was a natural blonde when we were just dating.'

'If I managed to get out of bed early enough on a Saturday morning to get to the hairdresser, then I would know, yeah.'

He laughed. He had perfect American teeth, a shade whiter than any Londoner would ever dare to go for fear it would look unnatural.

'You wanna play some pool? I seem to remember you're pretty crap at it.'

I knew the second I picked up a cue it would all be over and I wouldn't be leaving the hotel again until the following morning. He was the only guy I knew who could somehow turn pool into foreplay and I instantly forgot all about the American and the pathetic Christmas bonus.

After several rounds of lavender-infused deep purple-coloured martinis, we fell into the lift and kissed, before bashing our way along the corridor to his suite. But allowing a drunken narcoleptic anywhere near some of London's softest sheets is asking for trouble, and by the time he re-emerged from the bathroom I was on the brink of passing out.

'Ahh, so you only want me for my comfy bed? You should have said so; they're way more comfortable at the Four Seasons.'

The following day, after a blissful night's sleep on the shoulder of my favourite Yank, 6 a.m. sex among the breakfast room service trays, and a blue Adderall tablet crushed into my coffee ('this will wake you up, or at least get you through the morning'), I got to work ready to confront the American. When the 11 a.m. lull set in, I asked if I could have a word. The desk was pretty deserted as everyone was out getting lunch, but he insisted on dramatically walking the entire length of the room with me trailing along behind him, to go and sit in one of the glass offices. I explained as calmly as I could that I would not be accepting a couple of grand, half of which would be in shares that I didn't even want, 'to pay for Christmas', and that this was more insulting than receiving nothing at all.

He tried explaining that, as I was aware, business had slowed down and there was simply nothing in the bonus pot. He had become so predictable; I knew exactly what he was going to say, so I sat avoiding eye contact, watching cars speeding along through East London nineteen floors below us, barely listening to him. I knew that he wouldn't be saying anything of interest

224

and that I just needed to sit and wait for him to talk himself around. There was never any point in trying to argue with him; he seemed to be incapable of having a two-way conversation, preferring instead to speak over you for as long as possible. After a seemingly endless monologue on how much my work was appreciated, how screwed the market was and how much I could expect to earn in the future when it recovered, while I sat sulking in silence, he said he would speak to Leicester to see if they could sort something out. But the damage was already done. I knew that I would have to fight them every six months, every time bonus day came around, for every single penny that I was entitled to, and it wasn't a battle that I had the energy for. I worked for a company that would never play fair and I would never really win.

Christmas arrived just in time. I had been on the verge of resigning for the last few weeks and knew that at any moment I was likely to walk out, despite them having substantially increased my bonus. I was still lumbered with having to take half of it in shares, but it seemed like the best offer I was going to get.

Matt had mentioned that at least annually, if not every six months, he would refuse to come into work until they put an offer on the table that was vaguely in line with what he expected to receive. It was the only tactic that worked, as they couldn't afford for him not to be on the floor. Yet it was a game that had to be played every year; paying out what he deserved from the outset was too simple. The bonus struggle was an integral part of City life.

It had been a bad few months. Everyone had lost money and the Street was quiet, but the c-bombing continued regardless, courtesy of The Deviant. He was haemorrhaging money like everyone else – nobody was safe – but when he lost money he called as many people as possible cunts to make the day pass more quickly. He had recently switched banks, and his desk hadn't adjusted to his antics, so he was now whispering 'cunt'. Even Lena, who had been trading out of the New York office for a couple of days, got caught out when she had answered an unknown number on her mobile in the middle of the night only to have 'cunt' whispered down the line.

10:28:59 LENA KLEIN: good c-bombing

10:29:10 LENA KLEIN: bit stealthy tho when i'm in my deepest phase of sleep

10:31:03 LENA KLEIN: overnight

10:31:06 THE DEVIANT: u love it

10:32:10 LENA KLEIN: sounded like u were whispering

10:32:27 THE DEVIANT: i was

10:32:37 THE DEVIANT: was getting funny looks all day

10:33:28 LENA KLEIN: are they not familiar with your practices yet?

10:33:37 THE DEVIANT: not really

10:34:14 THE DEVIANT: the game today is to phone someone pretending to be their mate

10:34:21 THE DEVIANT: then c them

10:34:26 THE DEVIANT: most people fall for it

10:34:56 LENA KLEIN: best matesing followed by c-bombing? nice touch

Those who weren't busy shouting cunt at each other and hanging up, or pretending to be best friends with total strangers, and who were foolish or brave enough to show a bid would be hit immediately by Aggro Bank, who had begun selling everything they could in October. Their head trader was one of the few guys who seemed to have grasped the severity of the situation early enough and had marked everything down when there were still bids out there to hit.

Everyone else, especially some of the smaller players, was sitting on bulging books, still convinced that things would recover in January and determined that it wasn't worth lightening up so dramatically. They couldn't see the point in selling off perfectly good bonds and loans of companies that seemed to be having no credit problems because of what was viewed as being 'the American subprime problem'. That was how it was still being viewed: as something that was going on far away on the other side of the Atlantic that couldn't possibly affect high yield bonds, or anything else, in Europe.

The foreclosures were nothing to worry about, really. Hank Paulson, former Secretary of the US Treasury, was just scaremongering. And OK, Northern Rock had gone up in smoke, Merrills had revealed a 7.9 billion exposure to bad debt and were probably fucked, and Bear had lost a couple of funds, but surely the worst was over and there was no point selling at the bottom when everything would bounce back up soon enough? Everyone would go away for Christmas and come back in January to find the market had recovered and everything would soon return to normal. It had to.

CHAPTER 14

LA TRAVIATA

The market didn't improve; it began unravelling and falling apart. Stories were flying around about traders who, having been made redundant, decided to shit on their desks, or other people's, before smashing a few things, and were rumoured to have been sectioned. This was probably for the best, as I am not sure that it is ever possible to get past being the guy who smeared his own faeces all over the fixed income trading floor.

Stocks also shat themselves, suffering their biggest losses since 9/11. The Fed cut rates to 3.5 per cent, the biggest cut in 25 years. Crossover kept ballooning over 600 – something that was previously unimaginable. Hedge funds stopped buying. All of a sudden banks began to realize that they were sitting on billions of debt that they couldn't shift and that they should have marked it down in October and hit whatever bids were out there to decrease their exposure. But now it was too late and they were all stuck with huge books of tanking bonds and loans.

We kept ringing around every morning, asking for prices,

trying to keep the Street active somehow, but conversations with traders were becoming increasingly strange. It was like speaking to dozens of people with terminal illnesses who were making plans for the future, completely in denial that their number was up. All we could do was agree. We all knew the market was fucked but it didn't seem appropriate to reiterate it.

Many of the smaller banks were convinced they needed to ride it out; they owned good paper that couldn't possibly become worthless. If they could somehow keep their heads above water, it would all be fine. But as ever when it comes to traders, they seemed to be ignoring the wider economic picture: the desks they were a part of, and even the banks they were in, could disappear entirely, and their precious trading books would quickly become as worthless as their business cards.

Panic was slowly beginning to set in. No one knew who was exposed to the toxic CDOs, and which banks were likely to make the emergency calls to the government that would cause the entire market to start lurching around as it had after September's run on Northern Rock.

In a bull market, which we have been enjoying the benefits of in one way or another for years, nobody cares if there is zero transparency, or even bothers checking whom they are lending to, or what they in turn are sitting on, because the assumption is that the market will continue to grow regardless. Then a downturn sets in, and it quickly becomes apparent that the entire system is rotten and flawed – all the way down to the poorest of the poor Yanks and their horrific credit ratings.

Prices were now more or less all in the 80s. Loans that had been trading in the high 90s and all the way up to 103 when I'd started broking were now deemed 'distressed'. 'Par' no longer existed, and sending Bloomberg messages containing prices was now impossible because of the speed with which everything was moving.

Conversations were had solely by phone and trades were rarely posted, for fear of making things worse than they already were. If one trader decided to shift something to a distressed guy at 79 that was last offered at 90 months ago, it was best kept quiet. Posting it was at best rubbing salt in the wound, and at worst likely to trigger a mass sell-off. A sell-off would, of course, have been lucrative for us as middlemen, and for the various distressed traders lurking in the background waiting to pounce on anything headed sub 70, but only in the very short term.

The distressed market had been quiet for a long time, and it now looked likely to have a renaissance as high yield became distressed and investment grade became high yield. Investment grade no longer existed because nobody was investing.

Lena was permanently on the brink of having some sort of nervous breakdown. She was trading a book that was difficult to make money on in a bull market, let alone now, and kept having to be escorted off the floor by sales girls or the CDS trader she sat next to when she became hysterical. Today was no exception.

12:34:21 LENA KLEIN: got escorted off again
12:34:33 VENETIA THOMPSON: u taking p1ss?
12:34:37 VENETIA THOMPSON: why?
12:34:42 VENETIA THOMPSON: who escorted u out?
12:35:12 LENA KLEIN: i thought i'd crossed 40bps on a

bond i never trade, hate the name . . . then my buyer
who i've been working with for over a day on the trade
flakes and buys them away

12:35:18 LENA KLEIN: without giving me chance to
improve

12:35:32 LENA KLEIN: so am long 5m of some dog t1 i
would never have touched in a million years

12:36:01 VENETIA THOMPSON: argh

12:36:10 VENETIA THOMPSON: and what pushed over
edge?

12:36:17 VENETIA THOMPSON: did someone say
something

12:37:07 LENA KLEIN: the fact i've now probably lost
shedloads, have a position i can't move and all
management will be on my back

12:37:09 LENA KLEIN: just that

12:37:32 VENETIA THOMPSON: did u lose plot or just cry

12:38:04 LENA KLEIN: face in hands crying but badger
rushed me out

12:38:08 VENETIA THOMPSON: who? Why badger?

12:38:23 LENA KLEIN: sales girl who lost the trade. Cos
she once got caught taking a sh1t in her own garden

12:38:28 VENETIA THOMPSON: urgh

12:38:36 VENETIA THOMPSON: were u p1ssed with her
or not

12:38:47 LENA KLEIN: more her client

12:38:51 VENETIA THOMPSON: that sucks

12:38:58 VENETIA THOMPSON: u ok now?

12:39:06 LENA KLEIN: still crying quietly

12:39:58 VENETIA THOMPSON: sure there will be worse
losses

12:40:09 LENA KLEIN: I dunno. Could be 5 points in a day easy.

12:40:20 LENA KLEIN: god am angry. Should have carried on having hysterics and been sent home.

12:41:10 LENA KLEIN: keep expecting someone to stand up and fire me shouting 'you're an embarrassment to us all'.

12:41:20 VENETIA THOMPSON: sooner be an embarrassment than a kunt

The Big Swinging Dicks had all gone strangely quiet, and were now cowering underneath their desks waiting for the next bank to go bust or the next doom-laden announcement from the Chairman of the Federal Reserve, Ben Bernanke, to come booming out over the news. One or the other was bound to happen sooner or later; until then they were staying under-cover and leaving their desk assistants to field calls from clients and brokers.

Most of the banks had left their own clients for dead months ago and simply stopped sending prices. It was each man for himself; keeping some fund manager in Geneva happy was the least of everyone's worries. Masters of the Universe turn into pussies pretty quickly when things get uncomfortable.

Meanwhile, the Ferg had decided that it was time for a sab-batical. We had all known that, like Wayne and Stu before him, he had been unhappy for a while and wanted to move abroad and concentrate on his property empire, but it was still unex-pected when he announced his end date. I wasn't sure how the desk was going to function without him, or how I was going to make it through the day without our constant banter across the desk. I would miss him calling me Unit Bird. But first we

would somehow have to get through the transition period –
the fortnight before he finally disappeared. We now always
seemed to have an IB window where the Ferg, Lena and I
would talk as much shit as possible throughout the day.

13:57:35 THE FERG: I hate that fluffy idiot how crap must
he be to become a broker after trading at Aggro for 3
years. Ha ha. The fool.

13:58:24 THE FERG: I have 7 days left in this godforsaken
business. 'The Ferg: 14.5 inches choice. Get me a brass.'

Normally when someone leaves, whether they resign or are
fired, they leave immediately and are escorted out of the building by a security guard while someone is sent to retrieve their
possessions. But because the Ferg was theoretically going on
sabbatical – although we all knew that it was unlikely that he
would ever set foot on the floor again – he was working out his
notice period before his six months off officially began. Having
a broker on the desk who was leaving for six months in the sun
meant that morale was at an all-time low. Like having a dead
body propped up in a swivel chair, it would be impossible to
focus on anything else until it was removed.

The Ferg was scared. He'd reached his forties and only ever
known the bond market. He wasn't sure how he was going to
handle his transition back to society away from his City friends
and clients. He wasn't even sure whether he was going to enjoy
being at home all day. So many bookies of his generation had
tried retiring, only to resurface six months later once they realized they could play only so much golf and their families were
driving them insane. They missed the market and came crawling back. He'd seen them go through it.

I knew he wouldn't be back. He was different; he had always put his money straight into various investments, bypassing buying into the excessive lifestyle entirely because he had known that one day he would want to escape and take his family away from it all. It had always been part of the master plan and he had therefore always been prepared for it. He was strong enough to make the break; he just needed to be shoved out of the nest. I was going to miss him.

The American seemed to be slowly separating our business from the rest of the desk, dragging me down under the water with him. Knowing that the Ferg was leaving only made his paranoia worse. He knew that the Ferg's clients would be passed over to us at some point, and new relationships would have to be forged. But the American was convinced that the Ferg would try to sabotage the handover in some way, and make the possibility of any future business as difficult as possible. As a result, he had begun keeping information to himself, and only revealing colour to me, explicitly requesting that I didn't pass the information on to anyone else on the desk.

One afternoon, while we were finally about to trade something after days of silence, during a critical moment he decided that I had somehow been acting as the Ferg's informer, feeding him information and prices. He'd pushed his chair away from the desk.

'Shut your fucking mouth, you fucking stupid . . .'

The words tumbled out quietly, strangely controlled, but furious. Everything about his outburst was measured. His eyes had blackened into tiny holes, and were flicking between boring into me and staring at the floor under his desk. I looked back paralysed, feeling nothing at all other than a vague sense of disgust, finally seeing the man for what he really was.

I had been called a cunt, a fucking idiot and a bitch on numerous occasions by clients, but the American had never sworn at me directly. I thought that I was somehow impenetrable, that months of exposure to that sort of language and aggression had made me bulletproof. But I was wrong. He still had the power to flatten me, and for the first time in my year broking I felt physically intimidated. I didn't know what he was going to do next.

Ten minutes later, he stutteringly apologized, saying that it was a tense situation, and he was sorry. He coughed the words out, as if they were choking him; apologizing was so unnatural, it could only come clunking out of his mouth uncleanly. I kept staring at my Bloomberg inbox and didn't respond, like I'd had the shit beaten out of me and really didn't know what to say when some sort of reaction was needed.

Ironically, I hadn't told the Ferg anything, despite the fact that I was supposed to; we were meant to be working as a team, whether he was leaving or not. None of that mattered. The American would always work alone, and would never need anyone else.

It was 4.30 p.m. I wanted to go home, to get as far away as possible from the monstrosity who sat clipping his fingernails next to me. I had spent so long wanting to believe in this strange inscrutable man, wanting to prove to everyone that he wasn't the monster he was rumoured to be. But I'd simply got it wrong, and he was actually worse than I ever could have imagined.

Everyone always secretly wants to believe in the Devil. He's a more interesting character because he is fatally flawed, and therefore somehow more human. But he seduces: he makes you see light where there isn't any; he gains your trust and respect before he destroys you. It is easy to forget whom you are dealing with.

It was time to get the hell out.

I sent a Bloomberg to the Sicilian, who worked on the other side of the floor and had once presented me with a jar of pickled onions after I'd expressed my love for them. I asked him to meet me for a drink. I needed a confidant.

I gathered my things and left quietly, knowing only that I had to resign immediately. I got into an empty lift, hyperventilating, feeling the walls begin to close in as I dropped down nineteen floors to the bowels of the building, where I expected Abaddon to be standing waiting for me as the doors opened, but there was only the cheery security guard.

We had arranged to meet in a waterside bar on the other side of Canary Wharf, near the Four Seasons, where it was dark, windy and completely deserted. As I walked through the mall, past Square Pie, Space NK, where I had hurriedly stocked up on make-up before a client dinner when I forgot mine, and Toni and Guy, where I frequently stopped off for a blow dry before an event, everything faded. I knew that I was nearing the end of my time there.

I eventually emerged on the other side of the endless subterranean shops and interconnected escalators, everything flapping as I was slapped backwards and forwards by the wind, my hair swirling around and getting stuck to my lipgloss. I could barely see where I was going. It is easy to forget how windy Canary Wharf can get when you spend all day sitting high above street level, and simply walk from the Tube to your desk via the mall and never have to go outside. I wished that I'd gone outside more often; I'd been breathing the same sick air for too long.

He was sitting alone at the bar. I sat down next to him, and ordered a gin and tonic.

'So this is all very cloak and dagger. What's up, sweetheart? You look like you've seen a ghost.'

'I'm getting out.'

'OK. The American finally showed his true colours, eh, or did you just wake up and open your eyes this morning? I dunno how you coped for so long. He's not right, that one.'

We chatted for a while about my next move. And then I kissed him.

None of it really made any sense, but for a few minutes I felt like everything might be OK, that it didn't all have to end. He reminded me of everything that I had loved about the job: the Essex-boy ghost of broking past with brilliant banter, grinning straight at me and bearing a jar of pickled onions.

We walked back to the Tube like a couple, holding hands into the wind, making plans to go skiing for the weekend, saying goodbye somewhere near the DLR. I carried on through the deserted mall to the Tube. The day felt marginally less terrible. Embarking on another office fling seemed like the only way forward, and was as good a way to pass the time as any, but it turned out to be the last time I ever saw him.

There are always loose ends that need to be tied up. A few days later, I was taking a trader to the opening night of *La Traviata*; it seemed like a fitting end to it all.

I spent the day staring into my Bloomberg terminal, exchanging the odd email with the Sicilian and counting down the minutes until I could leave and head to the Royal Opera House. I wanted to forget that I had spent the entire day quietly wanting to slit my wrists and avoiding eye contact with the American.

We were sitting in the fourth row of the centre stalls – seats that I had previously only ever looked down on. I usually got the cheap seats in the stalls circle at the side, which had a restricted view because of the way they were angled, but I liked being close to the stage. From those seats I would look down into the stalls and could immediately spot the corporate tickets – those that had been expensed or made available at a cheap rate to law firm or bank employees. Those seats held mismatched couples wearing badly fitting trouser suits with comfortable work shoes or trainers; the women with hair messily tied back in whatever kind of ponytail they managed to form as they rushed late into the auditorium and the men frantically reading through synopses printed from the Internet. One or both of them would be asleep by the end of the first Act, having clapped when they weren't supposed to, coughed unashamedly and loudly whispered to each other throughout.

Now I, too, was the proud owner of two top-price £180 tickets that I had expensed, and was sitting there in my suit and my work shoes, next to a trader who had never been to the opera before but liked the idea of it, who was asking me what we were about to see, and whom I felt the urge to nudge when Anna Netrebko came on stage. It all felt wrong.

During both intervals we drank pink champagne over a plate of smoked salmon sandwiches and a bowl of crisps, just because we could. We were two City girls posturing, enjoying all that the opera had to offer, before dinner at the Ivy and returning home to our perfect Chelsea lives. But it was all

bullshit and always had been. I'd played the role of the cour-
tesan well. I wasn't dying of consumption but I might as well
have been. *Addio del passato.* I just wanted it all to be over while
I was still standing.

And then it was. I went to work the following morning, and
left at lunchtime to go and see my GP, who wasn't really mine,
but was the only person available when I had called to make the
appointment, knowing that I needed to see someone – anyone.
He had asked me what he could do for me and I'd instantly dis-
solved. I spent the next hour in the small windowless room
shaking and crying uncontrollably, as he passed me an endless
stream of tissues. He signed me off for ten days: nervous exhaustion and, after feeling my glands, probably the remnants of some
nameless virus lurking deep in my system. Being told by a
doctor that I was currently incapable of working was a relief.

He printed off a depression questionnaire and made me fill it
in. It seemed ridiculous ticking boxes to questions that made no
sense and yet apparently were the easiest way of diagnosing
depression. *How often do you think about killing yourself? Never?
Once a week? Between three and five times a week? Every day? All the
time?* I could barely hold the pen, and ticked the boxes randomly,
only half reading the questions. I didn't need a questionnaire to
tell me that I was depressed. He could write me a prescription
for some Citalopram if I felt that I needed it – not addictive. I
mumbled that I was just exhausted, and worked with the Devil.
He chuckled. I told him I wasn't joking, but he still carried on
laughing. I wasn't sure what I needed, but I was pretty sure that
a pill wasn't the answer. I hoped that if I had actually been in
need of medication, he wouldn't have given me the option. The
last thing a seriously depressed person needs is choices.

He wanted me to call a friend, for there to be someone at

home when I got back. He had the concerned face of a medical professional worried that I was going to throw myself under a bus the second I left the building. He didn't want to be responsible for sending me back out into Knightsbridge without even a prescription for anti-depressants, and then finding me spread across the road on Sloane Street.

But I didn't want to die; I just wanted to sleep, and to resign from the job I hated while I still had the energy to get the words out. He had no reason to worry. I didn't need the pills. I doubted whether they would even touch the sides anyway. If I had needed prescription drugs, I would have asked Mo. I wasn't sure whom I was trying to convince: the doctor, myself or both of us. But he seemed to be satisfied that I'd live to fight another day, and with a final reminder to make sure that I rested, he sent me on my way.

I was suddenly painfully aware that if I did get run over by a bus, everyone would think that I had indeed killed myself when they checked my medical records. I stood on the edge of the pavement totally paralysed for what felt like hours before I was sure that there weren't any buses coming and finally managed to cross.

I got home, sent an email to Dory explaining that I wouldn't be in for the next ten days. He replied straight away telling me to concentrate on getting better. I ripped off my suit, left it lying on the floor in the corner of my room, changed into a tracksuit, took a valium and quietly put myself to bed, where I stayed for the next forty-eight hours, getting up only for the occasional glass of water and trip to the bathroom. I was too tired to eat, and too desensitized to know if I was hungry; I probably wasn't. All I had done for the last year was eat. It was the last thing I needed to do now.

I kept having the same recurring dream: the American, wearing chinos and a pale green shirt, was slamming one of his phones against my skull, beating it until one side of my head caved in, only stopping when someone shouted for him down the squawk box, while I slumped in my swivel chair spitting out bits of broken teeth. Then a courier would arrive, wearing checkered trousers, and wheel me off the floor. I thought he was taking me away to hospital, but he pushed me to the edge of an empty elevator shaft. I always woke up as I started to fall.

I was glad of the dreams. They were so jarring that they ensured I was at least awake for long enough to remember to drink something, and occasionally even to brush my teeth and floss, which at the time seemed of paramount importance. Showering was completely off the cards; my oral hygiene was the only thing I could think about.

I must have repeated this cycle every few hours. I didn't look at the time, but I had nothing to get up for, so clock-watching seemed completely unnecessary. It had no bearing on anything whether it was 6 a.m. or 6 p.m. My blinds ensured the light didn't disturb me, but I wore a sleep mask anyway, just in case. There was something comforting about having my eyes covered.

By day three, I began to identify hunger once again and ventured upstairs to make myself some toast. It was mouldy, but I didn't care, and there was no butter, which would usually have sent me into a panic, but now it seemed irrelevant whether the toast was dry or not. It was light outside, but it could have been early morning or late afternoon. I returned a couple of calls to worried friends and family and went back to bed.

My parents were concerned, but probably less so than they

had been while I was at work escaping for a gin martini at 11 a.m. Safely ensconced in Chelsea, I was at least less likely to hurl myself drunkenly under a Tube or have a nervous break-down on the trading floor.

Chelsea is London's padded cell. Nothing that bad is ever supposed to happen in SW3, surely – only fluke incidents like someone crashing their Ferrari into a wall during the school run and taking themselves and a Filipino nanny out in the process, or bankers getting robbed at gunpoint on Cheney Walk every few years. We'd called the police only once, and they had arrived within thirty seconds – a detail that was reas-suring as I lay in the dark listening to the strange noises outside.

Eventually I migrated from my bed to the sofa, where I lay all day watching bits of daytime television and staring at the huge tree that towered over the garden opposite, drifting in and out of sleep. The only way that I was able to work out the time was by seeing what was on television. It would get dark early enough for me to have to endure only a few hours of day-light; if I made it upstairs to the sofa for a while I felt that I had at least achieved something.

Everything had finally slowed down. I wasn't worried about what was going to happen at the end of this ten-day reprieve. I had my pile of magazines and books, the tree and the sofa, and that was all I needed. Going back to work seemed like something that was never going to happen. And if it did, it would be happening to someone else.

At some point during the weekend before I was due to return to work, having worked my way through a stack of newspapers and old copies of *The New Yorker* and the *Spectator*, I started to feel like writing something to see if I still could.

Writing about broking seemed like as good a place to start as any. So I sent off a speculative email to the editor of the *Spectator* pitching an article, using the working title 'Essex and the City: When Posh Bird Met Barrow Boy'. When an email came back, completely unexpectedly asking me to write 1,150 words, I did.

I wrote continuously during Sunday afternoon and finally hit 'send' late that night. I hadn't moved from my position on the sofa, but I did manage to stay awake for the rest of the day and went to sleep at a normal time for the first time since I'd been signed off.

I figured I might hear back in a few weeks, or maybe never, but I had at least taken a step towards doing something that I wanted to do, and returning to work in the morning no longer seemed so horrifying. I could probably even keep going for another six months now, having briefly engaged my brain in something worthwhile.

Nothing had really changed when I returned to work. There was a gap where the Ferg used to sit, and I kept expecting him to stroll in and sit down, wearing one of his trademark purple shirts, but he was gone. I'd missed his leaving party.

Everyone was subdued. In the ten days that I'd missed there had been nothing but bad news, and there was now talk of a recession. For once I felt completely detached from all of the news stories popping up on Bloomberg, from the market commentary that was sent around every morning and from the various shouts coming from the head of the itraxx desk. If I hadn't known better, I would have thought that I had had a partial lobotomy.

Around mid-afternoon on Monday, I received an email from the *Spectator* informing me that they were running my article that week and it would be out on Thursday. It was the only piece of information that I'd reacted to all day. I now knew that I just needed to get through the next couple of days.

The American had been off the desk all day in meetings with Leicester and then Fabrizio, after Fabrizio hired an ex-trader to become head of LCDS (CDS for loans) without telling anyone. Considering most of the prices that we currently had in LCDS came from our clients, it seemed a little odd to find out about the new hire via an email sent only to Dory. The American was furious. After months of showing little interest in anything Fabrizio did, he finally lost it and went storming off across the floor and didn't return. Too bad I no longer gave a shit.

After my time off, I was finally able to see how stupidly invested I had become in the petty office politics and the power struggles. Now it all seemed so pointless and irrelevant. I didn't care whom Fabrizio had hired. He could have all of my clients; I didn't want them any more. I didn't care about the hours that I'd spent building up relationships, the evenings that I'd spent flattering their egos and making them think that they were the biggest traders in the Street, telling them that they were my favourite customers, or the times that I told them I was giving them first refusal on something when they were really bottom of the list.

It was all over.

CHAPTER 15

******* DELETE (********)
HAS LEFT THE ROOM

I spent most of Thursday morning fielding endless Bloomberg messages from strangers asking if it had been my article that they had just read. I never knew there were that many *Spectator* readers on Bloomberg.

Most of the messages had been automatically forwarded to the American, but on seeing they were personal he hadn't even bothered to read them. I was in a state of total panic every time a new message started flashing in front of me. I saw him open one message that mentioned both the *Spectator* and the article, but he had immediately clicked back to the news story that he'd been reading. It was probably so far removed from anything that he would've been expecting to happen that morning that even if the article had popped up in front of him, he wouldn't have realized.

Only Giles and the Sicilian had actually read it. Having kissed both of them at some point, I figured that I could probably

trust them more than everyone else. It was the logic of someone on death row. I was now sitting watching the back of Giles'
head as he read and re-read what I had written. It kept bobbing
up and down, and every so often he would turn around and
grin over his shoulder, eyes wild with a strange mix of shock,
amusement and fear. I tried avoiding making eye contact with
him, knowing that sooner or later someone was going to notice
that I was flushing and trying to stifle bouts of hysteria. It was
a moment that I knew I had to share with someone or I would
combust, and grinning across the room at each other was
enough.

I wanted to run to Waitrose and buy a copy. I'd barely had
a chance to check the website, not wanting anyone to see what
I was reading when they walked behind me. I kept the article
minimized at the bottom of my screen. I hadn't managed to get
beyond the title.

When the magazine rang about interest from one of the
Sunday papers, I ran off to the empty glass office at the end of
the floor to take the call – no one asked what I was doing. It
was like being lumbered with the full comedic weight of a fan-
tastic joke that I wasn't allowed to share with anyone else, and
it kept swelling up in my throat, threatening to erupt into a
wild cackling laugh at any moment.

My heart was pounding as I walked back to the desk; everyone was lost in copies of the *Sun* and reading the news online,
sipping tea. It was an ordinary February morning. Everything
looked the same as it had the day before, but was entirely different. I was giddy.

When the American had gone out to get his lunch, I'd messaged a couple of my favourite clients the link to the article. I
knew it was a bad idea, and I should have been trying to keep

it completely to myself for as long as possible, but I couldn't contain it any longer.

I spent the afternoon riding out the waves of hysteria and trying to ignore the mounting sense of impending doom. Giles reminded me that the Company was trying to go public, and the timing couldn't possibly have been any worse. He'd had no idea what was in the article until it came out, and I desperately wanted to speak to him about it and find out what he thought but it would have to wait until later that night.

Waiting for someone to see the article and let the American or the PR department know was like waiting for a stealth bomb to go off. I was watching the clock at the bottom of my screen, trying to behave as casually as possible, but my heart was pounding and I was beginning to sweat. I was sipping coffee every few seconds, and I now had the shakes. My stomach had also begun cramping – I'd needed to go to the bathroom for the last hour but didn't dare leave my desk in case in the five minutes that I was gone something catastrophic happened. It was a race against time and I really didn't know whether I was going to make it out of the building alive, or whether I was simultaneously going to shit myself and be fired on the spot. It was a strange day full of adrenalin but without a single trade having taken place.

Finally 5 p.m. arrived, and I walked out calmly, like a shoplifter, leaving the scene of the crime unnoticed. As soon as I got to the bottom of the escalators into the mall, I jogged into Waitrose, trying to expel some of my excess energy, but the store hadn't received its delivery of the magazine yet. I headed for the Tube, deciding that it was better to get back onto neutral territory in case the wolves were sent to drag me back to the floor that night.

I walked along the Kings Road from Sloane Square and stopped at Waterstone's to buy a copy of the magazine. I stood, flicking through it until I found the article, but my reading was interrupted by the incessant ringing coming from my BlackBerry.

I had several missed calls from unknown numbers, and there was one voicemail. I dialled 901 and waited. It was from Leicester. As soon as I heard his voice, I felt sick. He surely wouldn't be ringing me for any other reason. I'd been well and truly rumbled. Come in, number five, your time is up. His message was calm and surprisingly jovial: 'Venetia, Nigel Leicester. Can you please give me a call back as soon as you get this. Thanks.'

Game over.

If I wasn't standing holding a copy of the *Spectator* with an article in it in which I'd described the American as 'one of the most disliked and thickest skinned men in the City', I may have assumed from his tone that he was calling to check in to see how I was getting on – maybe even to arrange an appraisal or tell me that I was getting a larger bonus after all. I texted Giles, asking if anything had kicked off after I'd left: no reply. I needed to know what I might be dealing with. As I walked home, I tried calling him. No answer. I left a garbled voicemail that I really needed to speak to him.

I waited until I was safely ensconced on the sofa and had prepared myself before returning Nigel's call. I remembered Dory's words when I had got hooked for the first time. I dialled.

Stick to your story. Stick to your story. Stick to your story.

I knew it was serious when he answered immediately. By this time it was 6.30 p.m. – he would normally have left the office at 5 p.m. along with everyone else.

'Venetia? Thanks for calling me back. How's it going?'

'Umm, yeah, good thanks. How are you?'

'Good, good. Well, you must know why I'm calling. This thing you've written.'

'Thing?'

'Yeah. Come on now. You know what I'm talking about.'

I wasn't sure why I was playing dumb, as if I'd somehow forgotten about the article entirely, but it seemed better to feign amnesia for as long as possible.

'That sort of stuff just can't happen. You can't honestly have expected it to go unnoticed.'

'Nigel. I really didn't mean anything by it. I just. . .'

'Venetia, I don't want to discuss it now. You're not allowed to speak to anyone about this – not any of your colleagues or clients – and stay away from the floor. I don't want you to come in to work right now.'

'What? I don't understand. You're suspending me?'

'Just come straight in to see me and HR at 8.30 tomorrow and we'll sit down and have a chat about it.'

'You mean I'm banned from the floor?'

'Yes, for the time being. It's as much for your own safety as anything else. People are going to be hacked off and upset and we don't want you anywhere near them.'

'Do I need a lawyer or something?'

'No, it's not that kind of chat; don't worry. But you can bring a friend or get a colleague to sit in if you want.'

The conversation was over in seconds. He spoke calmly, as if it were the sort of thing he had to deal with every day, but his instructions betrayed his efforts to keep the conversation casual. Only on hearing that I was banned from the trading floor and not allowed to go in to work did I realize that the odds of getting fired were probably fairly high and they were taking this far more seriously than I'd imagined.

I'd asked if I needed a lawyer incredulously, and half in jest, but his straight reply was indicative of the seriousness of the situation. I could only assume that I probably would need one.

I slid off the sofa and flicked through the contacts on my BlackBerry, trying to decide whom to call. My mother was in Singapore visiting my brother, and my Dad was somewhere in Vietnam on holiday. Lena was skiing. Giles wasn't answering his phone and still hadn't returned any of my texts. I hadn't been in this much trouble for a while and didn't really know whom to call or ask to be my companion to witness the meeting.

My phone rang: Fitz. I got back up off the floor.

'Venetia. This is fucking hysterical.' He let out a laugh. 'I can't believe it. It's a brilliant article, by the way. But I'm sitting here reading this, and believe me, V, you won't be going back to work. You do know that, right?

'Should I still be keeping this to myself, by the way? I know you said no post before, but considering it's in the national press, it seems like the horse has already bolted somewhat.'

'No. Blast it out.'

'Are you sure? I mean I can literally click one button and send this to the entire credit market. You want me to?'

He sounded concerned, and had adopted a tone similar to the one my mother used when I was about to embark on something that could be deemed either genius or irresponsible.

'Just hit send. You're not setting off a nuclear bomb, Fitz, and I've got fuck all to lose. I'm not even allowed to speak to you, by the way, so seeing that I have already managed to break that rule, I might as well carry on. Just get it out there. You're only speeding up the process. It'll be all over the Street by next week anyway.'

I was kneeling on the sofa facing out the window, shivering like an overexcited dog. Chelsea drifted past. I wanted to call Dory or The Godfather to let them know what was happening, if they hadn't already been grilled by Nigel and decided that I was a lost cause. I couldn't find Dory's number, and dialled The Godfather. He hadn't been in all day, and when I got a foreign tone I suddenly remembered he was off somewhere watching a Spurs game. He answered, totally unaware of what had taken place, and I briefly explained what had happened. He chuckled in disbelief and told me to calm down; everything was going to be OK, and I'd probably just get a slapped wrist and a warning. I asked him whom I should get to go with me, and he said that if he was in the country he'd be there, but that I should call Dory.

I didn't want to ask Dory. I couldn't put him in that position, and I was almost too close to him. I didn't want him to hear what they had to say, or to hear the details of what I had done, which now felt like a crime I was about to stand trial for. I knew that he would be hurt that I had in some ways attacked the profession he'd given much of his life to. I already felt like I had let him down and didn't want to damage his opinion of me, or disappoint him, any further.

An email popped up on my BlackBerry. It was from Wayne: 'I hope u're ok after probably a day's grilling by those guys . . . If you need any help or advice if it gets messy let me know . . .'

He was the sort of guy whom you wanted on your side. I knew that I could ring him at any time and he would always have an answer to whatever trouble I'd managed to get myself into, because he'd probably been in the same position at some point over the years. But I was already fairly certain that this was the sort of problem that I was going to have to sort out alone. As tempted as I was to get him to come to the meeting, I held back.

CHAPTER 16

THE DEVIL MADE ME DO IT

It was a mess. I was caught somewhere between wanting to celebrate my first published article, and maybe getting the chance to embark on a career as a journalist, and feeling full of uncertainty about whether I'd actually done the right thing, whether I really wanted to leave the strange, warped safety of the City at all.

A week ago I'd decided I was going to stick it out as a broker for another six months at least. I'd just been having a bad few weeks and I'd been ill. Writing could wait. Now it was no longer a choice for me to make, or something I could control. It had been taken entirely out of my hands, which was oddly liberating.

The beauty of the Internet lies in the speed with which it allows you to forget an action. One click of 'send' and you can quite happily forget what you've written until it comes bouncing back days, or even weeks, later. There is none of the laboured writing by hand in ink and remembering to post the letter.

Once an article is on the newsstands, there are no retrac-
tions. As Richard Salter once wrote: acts demolish their
alternatives. The first thing that the head of HR and Leicester
asked me when I sat down was whether the article could be
pulled. If the comment had arisen in any other situation, I
might have laughed at their naivity. As I explained that it was
far too late for that, I had visions of the Company dispatching
its brokers all over the country, frantically trying to recover
every single copy.

'Can you get them to print a retraction then?'

'Err, no. Not really.'

'Why did you write it, Venetia?'

The devil made me do it?

I found it difficult to forget those first questions. As the HR
manager moved on, and read extracts of the article to me, I was
thinking only of her preliminary hopeful requests that this situation could in some way be rectified or erased. Herein lies the
problem with words: they don't disappear once they've been
released into the public domain. They cannot be contained or
retrieved, or cancelled like a trade, the bonds vanishing in the
process. Why two senior members of the Company failed to
understand this simple concept was all that I could think
about.

She kept reading, but it sounded to me like she was putting
emphasis in all the wrong places, like a schoolgirl trying to
read French, occasionally looking up at me theatrically over her
glasses to see my reaction, as if it was something she'd seen
done during police examinations and it seemed appropriate.
She'd made notes in the margin of the printout, and underlined
various sections of the article in red like a schoolteacher. I

wondered whether she had stayed up late last night doing her homework or whether it had been hurriedly done on the Tube that morning.

I wasn't sure what she was expecting me to do or say. Hearing my words read out was only making me wince. I wondered whether she wanted me to cry remorsefully, say that I was sorry and beg for forgiveness. Part of me wanted to shut her up and put her out of her misery, but all I could do was stare at her blankly, and answer her questions as evasively as possible. I was breathing as slowly as I could without having to gasp for air, playing my own game of that primary school favourite, Sleeping Lions, wondering if my pupils were dilating as I stared at her. I was detached again, like I'd popped several valium.

That morning when I'd got dressed, preparing myself for battle, pulling on Agent Provocateur's finest boned corset, a black Prada skirt, Lanvin shirt and Louboutin stilettos, something had shut down. I'd partially distanced myself already, when I found myself back on the trading floor after my time off, but I was now totally estranged. If I was going down, I was doing it in Prada and the most impractical underwear I could find. It was virtually bulletproof.

I'd gone alone, deciding that I didn't want any unnecessary variables or distractions in the room. It was either that, or turning up with someone totally unexpected to blindside them – like an important client.

Powering through the foyer, I bumped into a couple of the sterling boys, who shot me cheeky grins and conspiratorial nods, and continued on their way. I knew I wouldn't see them again. I didn't notice who was in the lift, and I didn't turn around to check. I was now *persona non grata*, so it was of little consequence whom I was ignoring.

Leicester intercepted me on the eighteenth floor as soon as I came out of the lift. It was somewhere I'd previously only ventured when I needed something from the HR team. I was taken to an office I'd never seen before and he offered me some water before the *grand dame* of HR made her entrance. It was her office, so I wasn't sure where she emerged from – maybe she just wanted to make an entrance.

Leicester remained fairly quiet throughout, only interrupting, visibly frustrated, when I'd said something particularly oblique, shattering their attempts at good cop, bad cop. She finally neared the end of the article, the second half of which was all neatly underlined. She must have used a ruler. I thought it sounded far longer than 1,150 words when it was read out. I wanted to uncross my legs, as I could feel my foot starting to go dead, but I'd seemingly lost the ability to alter the position I had adopted. I was frozen. If I hadn't been the only one playing, I would have won. I was a perfectly still, dead-legged, corset-clad sleeping lion. In hindsight I wished I'd given the character a slight limp when I'd come into the room, because I would now have one on the way out. My foot probably wouldn't regain consciousness until I was exiting the lift.

I was suddenly aware that she'd stopped talking. I'd obviously been asked a question. It was something like 'do you want to resign and make this easier for everyone?' but I couldn't be sure, as I'd been imagining myself jumping about on the desk, yelling manically, 'You can fire me, but you're going to have to catch me first, fuckers' and running off cackling down the corridor. The last thing I needed was hallucinations.

I shook my head as I slowly said no, as if I was thinking about it – which I was, because I didn't know what the sodding question had been. I apologized for not having been more helpful, and the meeting was adjourned. They would clearly need more time to decide what was to be done with me, and were maybe wondering if I was of sound mind, as was I. I just hoped I hadn't turned down something exciting, like a payoff – or a doughnut.

I was a bit disappointed that they hadn't fired me on the spot. I'd travelled all that way, sat for an hour in a corset, only to be sent home again and told they'd be in touch. Like an actor at an audition, there was nothing I could do but wait. I wondered what grounds for instant dismissal were, what I would have to have done probably killed someone or crapped on my desk. They were clearly following some convoluted HR protocol, which left no legal loopholes that could one day lead to me suing them for something like unfair dismissal.

I could've made it easy for them and resigned, but I wanted them to play it through and actually have to fire me if they wanted to get me out of there. I'd maintained throughout the meeting that I wanted to keep my job and get back to work as quickly as possible, thinking that this was the sort of curve-ball one throws in such situations. I was laying down the gauntlet for no particular reason. I hadn't really thought it through. It was either genius, or verging on insane. This is what happens when you don't talk things through with trusted friends before taking action. If Giles had answered his phone, he would've convinced me to behave sanely at least.

I waited for their next move. I wanted checkmate, but instead the next day I got a courier wielding a letter summoning me back for another disciplinary hearing with some different people. I wasn't sure whether they could physically force me to attend, or whether I could just disappear. I would've refused to sign for the letter if I'd been quicker and more conscious. The buzzer, violent and jarring, had gone off ridiculously early and I'd assumed it was a postman with a parcel. Before I knew what I was doing, or had fully woken up, I was signing for a letter. It could've been laced with a chemical weapon, and I'd have happily taken it. Keyser Söze in *The Usual Suspects* would never have done that. It was an embarrassing schoolboy error. There were lots of things I would've done differently: answering the door was just one of them but, in the grand scheme of the disciplinary hearing, was fairly insignificant.

Perhaps I should have taken notes the day before rather than seeing how shallowly I could breathe without passing out and imagining myself dancing around on the desk, my eyes narrowed throughout. I wasn't thinking logically. I was too busy trying to perform some sort of mind-trick and had forgotten what I was trying to achieve, if anything. At that moment I was just along for the ride: there in body, but my mind was doing cartwheels along the corridor towards the lift. I might as well have been on acid. Of course, I could also have been having some sort of nervous breakdown. Madness. Yes, I was mad. They couldn't fire me if I was mad. I needed help, not a disciplinary hearing.

And I also needed to go back to sleep. I took one last look at the letter, checking it for traces of anthrax, and let it float down onto my bedroom floor. I was fucked by now anyway if it had been poisoned – as was the poor Lycra-clad courier, but he'd been wearing cycling gloves and a face mask, so maybe he would be OK. Or maybe he was working for them and had been warned. He had looked familiar, with his tufts of ginger hair poking out, like he might have worked on the other side, on the swaps desk. Their desk was huge; he could've easily entirely escaped my attention previously and thus been the perfect candidate for an anthrax drop.

I should've paid more attention to their faces when I strolled around the other side of the floor to use their photocopier when ours was jammed. But I'd always been too busy looking straight ahead, hoping no one would start shouting abuse at me.

The Toad would always catch me on the way back, even if I'd managed to reach my destination relatively unscathed. His deep, rich bass voice-over tones of 'THERE SHE IS, OI, GORGEOUS' were impossible to ignore and I always stopped for a chat. But I'd never noticed whom he worked with, apart from the dark Frenchman who strolled around to our side of the trading floor, where it was quieter, to make calls. Their desk had always been a wall of noise: it was the island where the money was made, and they could always be heard roaring. And now I'd quite probably been poisoned. I should've taken heed of the courier's checkered cap. I knew they'd get me in the end. I popped a couple of Zolpidem left over from my last long-haul flight and dove under my duvet.

I woke up. It was pitch black. For a few seconds I thought that I'd gone blind. I was sweating, and had no idea where I was. I only realized when my phone started ringing and lit up the room, which I identified as my own. Yes, I was in Chelsea – at my flat. I wasn't dead or blind, but my phone was indeed ringing. Unknown number.

There was no chance in hell of me answering now. I felt nauseous whenever I heard its familiar calypso ringtone, whoever was calling, because it was the same sound my alarm made, and seemed instantly to trigger the beginnings of a familiarly dull, caffeine-withdrawal headache, which now constantly pursued me. I knew that it would develop into a fully fledged migraine if I didn't either knock back a double espresso or take pills immediately. The checkered cap and the fangs had faded away but I knew that they'd be back.

It turned out that it was 6 a.m. I didn't know how long I'd been asleep, or how many days had passed. Sitting up, I opened a text from Fitz saying that I'd been deleted from Bloomberg. There were lots of little stars instead of my name, and my header, the Oscar Wilde quote that had so perplexed the head of HR, 'one must always play fairly when one has the winning cards', had finally disappeared.

I didn't know whether it was today or tomorrow that I was due back in Canary Wharf for round two, or indeed what today was. Beyond finding the letter with the time and date of my next appearance, I had no reason to get out of bed: in limbo, grief without torture, *e vegno in parte ove non è che luca*[2], still to face the Grand Inquisitor.

I scrambled around in the dark for the letter and some Migraleve pills. Tomorrow, 10 a.m. With other people, whose names I didn't recognize. No Leicester or HR manager. I wasn't sure whether this was a good or a bad thing. They had either delegated, having given up on getting any sense out of me, or were bringing in others to do their dirty work, having already decided my fate.

The letter contained a worrying passage. They wanted to discuss the contents of my Bloomberg messages and personal emails. This probably could have been avoided if I'd resigned, but they'd clearly been forced to delve deeper into their bag of tricks. I wondered what particular section of the last fourteen months' worth of instant chat that had taken place between

2 'And to a place I come where nothing shines', Dante, *The Inferno*

me and countless friends they would find to be the most damning.

Lena and I had more or less discussed every single aspect of our lives in minute detail from the hours of 7 a.m. until 5 p.m., only breaking for lunch, ever since I'd discovered how to use Bloomberg's messenger service. I had not, of course, stopped to consider how these chats would resurface, and was strangely intrigued by what they might choose to read out. Most of it was full of expletives – kunt, fuk, sh1t – the careful removal and substitution of key letters ensuring that they all went happily undetected by Bloomberg's filtering system.

But there was no alert issued on 'think about when this might come back and bite you in the ass', 'can this be used against you in a disciplinary hearing?' or 'are you sure you want to talk about the size of that guy's cock?' warning. There probably should've been.

A lot can happen in a year, and I had unwittingly implicated everyone I'd ever chatted with or sent an email to, which was most of my clients, a load of random other traders scattered around the City, old university friends who'd turned up on Bloomberg and the guys I'd dated. They'd inevitably go trawling through all the replies. I should've known something like this was going to happen and distanced myself from everyone from the outset, and refused to correspond with anyone. I decided it would be better not to think about any of it.

The buzzer went off again.

This time it was another courier, with a large wad of A4 paper clamped together by a giant bulldog clip – the transcripts of my last couple of months of Bloomberg chat. I contemplated shredding it immediately. There was surely nothing in there that could, in any way, be beneficial to have been reminded of before the disciplinary hearing. It ran the risk of throwing me completely off kilter when I was already barely hanging on. It was as if I had suddenly found myself starring in a farcical, inverted City version of *This Is Your Life*, complete with all past sexual exploits, and all the things I would really rather have forgotten: it was the good, the bad and the ugly, but decidedly thin on the good.

The courier had played his part well, turning up to surprise me, but the smiling face of Michael Aspel was nowhere to be seen, and I knew that the only guest appearances would come from some HR cretin and a mystery man I might have worked with, but couldn't be sure from seeing his full name. Damn all those fucking nicknames. And no, Michael, Mr Courier – whoever the fuck you are – now is not the right time. I am not ready for the Big Red Book or the bulldog clip. I don't like surprises. This is not my life.

Never answer the door when you're not expecting someone. At best it'll be an out-of-work grisly miner with a ginger beard and a selection of tool kits, wielding a hammer; at worst it'll be someone in checkered Lycra cycling shorts holding a chunk of your past life in their hands, asking you to sign for it.

There was probably a funny side to be found somewhere, and things were getting so farcical that it was hard to take them too seriously. I left the parcel of papers on the kitchen surface and knocked back a couple of pink Migraleve tablets with a shot of Armagnac from the bottle by the kettle. If I was about to delve into that wad of paper, I would need to take the edge off. It was far too early in the morning to be reading about premature ejaculation.

I thought highlighting the sections that they'd be most interested in would be the most sensible thing to do, but my highlighter ran out of ink after only a few pages and I decided it was unwise to read any further. Now, if I sat there with it in the meeting, it at least looked like I'd made an effort and dipped the wad in fluorescence, or lithium. It would give me something to look at quizzically while they interviewed me.

The following morning I was back in Agent Provocateur and a different piece of Prada and sitting on the Jubilee Line for what I predicted might be the last time. I was hardly going to come all this way just to use the remainder of my gym membership. At least my wardrobe of black separates was getting an airing.

9.30 a.m. was an alien time slot to be travelling to Canary Wharf: the station was deserted. Everything looked completely different to how it always looked at 6.45 a.m.

I was tempted to head to the trading floor and see what happened, but I pressed 18 and made my way through the office, past legal, to the HR department. I was offered a glass of water again and asked to sit down. I then spent the next half an hour hearing extracts from my Bloomberg conversations read out by a different HR representative, and a senior broker whom I recognized from the floor and whom I knew as Eggy, which was, of course, not his name and explained why I hadn't recognized the name on the letter.

I couldn't help but notice the number of times I'd said to Lena, Giles, the Ferg, or whomever I was speaking to, that I wanted to kill myself or resign. Most of it was fairly nonsensical, but hearing the words 'I want to die' every few minutes was unnerving. Maybe I needed that prescription after all.

I wasn't sure why their examination of my chat transcripts was entirely necessary. It was obvious that they'd already made their decision as soon as Eggy began reading from a statement that had obviously been written days ago by someone else. They weren't his words. The only part that stuck was the final paragraph that he eventually reached: they had no choice but to terminate my employment, effective immediately, on grounds of gross misconduct. He barely looked up, clearly pained by the entire horrible episode.

He was no sadist. He wasn't part of senior management. He was one of us, the ground troops, and had sat behind me on a nearby desk for the last few months, occasionally turning around to tell us something, and now here he was, sitting hunched on my left in such wildly different circumstances. We'd never really spoken much, and I only remember one conversation that we'd had about laser eye treatment. He'd had both eyes done and thoroughly recommended it. But he was now reading as if he wished they'd been plucked out, and he didn't have to preside over this sorry mess.

Gross misconduct – such appropriate words to sum up the last fourteen months. Everything else was meaningless: the money I'd made for the Company, the new clients I'd brought in, the countless excessive and sleepless nights out with clients, the afternoon of horrific food poisoning. All of it now seemed so irrelevant; maybe none of it had really counted, and I wasn't sure whether I really cared. Gross misconduct erases all former good behaviour. I now had nothing to show for the last fourteen months other than a letter informing me of my instant dismissal, and a working knowledge of Soho's strip clubs. He shook my hand and said goodbye.

The HR girl in the stripy shirt escorted me out of the building. I walked through the barriers for the last time, and once I was safely on the other side, she stood smugly asking for my ID badge, the last remnant of the time I'd spent in that building. I'd always hated the photo printed on the front. My hair was scraped back into the tight ponytail that I'd worn during my first few weeks, my severe make-up perfectly applied. It had been my second ID card; the first was left in the back of a taxi, along with a pair of gold Jil Sander ballet shoes, after an illicit night out with Giles. I'd got Mark to ring around to try to locate the shoes the following day, but they were never found. I loved those shoes. I silently handed the ID card to her and walked away, out through the doors and back into the outside world. It was all over; I was free to go; free to do whatever I wanted, but I didn't know where or what that was.

I felt nothing at all for a good few hours, just numb and exhausted. I thought it was maybe how people felt after long drawn-out court battles – indifferent, as the process itself has drained you so savagely that you have nothing left within to react to the verdict, to remember what the desired outcome was.

I don't remember getting home – the Tube journey, the walk back along the Kings Road, the texts and emails I sent letting my family know what had happened, the cup of tea my flat-mate said she made me. I knew these things must have happened, and my BlackBerry confirmed that I'd sent the mes-sages, but I had no memory of writing them. When I read them back they were surprisingly lucid.

'Well, it's all over. Fired for gross misconduct, effective immediately. Will call you later, going home.'

I went straight to bed, putting on my sleep mask and earplugs. I wanted to spend the next twenty-four hours cocooned, safely hidden away from the outside world until I knew what I was going to do next. True to recent form, I was woken by the front-door buzzer once more. It was another courier, this time with a letter explaining why my actions con-stituted gross misconduct, in case there had been any confusion.

> 'Having considered all the information available, we have concluded that your actions constitute gross misconduct for the following reasons:'

The letter read like a bad answer to a GCSE English comprehension paper, with bullet points forming a list, marking each 'reason' for my dismissal. At the end of the second chunk of text were the words:

> 'The flippant remark which you made during your disciplinary meeting, upon our expressing serious concerns (regarding the content of your Instant Bloomberg Chats), namely that you were sorry that the Company was concerned, is noteworthy.'

Another bullet point followed:

> 'As for the article . . . we noted in particular your statement within it that you often turned up for work under the influence of alcohol. Similar insinuations are made in your Instant Bloomberg Chats. While we understand that your role requires a certain level of client entertainment it is your responsibility to ensure that this does not have a detrimental impact on your ability to carry out your normal duties.'

I went back to bed, hoping that this would be the last piece of badly written correspondence to turn up on my doorstep.

EPILOGUE

'Excuse me, can I take this stool?'

A familiar face turned round: it was Giles' uncle, who had once worked with us, staring back at me warmly. His facial hair had changed, but otherwise he looked the same· big, burly, long-haired and cashmere swathed. I didn't know what I was more surprised by, bumping into him, or bumping into him and his clients in the Groucho Club in Soho – an unlikely City boy hangout if ever there was one.

I hadn't seen anyone from my former life since Lena's leaving party last year. She'd invited the entire market to a pub in the City. I figured that it would be a good opportunity to catch up with a few people and headed down. Making a guest appearance was one of Lena's ex-bosses, Seb, whom we had both had a monumental crush on since first meeting him, and had even made a wager that one day, somehow, one of us would get together with him. We'd ended up at a club in South Kensington with a couple of Lena's old brokers and some guys from her bank, including one of her ex-bosses. We were at a table one last time, surrounded by the usual bottles of champagne and spirits. After months away from the market, it had been like stepping back in time, and I was soon drunker than I ever had been when I was a broker. I finally had no clients to worry about, someone else was pouring the champagne, and I was in the middle of the dance floor kissing Seb in full view of half the market – I'd completed the transition back to the other side. Lena high-fived me as she staggered across the dance floor. It was our last remaining piece of unfinished City business.

Now, months later, she was in New York, and I was in a bar chatting with Giles' uncle. I had never felt further away from my old City life, yet it had come hurtling back towards me when he'd turned round.

He'd been the only one who'd known about my relationship with Giles, and had kept it entirely to himself until it had all fallen apart, and I'd been suspended. He'd apparently come back from lunch one day to find half the floor roaring at Giles and assumed it was about us – which was correct, but until that point nothing had been confirmed or proven. Giles was busy keeping his head down, laughing it off and denying all knowledge, until the immortal words, 'Ohh, mate, so they finally found out about you and Venetia shagging?' boomed out during a lull, as he stood, taking off his jacket, and then slumped back into his chair, work done.

Having bumped into each other, I wanted to congratulate him for such superb delivery of the news, which quickly made its way around the entire floor. It had at least been a marginally better expression than 'Is that the bird Giles was hanging out the back of?', which I'd once overheard at a party.

We chatted for a few minutes, and it turned out that Dory had been tinned last year, and that The Godfather had retired four months ago. I was shocked, but the only people I would've been able to share the impact of the news with weren't around. The last remaining vestiges of the desk as I had known it had gone. I wondered what had happened to the giant jars of pickled onions and gherkins, and the cupboard where Dory kept the lost treasures of the desk from the decades when they were enough of a team to bring back ugly souvenirs and trinkets from holidays to form a desk collection. I thought about Dory, packing up his desk, emptying his drawers and the secret cupboard, and wondered whether he'd walked out clutching the onions and the pickles, the camel in the sombrero, the Eiffel Tower, the pyramids and the snow shakers, or just left everything behind for the cleaners.

I knew that Dory and The Godfather would be missed. They were the spiritual fathers of broking, believing in the profession and the markets when many others around them had lost faith, because they were driven by something other than greed. They were both in their fifties when I met them, and neither really needed to carry on working, but they did because they believed in the Company, in their colleagues and in supporting the younger generation blazing its way through.

They didn't panic when the credit crunch set in; they'd seen it all before, and knew that the market would eventually right itself over time. But there was a quiet resignation that the golden age of excess and irresponsibility was finally over and would never return. They'd seen the best of it and could now only watch as the City's towers began to crumble around them.

They were the two people I'd missed the most. I'd bought various cards and started writing to them on so many occasions to try to explain what had happened, but I'd always stopped, unable to finish. When I dropped round to my old

Chelsea flat in January to find a Christmas card from Dory and his family in a pile of post that hadn't been forwarded, I'd tried to write again. It was one of the many things that kept me awake at night, but all I'd ended up with was a drawer full of half-written greetings cards that I couldn't do anything with. I thought that one day I would pick one of them and finish it, and shred the rest, but it never happened.

Dory was one of the few people who had made the firm great; he'd believed in the Company when no one else had, and worked harder than anyone I knew. He had never been one of their top earners or provoked any of the venom that the American had, but he had been one of the guys who made up the firm's solid backbone and had been loyal to the end. Knowing that he'd been laid off only confirmed what I already felt about the Company: that it was rotten to the core and was finally turning on itself.

Without men like Dory, the City will cease to function. He was the closest thing to a moral compass that the firm had. He understood that broking was at times horrific, but it was also a gift, a privilege to be protected and not abused. The money that could be earned was like the sea: it didn't really belong to any of us and could flow in any direction at any moment. And now there was nothing left.

I didn't ask about the American; I knew that he would never have been fired or made redundant and would still be working away as he always had done. He was indestructible, only becoming more resilient with age. I heard he'd hired a girl to replace me – blonde, but her tits apparently weren't as good. There will never be another Airbags.

But we'd all moved on.

Months later I received a package from the States. It was

from the Company's head office containing details of the shares I apparently owned. I was fairly sure that getting fired for gross misconduct rendered any shares that I may or may not have held void, but it seemed like a fitting final piece of correspondence to receive, and at least it didn't come by courier. Maybe I really was still a shareholder.

The last year has proven that greed leads nowhere. It's a dead end. The City is full of people with nothing else to do but pursue money, who live for the hit of adrenalin that will continue to become increasingly difficult to get, until it finally disappears altogether and everything collapses.

It gets to the point when the job is no longer about the money; the cash made on each trade is just a by-product. What matters is the trade itself – the short, sharp hit of power that it releases and, like a gambler at a blackjack table, it is all too often too difficult to stand up and walk away. Even the smallest of men get to feel like a Big Swinging Dick on a trading floor.

I caught the final year of City excess. The Square Mile and Canary Wharf have now changed irreversibly; banks that I had assumed would be around forever have disappeared and those that remain are unrecognizable. Big Bad Bank and Aggro Bank have cleverly redefined themselves: they are no longer 'investment banks' but are now 'bank holding companies', and are far more tightly regulated. It's less glamorous, but far safer in the current climate.

The City was once something to be proud of: the UK had one of the world's finest financial centres. It is now nothing but a cause of contention; most markedly it was the target of protesters storming the Square Mile in April 2009, smashing the

271

Royal Bank of Scotland's windows, stealing and attacking anyone who made the mistake of wearing a suit to work.

Many of the traders whom I knew have been made redundant, a few have moved to funds and private equity shops, and the rest are getting used to working in the public sector with the majority shareholders of their banks now being the British taxpayer. Poached eggs have been removed from canteen menus, Post-it Notes are being phased out, pens are being rationed and stationery cupboards are kept locked. The lucky few who had negotiated guaranteed bonuses before the rot set in are sitting pretty and will still get their six-figure payouts – unless they happen to get lynched by a member of the public first.

As for the City's bookies, they are still entertaining as they always have done; ski trips went ahead as planned this year – the 'chalet from hell' lives on. While there are still traders to be wooed, brokers will keep taking them out, but I'm guessing that everything now tastes a little different.

The Kunt is still out there, although the last time someone checked, his Bloomberg status was red and had been for a while, so he's either been axed or some bookie has finally taken him out. Maybe I'll bump into him one day.

Emma and Brian's entire desk disappeared. Brian retired, and Emma emigrated to warmer climes.

The Ferg is still lying by a pool in Spain, living out the *Sexy Beast* dream.

Lena got made redundant, much to her relief, and is now living in New York. We still speak every day.

Word on the Street was that Leicester got reprimanded after a sly approach from another firm.

Giles met a girl, and is still a bookie.

Brad is still yelling at his sales team.

I never heard from the Sicilian, other than once receiving a missed call from him a year after I'd been fired. He didn't leave a voicemail. There was apparently a rumour going around after my demise that we'd fucked. We never did.

Toby is still single and still throwing his weight around at Aggro Bank. If he managed to survive dating a female broker, anyone can.

The Deviant is still the Biggest Swinging Dick out there, dropping the c-bomb whenever he pleases. He recently installed an espresso machine on his desk, but doubted it would survive longer than a day in the new puritanical regime.

Zippy's emails are still in circulation. He gives heavily to charity, and is rumoured to have opened an orphanage with those evil bonuses he once received.

The American is still out there – as disliked, misunderstood and indestructible as ever.

Mo moved to a fund after an unfortunate incident in which he was rumoured to have been found face down in a box full of cocaine one morning. He still does too much coke and samples many prescription drugs, and we still occasionally get lap-danced together over a glass of cheap wine after dinner at Nobu, paid for by him, and he always orders me a chocolate bento box without asking, and I never feel demeaned.

The City beats on.

GLOSSARY

Bid – the price a trader is willing to pay for a financial instrument. This will constantly change.

Bloomberg – a financial software, data and news company. In the City, most traders and brokers have Bloomberg running on one of their many computer screens to check information on different bond and stock prices, to send email or instant messages to other traders and brokers, to get the latest financial and non-financial news, to calculate interest and check exchange rates. There is a Bloomberg tool for everything, including restaurant recommendations and gift guides.

Bond – a debt security issued by corporations and governments. Bonds pay the holder a 'coupon' – an interest rate that can be fixed or tied to an index – until the maturity date.

Brass – a prostitute, as in 'get me a brass' or 'he's gone brassin''.

Broker (Inter-dealer broker) – also known as a 'bookie'. A middleman who takes bids and offers from traders within the secondary market and narrows down a price until it trades. Commission is taken on every trade.

CDO – Collateralized Debt Obligation – a term used to refer to a security (usually investment grade) backed by an underlying pool of other securities. A CDO can be comprised of any kind of debt instruments – usually bonds and loans

(CBOs and CLOs) but also mortgages (CMOs). The underlying securities all have different levels of risk attached to them, meaning that on the surface a security can appear high grade, but can actually be very risky.

CDS – Credit Default Swap – a contract between two counterparties that operates like an insurance policy for bonds or loans, offering protection should there be a 'credit event', such as a company defaulting on payments. CDS is the most widely traded financial derivative and can be traded with or without holding the actual asset. It is therefore possible, and widely used, to hedge or speculate against changes in a bond's value without owning the underlying product.

Chinese Wall – An information barrier within an organization that separates anyone with insider information from anyone who could use this information to their advantage e.g. investment bankers (who may have worked on a deal or made investment decisions regarding a deal) would be kept separate from traders.

Colour – information about the financial instrument or the price it is being offered or bid at that might be helpful to a trader.

Crossover – the high yield and sub-investment grade index that tracks around 50 companies and often indicates the general mood of the market.

Flat – Neither long nor short: equilibrium. Brokers should always be 'flat' in as much as they should never have positions one way or the other because they are middlemen. Traders are usually long or short but rarely flat, unless the market gets hairy and they are forced to 'flatten' their book, making sure they sell anything excessive and risky. Being 'flat' can also apply to single products, not entire books. So a trader may be flat in some random medical supplies company's bonds but short in something else. A trader may say to a broker, 'I'm flat' and mean he therefore has no interest in whatever price the broker is showing him, because he has completed all the buying and selling he currently needs to in that particular area.

FOK – Fill Or Kill – an ultimatum given by a trader to a broker, another way of saying 'this is the best I can do, get the trade done or take me out immediately'.

High yield bond – a bond that is issued below investment grade and therefore carries a higher risk of defaulting but also a higher coupon accordingly.

Hit – to 'hit' a bid is to agree to sell at the price the buyer is offering, thus making you the aggressor and, with a bond, the person who therefore pays the brokerage. You cannot hit an offer, only a bid. Saying 'yours' equates to hitting a bid.

Jub – a junior or trainee who is usually useless or stupid.

Lift – to 'lift' an offer is to agree to buy at the price the seller is currently offering, thus making you the aggressor and, with a bond, the person who therefore pays the brokerage. You cannot lift a bid, only an offer. Saying 'mine' equates to lifting an offer.

Loan – usually refers to a leveraged loan, which is a debt instrument. Loans are traded like bonds but they are a 'name give-up' product, meaning that when a trade takes place the broker tells the buyer and seller who their counterparty is and they arrange delivery of the loan between themselves. Loans are private, unlike most bonds, meaning that only holders of the loan can access information about the company.

Long – The opposite of being 'short'. If you're 'long' you usually have too much of something, often in the expectation that the price will go up and the financial instrument can then be sold for more than it was bought. If, however, the reverse happens and the price goes down, and you're stuck with millions of worthless crap, you're then 'long and wrong'. The same expression can be applied to women. 'I'm long a girlfriend', or sometimes when a broker has ordered too much food: 'long Nandos'.

Offer – opposite of bid. Where a seller will sell. This level will constantly change.

One shot – another way of saying FOK. 'Give him one shot at that level and then take me out.'

Paper – Term traditionally used to describe short-term unsecured instruments but generally used in the Street to describe any financial product being traded – whether bonds, loans, CDS, etc.

Room – whether a trader has any room to improve on a price. 'Does he have any room?' will give a broker a chance to say whether he or she thinks the price can be improved on or whether the offer or bid is stuck where it is.

Short – 'Going short' or 'being short' or 'shorting' is the opposite of being 'long' and entails selling financial instruments, often without actually owning them, usually to buy them back at a cheaper price and therefore pocket the difference. The same expression can be used in a more basic sense to say, 'I am short a drink' or 'I am short a brass' if it's something that you should have, but don't. You can easily get caught 'short' if the price goes up instead of down and you lose money instead of making it, having sold something for a lower price than it is actually available on the market.

Shovel/bugle – cocaine.

Spin – another expression meaning to 'work' a price widely among all your clients. 'Spin it' will usually be said after a market has 'cleared' and neither the buyer nor seller wants to improve for the time being and are happy for the broker to show it around to other traders.

Street – the secondary market. Originally referred to the Wall Street community, but now the term is used widely to refer to the market where investors buy and sell previously issued securities through a broker, as opposed to buying directly from the issuer in the primary market.

Tanking – when the price of a financial instrument goes down quickly and often unexpectedly.

Trader – someone who buys and sells financial instruments and derivatives at a bank or hedge fund in order to make a profit. All traders have 'books' and most have limits to the size of that book of instruments, i.e. what amount they can own at any one time and what risks can be taken overnight.

Work – to show a market around the Street to all your clients to try to get more traders involved. A market should only be worked when the buyer and seller are both happy for it to be shown around more widely. If they are not, they will say 'take me out' or 'I don't want it worked'

ACKNOWLEDGEMENTS

I'd like to thank my agent Simon Trewin for all his guidance and support. Thanks also to Sarah Ballard.

I'm hugely grateful to the team at Simon and Schuster, particularly Kerri Sharp and Emma Harrow.

Thank you to David Bartlett, Daisy Aitkens, Gayle Mackay, Jaspal Juj, Maggie Hitchens, Rachel Aarons and Richard Valtr.

I'd like to thank Mike Allen, a wonderful teacher and friend.

Thank you to Matthew d'Ancona and everyone at the *Spectator*.

There are many other people I would like to thank, but as they are still in the financial markets, I won't name them. You know who you are: thank you for everything.

Lastly, I really could not have written this book without the support of my family: thank you.